INDIVIDUALISM

AN ANALYSIS OF THE SYSTEM
OF SOCIAL SECURITY AND
SOCIAL WELFARE IN FRANCE

SOCIAL WELFARE

INDIVIDUALISM

 AN ANALYSIS OF THE SYSTEM
OF SOCIAL SECURITY AND
SOCIAL WELFARE IN FRANCE

SOCIAL WELFARE

by WALTER A. FRIEDLANDER

PROFESSOR OF SOCIAL WELFARE, EMERITUS
UNIVERSITY OF CALIFORNIA, BERKELEY

THE FREE PRESS OF GLENCOE, INC.
A DIVISION OF THE
CROWELL-COLLIER PUBLISHING CO.
NEW YORK
BUREAU OF SOCIAL & POLITICAL RESEARCH
MICHIGAN STATE UNIVERSITY
EAST LANSING

P R E F A C E

The interest in international relations has increased greatly during the past decades. We share with other countries the desire to gain a better understanding of the essential elements of our culture -- the economic and social fabric, the ideas and values of nations which have all become closer connected with one another through technical advances in communication, the expansion of world trade, and the exchange of scientific knowledge and cultural achievements all over this earth. Social welfare has contributed to this movement for international understanding and cooperation, together with the social sciences, economics, public administration, and international law. Social welfare and health services in all countries affect the daily life and well-being of individuals and peoples. They are based upon their culture, their political and social conditions, but they also influence the political and social structure, organization, and tendencies in these countries. The programs of social welfare and social security conserve, protect, and develop the human resources in each nation, and are interrelated to its political structure and its ideological development as well as to its economic and cultural life.

Planned international programs for the dissemination of knowledge and techniques in modern agriculture, industry, and other means of producing food, clothing, tools, and of eliminating hunger, disease, and suffering have been developed under the auspices of the United Nations and its specialized agencies, the International Labor Organization, the World Health Organization, the Food and Agricultural Organization, and the United Nations Children's Fund. They are supported by other international agencies and by numerous national projects and voluntary organizations. The rapid growth of scientific knowledge in medicine, public health, and chemistry, as well as in the social sciences, has caused a demand for an exchange of theoretical

49733

and technical knowledge as well as of practical experience in all the social services. Studies of a cross-cultural nature, the exchange of scholars and students, and observation visits among numerous nations have contributed to a growing desire to become familiar with the political, economic, and social conditions of other countries, to gain a deeper understanding of their culture, their values, and their sociological structure, with the aim of achieving closer cooperation and working together in a peaceful world.

In the area of social welfare, the awareness of the value of comparative studies and of the exchange of practical experience has been pronounced since the mid-nineteenth century. International congresses of charities, philanthropy, and corrections have been instrumental in the improvement of social services under religious, humanitarian, and public auspices since 1849. More recently, valuable publications of the League of Nations, the International Labor Organization, the United Nations, and its specialized agencies have spread information on the theory and practice of public health, public and private welfare services, and the prevention and control of crime and delinquency in many countries.

An interpretation of social welfare in France seemed desirable because it is difficult to understand the political, cultural, and social values of the French people. This has been convincingly demonstrated by the noted French political scientist, Professor André Siegfried in his "Approaches to an Understanding of Modern France" (in Edward Mead Earle, Modern France, Princeton University Press, 1951). He indicates that it requires serious study, sympathy, and patience to learn what lies under the surface of events and the legislative and societal structure of France.

The aim of this study is to explain the development, the present concepts, and the principles and practice of social welfare in France. It is based upon the author's studies and professional experience as an executive in a social agency in Paris from 1933 to 1936, and upon research studies carried out in France in 1951-1952, in 1956-1957, and in 1960.

vi

A historical analysis of the development from the medieval charities to the modern programs of public and private social services and of social security, social insurance, and family allowances seemed helpful for the understanding of the significance of the welfare activities for France today. The characteristic integration of both public and private health and welfare services is interpreted in Chapter 2, with explanation of the emphasis on protection of health and family life in the context of demographic conditions in the country. The field of child welfare services and protective and cultural activities are discussed in Chapter 3. The important role of private social agencies and other voluntary organizations in the preservation and protection of the health and the promotion of the well-being of the population are the topics of Chapter 4. The outstanding features of the French system of social security, particularly of the family allowances but also of the various social insurance programs in French social policies, required their analysis in Chapter 5. The concluding chapter presents a discussion of the professional development of social work in France, the changing methods of social welfare practice, and the education for social work.

In this introduction, some of the outstanding characteristics of the French system of social services and social security should be indicated. These characteristic traits find their explanation in the polarity of social forces which influence the cultural, political, and economic life of the French: the deep devotion to individualism, the desire for personal freedom, for intellectual, economic, and social independence, the strong concern for privacy in family life, affection for children, and the preservation of health. On the other side, the recognition that the striving for social security, above all in old age and sickness, cannot be fulfilled without a national program of aid to the needy and collective measures for health protection and the education of children which is reflected in the modern plan of social insurances and, above all, in the family allowances which play such a vital role in the economy of most French families with children. They provide an essential part of the total income of the working class and the middle class. This family allowance program deserves attention because we have not yet too seriously examined whether or not it might be a valuable solution to certain problems of our own social security system.

The French program of prevention of want through old-age and disability insurance, workmen's compensation, and financial support of various economically distressed groups of the population through public assistance is not basically different from our own policy. But the protection of the entire population against the contingencies of illness and disability by means of medical assistance and health insurance is quite different from the approach to these problems in the United States. In the area of health insurance, the French program requires that the insured patient, as a rule, assume the responsibility for paying a proportion of the medical and hospital expenses, but allows him free choice of physician, dentist, pharmacist, and hospital. The concept of social insurance protection was accepted in France only after the First World War because it was considered alien to French custom, just as the principle of social security was approved in the United States only after the Great Depression under the New Deal.

In contrast to this late development, France served as the pioneer nation in the field of family allowances. It is worthy of note that the main stimulus for the introduction of family allowances came from the private initiative of a few industrialists who envisaged the social necessity of family allowances for workers with large families, and their usefulness toward effective production. Another remarkable fact is that family allowances gained strong support from organized labor, neighborhood groups, consumer cooperatives, mutual aid societies and family associations after the program had been transformed into an integral part of the social security system on a legal basis.

In view of the numerous difficulties which the many private charities, voluntary welfare organizations, and public health and welfare authorities face in their attempt to coordinate their services and activities -- a problem well known in the United States -- it is of interest to observe how successfully the "Coordinated Family Service" is operating in most larger cities and even in rural regions (Chapter 4). This united family casework service has greatly increased individual counseling, economic support, ealth education, guidance, and social protection for the French population through the cooperation of public and private social and health agencies. In this connection, the participation of the social insurance and family allowance authorities, in cooperation with public welfare departments and religious and non-sectarian private organizations gives a provocative example of future desirable developments. In this coordinated program we find again an example of the possibility of maintaining high ideals of individual freedom and independence of social organizations, but combining with them the readiness for wholesome cooperation and collective action required for the well-being of fellow men.

In the preparation of this book, the author gained encouragement and invaluable help from his wife, to whom he owes deep gratitude. He is also indebted to the University of California for assistance in the research for this study, and to the United States Fulbright Commission whose grant enabled him to carry on part of this research. The author wishes to express his gratitude for critical comments on the manuscript and support in its final form to Dr. Frank A. Pinner, Director of the Bureau of Social and Political Research, Michigan State University, to Hilda Jaffe, Editor of the Bureau, and to several colleagues of the faculty of the School of Social Work, Michigan State University, and of the School of Social Welfare, University of California. His thanks are also due to Miss Helen Graham, Mrs. Mary Trumpener, Miss Patricia Seawell, and Miss Aura Cuevas who helped in the writing of the manuscript.

W. F.

L i s t   o f
T A B L E S
a n d
C H A R T S

C O N T E N T S

CHAPTER 1 THE HISTORY OF CHARITIES IN FRANCE

EARLY DEVELOPMENT

During the Middle Ages relief to the poor was a function of the church whose priests and bishops were considered the guardians of the destitute and helpless. Under the reign of the Merovingian kings, the "Conciles," [church councils] pronounced that the bishop should feed and clothe the poor and that the churches should use one-quarter of their revenues for the care of the poor and the sick. Each parish was to give relief only to its resident paupers to discourage vagabondage. During the feudal periods the bishop supervised the charities in his diocese. Collections were taken up at regular church services; after the Sunday service the priest distributed alms, food, and clothing to the poor.

In the ninth century Charlemagne and Louis the Pious assumed a protectorate over all paupers and allocated royal subsidies to local parish churches unable to carry the financial burden of poor relief. A royal decree ("capitulaire") of 806 under Charlemagne required the lords to care for the poor on the manor and the townships to procure food for the destitute; it prohibited paupers from moving from one place to another.[1] Each monastery

---

1. René Sand, Le Service social à travers le monde (Paris: A. Colin, 1931), pp. 20 and 22.

had to maintain a guest house for travellers and old men, while old women found refuge in convents. In the eleventh and twelfth centuries the bishops founded clerical institutions and alms-houses called hôtels de Dieu for the care of orphans, abandoned children, the old, the infirm, the disabled, the sick, and homeless pregnant women.[2] With the spread of epidemics and contagious diseases such as leprosy, smallpox, and the plague during the Crusades, the almshouses were unable to care for the mass of patients, so that several cities were forced to establish municipal hospitals.[3] Various monastic orders, such as the Franciscan Brothers, the Béguines, the "Hospitallers" under Guy de Montpeliers, the Order "de la Vie Commune, " the Soeurs de la Pénitence, and Filles de Saint-Victor, devoted themselves to charitable work.

Two contradictory trends appear in the policy of medieval charity in France. The royal dynasty and the church followed the Roman tradition of a uniform central authority, exercising control over the entire country. On the other hand, the French people in the provinces had inherited the Germanic tribal desire for independence which resulted in the desire for local responsi-bility. As a result of these divergent tendencies, a church council in Paris in 829 insisted that the king was obliged to grant subsidies to the charities of the local churches. Thus a certain cooperation between the royal administration and religious charities developed, leading to some control by the king's offi-cials over the clergy's administration of charitable institutions.[4]

---

2. The term "hospital" [hôpital] was also used at this time, but meant a charitable institution for all needy persons, whether sick, aged, infirm, or helpless children.

3. French cities followed here the example of Italian municipalities which established asylums in the ninth century; the hospitals were frequently financed by special endowments of wealthy citizens (see René Sand, The Advance to Social Medicine [London: Staples Press, 1952], p. 355).

4. L. Pasquier, "Assistance Publique," La Grande Encyclopédie (Paris, 1937), IV, 266.

As in most European countries, one of the serious problems in France was created through the vagrant beggars. As early as 806, Charlemagne ordered that every lord should feed the poor on his manor and not allow them to go begging elsewhere.[5] But neither the lords nor the churches and religious institutions were able to prevent vagrancy. The number of migrant beggars increased regularly during wars, famines, and floods. Because a large proportion of the serfs and farm hands received such a meager wage that their standard of living differed only slightly from that of beggars who moved through the country without hard labor, many serfs and peasants joined the beggar bands. In the eleventh century the parish system of relief through the local church broke down and left the responsibility to charity institutions and monastic and lay orders. The religious fervor of the Crusades inspired donations and bequests to churches for the establishment of charitable institutions, the donor hoping to secure the salvation of his and his family's souls.

With the decline of feudalism, many paupers and sick people were deprived of the support which they had received from the lord of the manor. New hospitals and almshouses had to be established to fill this gap.[6] The ruling aristocracy was no longer willing to make large donations to the church, and the religious orders and hospitals lost influence with the decrease of gifts for their work. A veritable army of beggars and vagrants, increased by wars and political struggles, became the curse of the country. Brutal attempts at deterrence of the tide of vagabonds, such as the pillory, the stocks, branding, and whipping, had little success.

_____

5. Shelby McCloy, Government Assistance in 18th Century France (Durham, N. C.: Duke University Press, 1946), p. 260.

6. During the fourteenth century, the hospitals ceased to serve as hostelries for travellers because inns were built, and gradually the hospitals admitted sick and destitute persons in increasing numbers.

THE PERIOD OF THE MONARCHY

Under Louis IX paupers and invalids had to be registered in their community in order to receive food and clothes, and after the Hundred Years War (1337-1443) several royal decrees repeatedly prohibited begging and vagrancy. But these legal measures remained ineffective because the vagrants could not get regular work and found shelter in the monasteries, convents, and church guesthouses. These, as clerical institutions, were not under the jurisdiction of the king and thus could discharge their religious duty of almsgiving and asylum to the poor. [7]

Certain problems developed from the fact that there was some abuse of the ecclesiastical system of charities, that funds and property were diverted from their intended function. The clergy, administering hospitals, almshouses, and orphanages, was accused of neglecting the poor, letting the buildings decay, and using the major part of the gifts and revenues for itself. The Council of Vienna in 1311 ordered, therefore, that hospitals should be placed under the supervision of well-to-do laymen who must render account of all financial operations to the bishop every two years, and a papal decree of Pope Clement V of 1311 organized lay boards for the supervision of almshouses and hospitals. [8] Monasteries and larger cities maintained lazar houses for lepers outside of the city walls. Merchant guilds and craft and trade brotherhoods organized mutual aid societies for members and their families. At Nîmes a wealthy citizen in 1492 left his property for the legal defense of the poor, a fore-runner of legal aid societies.

Meanwhile the drift from the country to the towns was accelerated by crop failures, famines, floods, and wars. Rural workers and sharecroppers, often in conflict with their lord, as well

---

7. H. Dérouin, A. Gory, and F. Worms, Traité théorique et pratique d'assistance publique (Paris, 1900), p. 14.

8. During the following centuries, various royal decrees ordered the transfer of the administration of hospitals and almshouses to civil commissioners, but had only limited success. Ibid., pp. 9-10.

as crippled soldiers and beggars poured into the towns. They were all called "vagabonds." Statutes repeatedly stipulated that an able-bodied, unemployed beggar should be returned to his home parish and if he refused, be punished by branding or by confinement to the galleys from two years to life. In the seventeenth century, arrested vagrants were sentenced to hard labor in special depôts de mendicité [workhouses]. The vagrants often organized in bands, used a special slang, threatened force if their begging did not arouse sufficient pity, and infested the countryside soliciting food and clothes. Farmers did not dare to refuse alms because they were afraid of being robbed or of having their houses and barns set on fire. This beggars' army was constantly supplied with new recruits because the craft guilds refused to accept outsiders as apprentices. The slow development of manufacturing and industries before the French Revolution and the starvation wages of rural workers and share-tenants drove many unemployed into the ranks of the beggars.

Between the sixteenth and eighteenth centuries, the trend toward a separation of charities from the control of the church became stronger. In 1525, the cities of Mons and Ypres organized a municipal relief administration, and Paris followed in 1544 with a "pauper office" in each of her boroughs, while a Grand bureau des pauvres [central relief office] was established in 1550.[9] Relief distribution alleviated only the most elementary needs of the paupers. The civil spirit of local autonomy, which had suffered in the Middle Ages, grew again and was recognized in royal decrees confirming the municipal responsibility for the care of the poor and the sick.[10] In 1566, the royal Edict of Moulins established the principle of "settlement," and authorized a municipal poor tax to raise money for poor relief; this statute preceded by six years the famous poor-tax law of Queen

---

9. Baron Dupin, Histoire de l'administration des secours publics (Paris, 1821), Chapter 1.

10. René Sand, Le Service social à travers le monde, p. 21; Carl R. Steinbicker, Poor Relief in the Sixteenth Century (Washington: Catholic University of America Press, 1937), p. 73.

Elizabeth of England, enacted in 1572.[11] Other cities and towns followed the example of Paris and organized bureaux des pauvres [poor-relief bureaus]. When taxed for the costs of poor relief, local citizens also asked for control of relief by their own city council.

Exceptional treatment was granted to disabled and aged soldiers who, beginning in the late Middle Ages, were maintained in monasteries as oblats at the expense of the royal court. The Hôpital Bicêtre in Paris served as a veterans' asylum, and the noted Hôtel des Invalides was established in 1674 as a home for disabled and aged war veterans. Other veterans received royal pensions in their own homes.

The great reformer in the field of charities in France, in the seventeenth century, was St. Vincent de Paul (1576-1660). Born at Pouy, he was ordained a priest in 1600. On a voyage to his first parish in Narbonne he was captured by Barbary pirates in the Mediterranean and was sold as a galley slave in Tunis. After seven years of suffering he succeeded in converting his master, a former Italian merchant, and escaped with him to Italy. When Father Vincent returned to France, he had gained insight into the unbelievable conditions under which the unfortunate galley slaves lived; consequently, he devoted his special concern to families of galley slaves and other convicts. His sermons emphasized the religious duty of charity for the destitute, the sick, blind and lame, the galley slaves and their families, and deeply impressed his audiences. He soon became famous for his preaching and influenced the ideas of many young priests. Father Vincent recognized the need for a fundamental change in the system of church charity for the poor, and saw that the scanty alms distributed to the destitute did not relieve them from economic and moral deprivation. Thus he insisted that a charity contribution must entail a real sacrifice, and he encouraged the wealthy aristocrats in his audiences to give more

---

11. It is characteristic that under the English statute of 1536 paupers could receive relief in their parish after they had resided three years in the county, while the French statute required merely residence, not several years of domicile.

generously. This made a reform of charity methods possible as large endowments by members of the gentry were made. But Father Vincent was not content with material gifts alone.

In 1617, he organized, with the support of the Countess de Joigny, whose children he taught, a religious lay order, La Confrérie de charité [The Sisterhood of Charity]. It was composed of well-to-do upper-class women who visited the homes of poor families to distribute food and clothes, and to comfort the women and children. The ladies also visited patients in hospitals and brought them gifts. After some years, a brotherhood of similar character was founded whose members paid regular visits to male patients in the hospitals and asylums. However, the work of these volunteers did not suffice. Their social and personal obligations prevented them from devoting sufficient time to charitable work; and their lack of understanding of the fate, feeling, and suffering of the poor easily created shame and resentment. Father Vincent decided, therefore, to train young peasant women willing to devote themselves to charity work to serve in hospitals and to visit the sick and the poor. This lay order was first called Les Servantes des pauvres [Servants of the Poor] and was organized with the help of Father Vincent's able assistant, Madame Louise de Marillac; when he moved to Paris, in 1633, the name was changed to Les Filles de charité [The Daughters of Charity].12 This order was the forerunner of professional social workers in France. Father Vincent established a school in Paris for training in nursing and charity visiting, and the order soon spread to the provinces of France.

To satisfy his desire to help the galley slaves and their families, Father Vincent founded a special hospital for them at Marseilles. He also became interested in the fate of abandoned and illegitimate children and foundlings after observing the deplorable conditions in a foundling asylum, Maison de la couche

---

12. Today the order is known as Les Soeurs de charité, Les Soeurs grises, or Soeurs de Saint Vincent and plays an important role in France. Baron de Gérando, De la bienfaisance publique (Paris: Renouard, 1839), IV, 478-483.

in Paris, where the children suffered from hunger, cold, and
exploitation and usually died at an early age. Other children
were sold to beggars and were mutilated to solicit the pity of
the passers-by. To counteract this abuse, Father Vincent
founded, in 1638, a foundling asylum in Paris, the Hôpital des
enfants trouvés, the first orphanage which also received illegitimate children; it was recognized as a charitable institution by
the king in 1642 and endowed with a royal annual subsidy. At
the time of Father Vincent's death, 1660, the order of the Filles
de charité owned 28 charitable institutions in France, among
them orphanages and foundling asylums, hospitals, and homes
for the aged and infirm. [13]

A Protestant contemporary of Father Vincent, Théophraste
Renaudot, established in 1629 the first employment service, the
Bureau d'adresses, in Paris and a confidential charity exchange,
the Bureau de rencontres, where people in distress asking for
aid were referred to persons willing to help them. He finally
founded, in 1637, a people's pawn shop where loans were given
at only three per cent interest.

During the subsequent period of the absolute monarchy, there
was a strong tendency toward a centralization of power in all
areas of government. Local authorities were no longer encouraged to act on their own initiative in charitable work. The
existing asylums and hospitals were too small to meet the growing needs of their inmates. These facts induced Louis XIV to
centralize the method of poor relief by abandoning most of the
relief to people in their own homes and by establishing in Paris,
in 1656, a large institution, the Hôpital général, [14] following an
earlier example of the city of Lyons in 1531. It became a shelter
for the sick, invalids, paupers, and beggars who were forcibly
brought there, and a stream of destitute people from all parts

---

13. After Father Vincent's canonization, his name was changed to Saint
Vincent de Paul. Léon Lallemand, Histoire de la Charité (Paris, 1910-1912), I, 16.

14. This hospital is now La Salpêtrière and serves as one of the training hospitals
for the medical school of the University of Paris (Sorbonne). See also, Gérando,
op. cit., IV, 486-488.

of the country came to this refuge. Officials of provinces who desired to save expenses sent foundlings and orphans also to this hospital. Finally the mass movement of beggars was stopped by armed guards at the gates of Paris, and a royal edict of 1662 ordered the establishment of a general hospital in the capital of each province to prevent the further attraction of paupers and vagrants to Paris. Meanwhile the beggars in Paris objected to their internment in the hospital, and riots in the streets occurred between them and the guards. The populace was in sympathy with the beggars and helped them to escape and to hide.[15]

The Hôpital général in Paris, like other hospitals, was financed by endowments, gifts, legacies, foundations, special taxes, and municipal grants. Charitable institutions were exempt from taxes and had income from lotteries and the privilege of selling fish and game during the Lenten season.

Beginning in the sixteenth century, work relief was used on a substantial scale. Ateliers de charité [charity workshops] provided work for paupers, vagabonds, and other unemployed. Established first in Paris as an emergency measure, then in other large cities, these workshops in times of economic crisis and famine attracted large numbers of the poor from smaller towns and villages who were often desperate and turned to rioting and plundering. As a result, beginning in 1770, small charity workshops were set up in various parishes of each province. In some workshops new industries, such as carpet-making, spinning, and weaving, were introduced with the help of foreign instructors brought from England and Belgium.

The threat of famine, floods, contagious diseases, the bubonic plague, dysentery, typhus, smallpox, and scarlet fever, remained a serious health problem for France. In order to prevent riots grain, rice, beans, barley, and new seeds were distributed. A royal decree of 1709 gave general permission to anyone to cultivate untilled waste land and to harvest its crops, regardless of ownership.

---

15. Léon Lallemand, op. cit., IV, 356.

Contemporary writers described the appalling conditions of the poor in rural areas. Massillon in his book Carême observed in Sermon XXV, "Sur l'aumône": "Innumerable people died, literally, of hunger, and many more perished from disease caused by utter destitution" (1709). [16] In rural provinces peasants lived in dire poverty, without bedding or furniture, and farm hands were forced to live off grass and herbs like animals in the fields. [17] In some cities public kitchens served rice and soup to all the hungry.

Medical care played an important role in the development of charities during the seventeenth and eighteenth centuries in France. Frequent epidemics made it necessary to send doctors, pharmacists, and nurses to stricken regions. Louis XIV began to send annually to the provincial governments medicines and drugs for free distribution. The Royal Society of Medicine was founded in 1776, and aided in the fight against epidemics by giving advice to local physicians in the provinces. In order to prevent further epidemics, a royal order of May, 1776 directed that graves and cemeteries be removed from the floors of the churches and placed outside the city walls. The high mortality rate among mothers and infants induced the surgeons in the public hospitals to train midwives, and systematic courses were developed by Madame de Coudray. [18] The Hôtel des consultations charitables in Paris was a pioneer clinic where 20 physicians gave medical examinations, advice, and treatment free of charge to patients who were unable to pay.

In spite of medical progress, in asylums and hospitals five or six patients were placed in one bed though they suffered from different, sometimes contagious, diseases. Only patients

---

16. Le Duc de Saint-Simon, Mémoirs (Paris: Charnel, Hachette, 1864), IX, 334.

17. René Sand, The Advance to Social Medicine, p. 375; Camille Bloch, L'assistance et l'état en France à la veille de la Révolution (1764-1790) (Paris, 1908), p. 8.

18. René Sand, The Advance to Social Medicine, pp. 376-377.

afflicted with itch were isolated in a "pest hospital" ward. Bedding was changed infrequently, and inadequate ventilation, bathing and toilet facilities led to bitter criticism by the patients, their families, and other citizens. As a result, hospitals for general medical and surgical care were later separated from those for contagious diseases. In Paris, La Salpêtrière served at the same time as a detention home for delinquent and sick women and girls, as an orphanage for young boys, and as a central station for wet nurses; its 8,000 patients included old and blind people, crippled children, imbeciles, epileptics, paralytics, and the insane. During the second half of the eighteenth century, foundlings and orphans were farmed out to families in rural districts.[19] Boys were apprenticed; if they did not work well, they were discharged, often to get into bad company and to become criminals. Girls were taught cooking, spinning, weaving, and lace-making, and were hired out as domestic servants.

Prostitutes and patients with venereal diseases were forcibly committed to hospitals and held in cells behind iron-barred windows.[20]

CARE OF THE MENTALLY AND PHYSICALLY HANDICAPPED

The fate of the insane and mentally deficient was even more appalling. An asylum open to mentally ill patients from all provinces had been founded in Charenton by King Louis XIII in 1641 and was maintained as a national institution under changing governments,[21] but until the eighteenth century the treatment of

---

19. Ibid., pp. 381-384.

20. The statutes against prostitution in France began under Charlemagne; prostitutes later were placed in convents for penitent women. But many cities such as Toulouse, Montpelliers, and Avignon maintained prosperous brothels. In 1778, compulsory registration and medical examinations of prostitutes were instituted. Dérouin, op. cit., pp. 19-21.

21. Charles R. Henderson, Modern Methods of Charity (New York: Macmillan, 1904), p. 538.

the insane and the feeble-minded was as deplorable in France as in other countries at that time. The insane were usually placed in poorhouses, but some were put away in workhouses and even in prisons; others were in hospitals with chronically sick patients, old persons, children, vagrants, and prostitutes. Sometimes the unruly insane were detained in special wards or chained to the walls in cellars and dungeons. There was no medical treatment as a rule, but in a few hospitals in Paris a first attempt was made to cure mental diseases by cold and hot baths and by excessive blood-letting. In general, lunatic patients were kept locked day and night in cells, shackled or in strait-jackets. If they were violent or resisted orders, they were flogged, beaten, and starved.

The reform of this cruel treatment of the insane began through the initiative of Dr. Philippe Pinel[22] in the 1770's. He had been educated for the priesthood, but changed his studies to philosophy, science, and medicine, and became one of the leading physicians and the first psychiatrist of his time. While on the staff of a small hospital, Maison de santé belhomme, in spite of strong opposition from the other physicians in the hospital he advocated the abolition of the brutal mistreatment of the insane patients and introduced a therapy of nursing, diets, and occupation in simple types of work. In 1775, Pinel was appointed head physician of the mental hospital for women, La Salpêtrière in Paris, where he immediately changed the inhuman methods of treatment and introduced scientific studies of insanity. In October, 1793, after the victory of the Revolution, two of his personal friends became members of the board of hospitals in Paris and appointed him chief physician of the largest hospital for psychotic patients in Paris, La Bicêtre. There he applied the same methods he had used in La Salpêtrière; he immediately removed the chains from patients, many of whom were considered dangerous by other physicians and their attendants, but no violence occurred. He discontinued the excessive blood-letting

---

22. Shelby McCloy, op. cit., pp. 225-226; Albert Deutsch, The Mentally Ill in America (New York: Columbia University Press, 1949), pp. 88-92.

and drugging and developed a considerate, though firm, method of medical therapy which was called "traitement moral. "[23]

The fate of the feeble-minded in France was very similar to that of the insane until the end of the eighteenth century. If harmless, they remained with their families where they were often neglected and badly treated, hidden in barns, attics, or basements so that the neighbors would not see them and bring shame upon the family. Sometimes they were thought to be without human emotions and left in unheated rooms in the winter or with animals in the stables. Unruly feeble-minded persons were thrown into almshouses or jails, just as in our country before the reform initiated by Dorothea Dix in the nineteenth century. The first recorded attempt to influence and educate a feeble-minded person occurred in 1799, when Dr. Jean Marc Gaspard Itard, chief physician of the National Institute for the Deaf and Dumb in Paris, began to treat an idiot child. The boy had been found roaming like a little animal by hunters in the woods near Aveyron. Dr. Itard tried to educate the child, but he abandoned his experiment after five years when it was plainly unsuccessful. Other French physicians continued the endeavor to educate idiot children; most prominent among them were Dr. Ferret at La Bicêtre in 1828, and Dr. Fabret, in 1831, at La Salpêtrière. Two years later, in 1833, another physician, Dr. Voisier, opened a small private school for idiot children in Paris. These experiments were unsuccessful, but Dr. Edouard Seguin began to study the causes of mental deficiency and tried to determine what kind of training could be given to feeble-minded children. In 1837, he founded in Paris at his own expense a private institution, the Hospice des incurables, which aroused considerable attention. In 1844, he received a high commendation from the French Academy of Science, the Academy feeling that his methods gave serious promise for effective

---

23. It seems that similar methods had been used earlier by a Scotch physician, Alexander Hunter, at York in England, but they became known in France only in 1790 (McCloy, op. cit., p. 228). When Benjamin Rush, the "Father of American Psychiatry," came to Paris to study medical treatment of lunatics, he was greatly impressed and influenced by Pinel's work and personality. Dr. Rush brought Pinel's ideas and medical methods to Pennsylvania.

training of mentally deficient children. Dr. Seguin became widely known throughout Europe, and, in 1848, was invited to visit the United States where he became a missionary for the treatment and education of feeble-minded children. He addressed medical societies and several legislatures, and encouraged the establishment of special schools for mentally deficient children in Massachusetts, New York, Connecticut, Ohio, and Pennsylvania. [24]

In France, however, the high hopes that effective education of the feeble-minded would enable them to work and earn their own living were not realized. The most seriously afflicted group, the idiots, and the majority of the imbeciles remained so severely handicapped that they could not be safely returned to their families, and were unable to earn, even partially, their living.

Throughout the Middle Ages cripples represented a substantial proportion of recognized beggars. Because severely crippled persons, particularly children, aroused sympathy in the hearts of the passers-by, some parents or guardians mutilated children to use them as beggars. [25]

As early as 1784 the first school for the treatment of crippled children was founded in Paris as was, in 1853, a private orthopedic hospital. Other asylums for cripples were established by private charitable societies to give custodial care, but no attempt was made to rehabilitate and educate the patients or to make them self-supporting. No one recognized that the cripple's suffering is based not only upon his physical weakness and the handicap of his deformity, but also upon his feeling of inferiority, his continuous dependency, and the social attitude of superiority of his normal associates. [26]

---

24. Walter E. Fernald, "History of the Treatment of the Feebleminded," Proceedings of the 20th National Conference of Charities and Correction, 1893 (Boston), p. 203 ff.

25. Joan Rose Chusman, "Cripples," Encyclopedia of Social Sciences, IV, 593.

26. For present methods of rehabilitation in France see "Le reclassement professionnel des handicapés," Actualités sociales hebdomadaires, April 4, 1958; and Alfred Spire, "Le réclassement des dimunués physiques," Droit Social, 21, No. 3 (March, 1958), 158-162.

In the seventh century, a hospital for the blind had been established by Bishop St. Bertrand of Le Mans, and during the eleventh century William the Conqueror founded hospitals for the blind and the disabled at Cherbourg, Caen, Rouen, and Bayeux.[27] In the thirteenth and fourteenth centuries other private hospitals for blind patients were established at Chartres, Strasbourg, and Tournai, while religious orders and brotherhoods organized relief and care for blind people in their homes. The most noted institution for the blind in France, the Hospice national des quinze-vingts in Paris, was founded by King Louis IX in 1254.[28] It is reported that the king, deeply moved upon learning that a group of blind people had organized a mutual aid society, donated a house as a permanent asylum for the blind. Here a sizeable number of crusaders who had been captured and blinded by the Saracens were hospitalized. This hospital for blind patients in Paris still has its three hundred beds today, provides clinical treatment to out-patients, and serves as a consultation center for other hospitals outside the capital. (Blind persons who cannot be cared for by their own families are placed in general hospitals or in nursing homes or old-age institutions.)

The first attempt to educate the blind was made by Valentin Haüy (1743-1822), the son of a poor weaver, who had attended a monastic school and worked as an interpreter. After studying the work of the blind English mathematician Saunderson, he became interested in teaching the blind when he observed a group of blind musicians playing in a street coffee house in Paris. Following a method invented by a blind contemporary, Mlle de Sélignac, Haüy developed a system of characters in relief on paper. In 1784 he found a helpless blind 16-year-old boy, François Lesueur, begging in the street. Haüy taught him to read and speak, using his new system, and the child made rapid progress. In 1786 Haüy published his report, Essai sur l'education des aveugles,

---

27. McCloy, op. cit., p. 228.

28. "National Hospital of the Three Hundred," which the king gave to blind persons, not merely to blinded crusaders as the legend has it.

and a group of citizens became interested and asked him to
teach 12 blind children at the school of the Philanthropic Society
in Paris. Lesueur soon became an instructor on the faculty of this
same school. The children were taught several disciplines, the
main emphasis being on music, for which the children showed
a particular gift.[29] In 1790, due to financial difficulties, the
school was combined with that for the deaf-mutes, and Valentin
Haüy was appointed director of both. The merger of the schools
and the lack of funds, however, seriously endangered progress
in the education of the blind. In 1791, Haüy succeeded in per-
suading the Constituent Assembly to designate all needy blind
children as "wards of the nation."

In 1825, Charles Barbier invented a system of cells with
12 points to represent in various combinations the letters of
the alphabet. This system was simplified in 1829 by Louis
Braille, a blind young instructor at the school for the blind in
Paris. Braille's method consisted of a raised type of script
which the children could learn to write as well as read and which
now has been accepted in most countries of the world.[30] Other
schools for the blind operate at Nancy, Lille, Marseilles, Lyons,
Arras, Soissons, Poitiers, and Saint-Hyppolyte (Gard). Initially
they were private schools, maintained with public subsidies; but
since the General Education Act of April 15, 1909, they have
been administered by the government, and all blind children in
France are entitled to free special education.[31] In the sixteenth
century, a Spanish Benedictine, Don Pedro Ponce, educated a few
deaf-mute children and gained a reputation for his skill, but

---

29. The studies included reading, writing, grammar, arithmetic, history,
geography, music, spinning, ribbon-weaving, ropemaking, leather-work, and
book binding, and the school was chartered a national public school for the blind
in 1789 (McCloy, op. cit., p. 432).

30. Louis Braille, born in 1809, was admitted to the school in 1819, and became an instructor in 1827, at the age of 18.

31. See also Pierre Henri, L'Adaption des deficients visuels à la vie sociale et
professionnelle (Paris: Service de documentation pour la réadaption professionnelle,
1957).

it was not until the eighteenth century that the first scientific method of teaching deaf children was developed by Jacob Rodriges Pereire in Bordeaux. He devoted his life to this task and achieved remarkable results. In 1750 he submitted a report describing his methods of instructing deaf-mute children to the Royal Academy of Science which received great attention. He worked with his students individually, not in groups.[32] In 1760 the Abbé Charles Michel de l'Epée (1712-1788), utilizing Pereire's method and with the aid of his brother, founded the first school for deaf-mute children in Paris. In a few years the school had gained international fame. Although originally maintained from the personal property of the founders, tuition fees, and private donations, the Abbé's school has received subsidies from the national government since 1785. Pupils of Charles de l'Epée established similar schools at Angers and Bordeaux, and, later, in various countries of Europe.[33]

THE PERIOD OF THE REVOLUTION

Private religious charities played a very important role in caring for the poor and the sick until the time of the Revolution. In spite of tensions between church and secular authorities, the churches received large donations and distributed alms to the poor. Clergymen remained influential members of boards of hospitals, asylums, and schools. Religious orders administered the entire field of home nursing, smaller hospitals, and asylums. Fraternal orders and mutual aid societies assisted their members and families in times of need, and some philanthropic societies gave relief to orphans, prisoners and their families, and to unmarried mothers.[34]

The Revolution of 1789 started the third period of charities in France. Montesquieu, Diderot, Voltaire, and Rousseau advocated

---

32. McCloy, op. cit., p. 429; René Sand, op. cit., p. 410.

33. McCloy, op. cit., p. 431.

34. Ibid., pp. 448-455; the first non-denominational "société philanthropique" in Paris was founded in 1780.

as a political philosophy that the state should guarantee its citizens personal freedom and dignity, and should assume the responsibility for the support of the destitute. The principles of the French Revolution included human equality, liberty, and justice; poverty should be abolished by social reform. They promised opportunity for work and education, and attempted a program of public assistance for those unable to work. [35] As the church and the clergy were closely linked with the royal regime, religious institutions suffered together with the nobility, and the institutions and church property were confiscated. Meanwhile, the National Assembly pronounced society responsible for the relief of the poor and sick and established the following fundamental program: [36]

1. Because poor relief is a national debt, hospitals, foundations, and endowments for the poor shall be sold for the profit of the nation;

2. Society has to provide maintenance for destitute citizens at the place of their residence either by employment or by granting the means of support for those unable to work;

3. Medical care for the population shall be secured by a licensed physician serving in each cantonal district;

4. Parents who are financially unable to support their children shall receive public aid from the nation.

The internment of the poor in almshouses and hospitals was to be abandoned, and outdoor relief given to the poor in their homes, administered by a bureau de bienfaisance [welfare bureau].

However, the political unrest of the Revolution and the subsequent wars did not permit the realization of these principles. In

---

35. Jean Pillu, L'organisation de l'administration générale de l'assistance publique à Paris (Paris: Sirey, 1934), p. 17.

36. René Sand, Le Service social, pp. 73, 86; Camille Bloch, op. cit. pp. 46-51.

In 1792, a severe famine broke out and forced the Revolutionary government to confiscate all grain not needed for seed, and to control its sale from storage houses.[37]

In 1794 the property of religious hospitals, orphanages, and asylums was "nationalized, " their endowments were confiscated, and local customs dues and indirect taxes which had been the main resource for the maintenance of hospitals and charitable institutions were abolished; deprived of their revenues they could no longer care for their patients and residents. But the communities had no resources to finance public relief, and many did not succeed in setting up any relief administration at all. In 1796, therefore, the confiscated church property was given over to lay hospitals and asylums, and in 1800 the old taxes were restored in order to finance them. National subsidies for the support of the destitute in their own homes made it possible to maintain some municipal outdoor relief.

The government also attempted to improve medical care and public health conditions, organizing free courses in midwifery and maternal care, and sending surgeons, physicians, nurses, and hospital attendants into regions suffering from epidemics. In 1799, physicians Pinel and Aubert introduced vaccination with the aid of the British medical authority, Dr. Woodville, who came to Paris for the purpose despite the war between England and France. Nurses visited the homes of the sick, and new hospitals were built.

In 1811, an important change in poor relief practice was introduced by Napoleon with the establishment of the Assistance publique, a uniform public assistance administration. Under the direction of the Ministry of the Interior, each département set up a division of public assistance. Home relief to the poor was rendered by a local bureau de bienfaisance [welfare bureau].[38] The standard of poor relief varied among the different communities and

---

37. McCloy, op. cit., pp. 46-48; Camille Bloch, op. cit., p. 63.

38. Before the Revolution, most communities had a parish bureau de charité [poor relief committee] with the local priest as chairman. Dupin, op. cit., pp. 17-24.

provinces. Local communities refused relief to non-residents, but Napoleon established dépôts de mendicité [workhouses for vagrants] in several cities.

After the restitution of the royal regime under the Directoire, the religious orders expelled by the Revolution were recalled and their hospitals, almshouses, orphanages, and asylums returned to them. In the local communities biens des pauvres [poor-relief chests] gave relief to the poor. Public control over religious charities, however, still continued, and lay commissions appointed by the municipal and departmental councils supervised hospitals, asylums, and orphanages.

In 1851, the first monts-de-piété [philanthropic loan societies] were founded. They gave loans to self-employed persons impoverished by sickness, accidents, or misfortune, in order that they might become self-supporting again. After investigation, loans were granted without security, with moderate interest rates and easy terms of repayment in installments.

During the Middle Ages, craft guilds and merchant associations in France played a less important role than in England and Germany. Commercial insurance companies were founded at the beginning of the nineteenth century, and in 1850 voluntary insurance companies received legal status. At the same time sociétés de secours mutuelles [mutual-aid societies] were established among workers on the basis of their trade and industrial affiliation or neighborhood. They provided benefits to members and their families in case of sickness, accidents, unemployment, maternity, and old age, and were often supported by public subsidies. On a national scale the sociétés were recognized as privileged, non-profit institutions by a law of April 1, 1898.

ILLEGITIMATE CHILDREN AND CHILD LABOR

Until the Revolution, there was widespread discrimination against illegitimate children in France. Except for one special home for them in Paris, orphanages and foundling asylums refused to receive children born out of wedlock. However, in 1793, a statute of the Revolutionary Assembly changed the official attitude and provided that these children, as "natural children of the fatherland, " should receive the same public aid as needy legitimate children. The Code Napoleon prohibited the search for the father of an illegitimate child, with the result that the child and his mother usually could not get financial support from the father for the child's education and maintenance even if the mother was without means. This legal provision was abolished in 1922; it is now possible to search for the father, file a paternity suit, and force him to support the child.

With the beginning of industrialization in France at the end of the eighteenth century, children were employed in workshops, mills, and mining industries. Although children had worked in agriculture earlier, their widespread use and exploitation in industry made protective child-labor legislation necessary. The first such provision was a decree of 1813, prohibiting the employment of children under ten years of age in the underground galleries of mines.[39] However, no minimum age was established for the employment of children in any other type of work, nor any limit set on working hours although the usual working day in industry was 14 hours. In all types of manufacturing and craft work, children as young as seven and occasionally even four and five years old were employed.

The Factory Law of March 22, 1841, the first attempt to regulate working time, limited the daily working hours to eight for children between eight and 12 years of age, and to 12 for children 12 to 16 years old, but applied only to workshops and factories using mechanical power (water or steam) or continuous furnaces, or employing 20 or more workers. Employment of children under eight was no longer permitted in factories and industrial shops, and night work was prohibited for children under 13. A certification of the child's age was issued by local civil authorities, but children under 12 had to attend school, and no Sunday or holiday work was allowed for those under 16 years

---

39. Decree of January 3, 1813. The preceding English statute of 1802, "Act for the Preservation of the Health and Morals of Apprentices and Others Employed in Cotton and Other Mills," limited the working hours, but had not required an age limit, even for children working in the underground mines. (Gaston Chauderlot, De La Protection légale des Enfants et des Adolescents [Paris, 1911], p. 14.)

of age.[40] Unfortunately, the provisions of the law of 1841 were rarely enforced. In most départements no inspectors for the supervision of child labor were employed, and no national funds were allocated for the administration of the law. The population remained indifferent, and many workers' families were hostile to the statute because they saw in it only an attempt to deprive them of their children's earnings.

After the Franco-Prussian War of 1870-1871, however, more effective protection was secured by a new Factory Law of May 19, 1874, which prohibited the employment of children under ten in several branches of industry, factories, and workshops, and of boys under 12 and all girls and women in the subterranean galleries of mines and quarries. Dangerous and unhealthy occupations were prohibited for children under 16. The law provided for the appointment of factory inspectors and mining inspectors by the national government, and children needed a municipal work permit before they could be employed.

THE PERIOD OF THE THIRD AND FOURTH REPUBLICS

In the Franco-Prussian War of 1870-1871 heavy losses in manpower through death and injuries caused social problems; the country had suffered from the destruction of fields and factories and through military occupation. In the aftermath of the war, the lack of housing and disrupted agricultural and industrial production demanded a more effective system of health and welfare services.[41] A national commission examined the relief system and found that the local bureaux de bienfaisance lacked uniformity of standards and policies. In 1886, a national board, the Directoire de l'assistance publique [Directorate of Public Assistance], was established to supervise and coordinate all branches of relief.

---

40. The English Factory Act of 1833 protected only children under nine in textile mills. A wider range of factories was not reached until the Factory Act of 1844 in England, but the inadequate enforcement of both the English and French statutes made the value of their provisions questionable.

41. Léon Lallemand, op. cit., Vol. I, Chapter 4.

Two years later, in 1888, this board was enlarged and renamed the Conseil supérieur de l'assistance publique [Superior Council of Public Assistance]. It was composed of 60 members, including experts in the field of charitable work and representatives of government agencies. The main policies developed by the Conseil were: public aid was to be given to indigent persons only if they had no other resources; it was to be administered and financed by local authorities. Classified as groups in particular need were orphans, abandoned children, the insane, the aged, the infirm, and the sick. Surveys of the Conseil supérieur revealed that the aged and infirm were often neglected and did not receive adequate care, especially in rural regions.

The first notable result of the findings was that Parliament recognized the need for a reform of medical care. In 1893, it passed the Loi nationale de l'assistance médicale gratuite [National Law for Free Medical Assistance], providing for medical treatment and hospitalization for patients unable to pay for those services, although not in other financial distress. This law was the first of its kind in Europe: it meant a definite departure from the old concepts of the poor laws; it created the category of medically needy persons. The payment for medical examination, treatment, surgery, hospitalization, and medicines in France differed from the health insurance measures in Germany and Austria; the French practice did not include indemnity payments in addition to medical care provided under health insurance programs. The aid offered to the medically needy preceded by decades similar practices for patients of low income in the United States.

The network of public relief agencies in the country was expanded, and new national regulations led to more uniform relief practices. The local bureaux de bienfaisance gave outdoor relief and paid the expenses for medical care. The administration of hospitals, orphanages, and asylums remained separate from the welfare bureaus; they were managed by their own boards and supervised by the département. [42]

---

42. The département is in size of population comparable to the county in England and the United States, but has a greater autonomy in administrative and personnel matters.

In contrast to the other départements, in Paris charitable institutions and hospitals, medical assistance, and outdoor relief were administered by one single agency, the Assistance publique centrale. Its Comité de surveillance [Supervisory Committee] was composed of 33 members appointed by the Minister of the Interior. [43]

The centuries-old tension between the church and the government in the fields of education and charity culminated in the constitutional amendment on the separation of church and state in 1904. It brought fundamental changes in the relationship between the numerous religious charities and the public relief authorities. Until this time, the expenses for charitable institutions, hospitals, and asylums had been subsidized by government authorities. The salaries of the priests and clergy who administered charitable institutions were paid from tax funds. These subsidies were now withdrawn. Several religious orders left the country, and departmental governments had to take over the management and the financing of hospitals and asylums. In spite of these changes, however, private social agencies, both sectarian and non-sectarian, are still numerous and play an important role in the field of social welfare in France.

During the First World War relief activities conducted by American social agencies, particularly the American Red Cross, brought professionally trained social workers to France. They emphasized the value of social investigations, diagnosis, and environmental and personal adjustment. Some French social agencies became interested in the establishment of casework services. The first agency, Le Service social pour l'enfance en danger moral, was set up in Paris in 1923 with the help of an American social worker, Miss Chloe Owing. For years it played a pioneer role in the French casework field. The training of social workers in schools of social work after the First World War made it possible for an increasing number of agencies to employ a professional staff. More recently, public

---

43. Jean Pillu, op. cit., Chapters 2 and 3.

relief agencies and institutions have followed the example of private organizations and employ trained social workers.

The Second World War again brought a period of severe devastation and deprivation. The deportation of millions of soldiers as prisoners of war and forced laborers to Germany, the destruction and evacuation of battle areas, and the interruption of the economic and political life of the nation created the severest problems. [44] After the war, the social services faced a most difficult task and played an essential role in the recovery of the nation.

SELECTED BIBLIOGRAPHY

Balch, Emily Greene. "Public Assistance of the Poor in France " Publications of the American Economic Association, Vol. VIII, Nos. 4 and 5. Baltimore, July and September, 1893.

Bloch, Camille. L'assistance et l'état en France à la veille de la Révolution (1764-1790). Paris, 1908.

Brinton, Crane. French Revolutionary Legislation on Illegitimacy, 1789-1804. Cambridge, Mass.: Harvard University Press, 1036.

Dérouin, H., A. Gory and F. Worms. Traité thèorique et pratique d'assistance publique. Paris, 1900.

Dupin, Baron. Histoire de l'administration des secours publics, ou analyse historique de la législation des secours publics. Paris, 1821.

Ferdinand - Dreyfuss, F. L'Assistance sous la Législative et la Convention, 1791-1795. Paris, 1905.

Gérando, Baron de. De la bienfaisance publique. Paris: Renouard, 1839.

Henderson, Charles Richmond. Modern Methods of Charity, An Account of the Systems of Relief, Public and Private, in the Principal Countries Having Modern Methods. New York: Macmillan, 1904.

Lallemand, Léon. Histoire de la Charité. Paris, 1910-1912.

44. Jacques Parisot, Le Comité Français de Service social: Historique de son action (Nancy: Berger-Levrault, 1947), pp. 40-64.

Laporte, André. L'Assistance publique et privée en France. Paris: Librairies Techniques, 1952.

Maclean, Annie Marion. "France, " in Charles R. Henderson, Modern Methods of Charity, supra, pp. 512-535.

McCloy, Shelby T. Government Assistance in Eighteenth Century France. Durham, N. C. : Duke University Press, 1946.

Matthews, Ronald. The Death of the Fourth Republic. New York: Praeger, 1954.

Parisot, Jacques (ed.) Le Comité Français de service social: Historique de son action. Nancy: Berger-Levrault, 1947.

Pasquier, L. "L'assistance publique, " La Grande Encyclopedie, Vol. IV. Paris, 1937.

Pillu, Jean. L'organisation de l'administration générale de l'assistance publique à Paris. Paris: Sirey, 1934.

Sand, René. L'économie humaine par la médecine sociale. Paris: Rieder, 1934 (2nd ed., 1941).

_____. Le Service social à travers le monde: Assistance, prévoyance, hygiène. Paris: Armand Colin, 1931.

Recalde, Abbé de. Abrégé Historique des hôpitaux. Paris: Guillot, 1784.

Tollet, C. Les édifices hospitaliers depuis l'origine jusqu'à nos jours, De l'assistance publique et des hôpitaux. Paris, 1892.

Wells, Carlotta. "Social Work in France, " Social Service Review, I, No. 4 (December, 1927), 537-556.

Wickwar, W. Hardy. "The Welfare Map of Europe, " Social Service Review, XX, No. 2 (June, 1946), 141-149.

CHAPTER 2 THE ORGANIZATION AND
PROGRAM
OF SOCIAL WELFARE
AND HEALTH SERVICES

ORGANIZATIONAL STRUCTURE

In France, as in most industrial countries today, social security is provided by three major social service programs.[1] The first is a system of family allowances, social insurance, and various pensions guaranteed as a legal right to all persons eligible under statutory provisions. The second program includes public assistance of categorical and general nature provided by local and departmental authorities to persons in economic and medical need.[2] The third comprises health and welfare services under public and private auspices designed to protect the entire population against ill health, the spread of communicable diseases, and emotional and social maladjustment; it is designed to improve the standard of living and to insure the healthy development of children and young people.

---

1. The analysis in this chapter emphasizes the health and welfare services under governmental auspices, but the activities of private social agencies are closely connected with public services.

2. The delineation between social security and public assistance is not agreed upon in French social theory. Some writers are convinced that a distinction between the various categories of social security will be abandoned in the future; see André Laporte, L'assistance publique et privée en France (Paris: Libraries Techniques, 1952), p. 3.

The great devastation of World War II, with the occupation of the country by German armies and the division of loyalty between the Vichy government and the Resistance movement, severely affected the social fabric of France. The people suffered not only the military defeat and surrender of their armies, war injuries, mass internment, and diseases, but also malnutrition and poverty.[3] The healing and reconstruction process required economic recovery and social and health services for the stricken population.

The present territory of France covers an area of about 212,000 square miles, approximately the same as the states of California and Washington combined. Its population of about 44 million lives in 38,014 communities and includes only minor linguistic and ethnic minorities: the Bretons, Provençals, the Germans in the Saar and Alsace, and the Catalans and Basques in the Pyrenees. The population is divided about equally between rural and urban dwellers. Income from gainful employment or self-employment is derived from:[4]

Agriculture, forestry, and fisheries	28.9%
Industry	34.9%
Commerce	13.9%
Professions and public service	11.8%
Transportation services	4.7%
Nursing and domestic service	5.0%
Unknown occupations	0.8%

The total labor force is about 20 million persons, of whom 66.3 per cent are workers and employees, 20.6 per cent employers

---

3. Other destructive forces against the economy and national spirit of France after the end of World War II were the Communist strikes and sabotage, the fight between the trade unions, and the shameless exploitation of the population by the greed of merchants and shopkeepers. Ronald Matthews, The Death of the Fourth Republic (New York: Praeger, 1954), pp. 244-257.

4. Annuaire Statistique de la France, 1956 (Paris: Imprimérie Nationale, 1957), p. 4.

and self-employed persons, and 13.1 per cent unpaid members of the family of the second group.[5]

Only 28 cities have a population of 100,000 or more inhabitants, but 31,000 small villages have less than 1,000. Of the total working population, 56 per cent receive wages or salaries; less than one-half of the urban population works for others, while the majority are independent merchants, shopkeepers, salesmen, craftsmen, artisans, or professionals. Among the rural population the majority are farmers on their own small holdings, particularly in the South, or are share-tenants obliged to give one-half of their products to the landlord.

Following an old tradition, public administration in France is highly centralized. The country is divided into 16 regions and 89 départements. The regional districts, comprising five to seven départements, have mainly coordinating and supervisory functions for communication and administrative planning. The essential functions of administration of social welfare are performed by the départements and the communities. The prefects [governors] of each region and of each département are appointed by the President of the Republic upon the recommendation of the Minister of the Interior. The subdivisions of the départements -- 281 arrondissements and 3,028 cantons, as well as cities and towns, enjoy within their local jurisdiction marked rights of self-government.

Civil service plays an important role in the social services in France.[6] It dominates, as a unified system, the central administration of the national government, as well as the regional, departmental, and municipal public services. Civil service officials are appointed on the basis of competitive examinations. They enjoy, after a probationary period, the advantages of positions with tenure, the probability of regular

---

5. United Nations, Report on the World Social Situation: West European Social Conditions (New York, 1957), p. 94, Table 2.

6. P. Chatenet, "The Civil Service in France," in William A. Robson, The Civil Service in Britain and France (London: The Hogarth Press, 1956), pp. 161-169. The statute on civil service of October 19, 1946 grants trade-union rights to civil servants.

CHART   STRUCTURE OF HEALTH AND WELFARE
I   SERVICES IN FRANCE

MINISTERE DE SANTE PUBLIQUE ET DE POPULATION
[Ministry of Public Health and Population]

DIVISION CENTRAL
LEGISLATIVE SERVICE / BUDGET / PERSONNEL POLICY

DIRECTOIRE D'HYGIENE
PUBLIQUE ET DES HOPITAUX
[Directorate of Public Hygiene and Hospitals]
PUBLIC HEALTH SERVICES / CONTROL OF DISEASE
/ CONTROL OF ALCOHOLISM /
CONTROL OF PROSTITUTION

DIRECTOIRE DE POPULATION
ET D'ASSISTANCE PUBLIQUE
[Directorate of Population &Public Assistance]
POPULATION MOVEMENT/NATURALIZATION/SOCIAL
WELFARE POLICIES/PUBLIC HOUSING/PUBLIC SUBSIDIES
/ COORDINATION WITH PRIVATE SOCIAL AGENCIES

DIRECTION REGIONALE
D'HYGIENE PUBLIQUE ET
DES HOPITAUX [Regional Public
Hygiene and Hospital Administration]
ADMINISTRATIVE SUPERVISION of HEALTH SERVICES

DIRECTION REGIONALE DE
POPULATION ET D'ASSISTANCE
PUBLIQUE [Regional Population
and Public Assistance Administration]
ADMINISTRATIVE SUPERVISION of WELFARE SERVICES

DIRECTION DEPARTEMENTALE D'HYGIENE PUBLIQUE
[Departmental Public Hygiene Administration]

DIVISION DEPARTEMENTALE
D'HYGIENE PUBLIQUE ET DES
HOPITAUX [Departmental Division
of Public Hygiene and Hospitals]
ADMINISTRATION OF HOSPITALS AND PUBLIC
INSTITUTIONS / SUPERVISION OF MUNICIPAL
HEALTH SERVICES / VITAL STATISTICS

DIVISION DEPARTEMENTALE DE
POPULATION ET D'ASSISTANCE
PUBLIQUE [Departmental Division of
Population and Public Assistance]
ADMINISTRATION OF PROVINCIAL INSTITUTIONS
(OLD-AGE HOMES, ASYLUMS, ETC.) / SUPERVISION
OF MUNICIPAL WELFARE SERVICES

Local (Municipal) Administration

BUREAU D'HYGIENE PUBLIQUE
[Bureau of Public Hygiene (local health office)]
CONTROL of COMMUNICABLE DISEASE and EPIDEMICS
/ SANITARY CONTROLS / CONTROL of ALCOHOLISM /
VACCINATIONS

BUREAU D'AIDE SOCIALE
[Bureau of Social Aid (public welfare dept.)]
GENERAL AND CATEGORICAL PUBLIC ASSISTANCE
/ CHILD WELFARE SERVICES /
AID TO LARGE FAMILIES / INSTITUTIONAL CARE

CHART   FUNCTIONS OF THE BUREAU D'AIDE SOCIALE
II   (Municipal Bureau of Social Aid [Public Welfare Dept.])

MUNICIPAL COUNCIL
Office of the Director of the Bureau of Social Aid

CATEGORICAL
PUBLIC ASSISTANCE
OLD-AGE ASSISTANCE
/ DISABILITY ASSISTANCE /
MEDICAL ASSISTANCE
/ AID TO DEPENDENT CHILDREN /
MATERNITY ASSISTANCE

SPECIAL
TYPES OF ASSISTANCE
GENERAL INDIGENT AID
/ AID TO LARGE FAMILIES /
BIRTH PREMIUMS
/ NURSING BONUSES /
OTHER MATERNITY BENEFITS

CHILD WELFARE
SERVICES
CASEWORK IN FAMILY / FOSTER-
FAMILY CARE / CHILDREN'S HOMES
/ ADOPTION SERVICES / TEMPORARY
CARE FOR CHILDREN / PERMANENT
CARE FOR CHILDREN

**CHART III
ORGANIZATIONAL STRUCTURE OF
SOCIAL SECURITY IN FRANCE**

MINISTERE DE TRAVAIL ET DE SECURITE SOCIALE
[Ministry of Labor and Social Security]

CONSEIL SUPERIEUR
DE SECURITE SOCIALE
[Superior Council of Social
Security (Advisory Board)]

COMITE TECHNIQUE
D'HYGIENE ET
DES SERVICES SOCIAUX
[Technical Committee of
Hygiene & Social Services]

DIRECTOIRE GENERALE DE SECURITE SOCIALE
[General Directorate of Social Security]

DIRECTION des ASSURANCES SOCIALES [Social Insurance Administration]	DIRECTION des ASSURANCES DE MALADIES [Workmen's Compensation Administration]	CONSEIL SUPERIEUR DES ALLOCATIONS FAMILIALES [Superior Council of Family Allowances]
NATIONAL SUPERVISION / REGULATIONS / APPROVAL OF VOLUNTARY UNEMPLOYMENT INSURANCE PLANS	NATIONAL SUPERVISION / REGULATIONS / ACCIDENT PREVENTION	NATIONAL SUPERVISION / LEGISLATION / REGULATIONS

FONDS JOINT D'ACTION
[Joint Action Fund]

DIRECTION REGIONALE DE SECURITE SOCIALE
[Regional Social Security Administration]

CONSEIL REGIONAL
DE SECURITE SOCIALE
[Regional Council of Social
Security (Advisory Board)]

CAISSE REGIONALE DE SECURITE SOCIALE [Regional Social Security Fund]	CAISSE REGIONALE DES ASSURANCES DE MALADIES INDUSTRIELLES [Regional Workmen's Compensation Administration]	CONSEIL REGIONAL DES ALLOCATIONS FAMILIALES [Regional Council of Family Allowances]
ADMINISTRATION OF REGIONAL BENEFITS / SUPERVISION OF PROVINCIAL (DEPARTMENTAL) BENEFITS	ASSESSMENT, COLLECTION AND DISTRIBUTION OF HEALTH BENEFITS	SUPERVISION OF PROVINCIAL (DEPARTMENTAL) FAMILY ALLOWANCES

DIRECTION DEPARTEMENTALE DE SECURITE SOCIALE
[Departmental Social Security Administration]

CAISSE PRIMAIRE DE SECURITE SOCIALE [Primary Social Security Fund]	CAISSE PRIMAIRE D'ASSURANCE DE MALADIES INDUSTRIELLES [Primary Workmen's Compensation Fund]	CONSEIL DEPARTEMENTAL DES ALLOCATIONS FAMILIALES [Departmental Council of Family Allowances]
OLD-AGE AND DISABILITY INSURANCE BENEFITS / HEALTH AND MATERNITY INSURANCE BENEFITS / NATIONAL SOLIDARITY FUND / SUBSIDIES TO UNEMPLOYMENT INSURANCE PLANS / SOCIAL SERVICE DIVISION	INDEMNITY BENEFITS / REHABILITATION SERVICES	PUBLIC FAMILY ALLOWANCE FUNDS / PRIVATE EQUALIZATION FUNDS

advancement in rank and salary, and life pensions after retirement. Unfortunately, the tenure position of civil servants
sometimes causes an apathetic attitude toward the public and a
lack of flexibility that is detrimental to effective performance.

THE ADMINISTRATION OF SOCIAL SERVICES AND PUBLIC HEALTH

On the national level, the administration of the social insurances and family allowances is under the jurisdiction of the
Ministère de travail et de sécurité sociale [Ministry of Labor
and Social Security], while public assistance, health, and welfare
services are under the jurisdiction of the Ministère de santé
publique et de population [Ministry of Public Health and Popula-
tion]. Legislation, rules, and regulations are the same for the
entire country, but individual benefit rates in public assistance
and services vary according to local conditions and standards
of living. The Directoire d'hygiène publique et des hôpitaux
[Directorate of Public Hygiene and Hospitals] establishes the
principles and regulations for public health measures; the control
of tuberculosis, cancer, venereal diseases, alcoholism, and
prostitution; the standards for hospitals and clinics; and the
control of drugs and medicines. The Directoire de population
et d'assistance publique [Directorate of Population and Public
Assistance] is in charge of population movements, of naturaliza-
tion, and of social welfare policies. A special section of this
division develops principles for cooperation between private and
public health and welfare services, and for government subsidies
to private social agencies.

The regional authorities and the départements supervise
the operations of the bureaux d'aide sociale and of public and
private local social institutions (such as orphanages, homes for
the aged, and children's asylums). Cities and towns administer
general relief.

Until 1953 the administration of public assistance was divided
between two agencies, the Bureau d'assistance publique [Public
Assistance Bureau] and the Bureau de bienfaisance [Welfare
Bureau]. The Bureau d'assistance publique administered categorical assistance to the aged and sick and to needy children. The

Bureau de bienfaisance provided general assistance (indigent aid) and applicants were referred to private agencies whenever possible.

Where there was no Bureau de bienfaisance, the Bureau d'assistance publique also gave general relief to applicants. The existence of two local social agencies in the field of public assistance with overlapping functions was expensive, and led to rivalries and confusion.[7] In 1953, the two categories of local welfare offices were merged. The combined agency is now called the Bureau d'aide sociale [Bureau of Social Aid]; it receives applications for assistance, and administers financial help, medical care, and aid in health and personality difficulties. It cooperates with private social agencies whose initiative it encourages.

People in economic need are eligible for public assistance if their property, income, and resources, including support from relatives, are insufficient to maintain them. Pensions, allowances to war veterans, and family allowances are not dependent upon financial need.

SOCIAL ASSISTANCE TO PERSONS IN NEED

Since the French Revolution, aid to indigent persons has been considered primarily the responsibility of government. Private social agencies either supplement public financial assistance or help persons not eligible for public aid, such as non-residents and foreigners. Today the fundamental principles and standards of social assistance are established by national legislation and regulations. In the framework of these provisions, the local conseil municipal [municipal council] determines the procedure and the scale of assistance to individuals and families in economic distress. The amount of assistance considered necessary to

---

7. André Berthet, Le Problème de l'assistance et le rôle social des bureaux de bienfaisance (Lyon: L'Effort, 1935), p. 114.

maintain the applicant is determined by the bureau d'aide sociale after an investigation of the client's circumstances. The applicant must first use his own resources before he is entitled to public relief. All income from property, annuities, or gainful work is deducted. Small savings and casual income, especially of persons over 70, are disregarded in order to preserve the applicant's self-respect. As thrift is highly regarded in French culture, it is not considered good policy to force applicants to exhaust their small savings entirely. Financial aid granted by private social agencies is usually given with the aim of supplementing public relief; charity aid is therefore not deducted from public assistance payments, a practice different from that of some American welfare departments.

If the client is dissatisfied, he may appeal to the municipal council, and against the council's decision to a cantonal "appeal commission." Relief is usually granted in cash, but some social aid bureaus and private agencies render relief in kind, dispensing food, clothes, and fuel.

The financial burden of general relief is placed upon the local community, [8] as in some states in the United States. The funds for general relief are derived from three sources: 1) a general poor-law tax; 2) local revenues and taxes on theaters, movies, concerts, dance halls, other amusement facilities, and cemetery concessions; and 3) bequests and donations by individuals and foundations. An important factor in the prevention of destitution are associations familiales [family associations] and mutualitées familiales [self-help cooperatives] in France, organizations of family groups in the same neighborhood, of the same trade, occupation, or profession, or sometimes of members of a labor union. [9] They encourage social legislation, set up low-price consumers' stores, non-profit loan societies, community

---

8. André Laporte, op. cit., Fasc. 225, p. 10; Emile Graille, Services publics d'Assistance (Paris: Receuil Sirey, 1947).

9. Robert Garric, Réponse Française à VIIe Conférence Internationale de Service Social (Toronto, 1954), pp. 6-8.

centers, and legal aid services which save their members from economic dependency.

CATEGORICAL PUBLIC ASSISTANCE

As the local community has the responsibility for the support of indigent persons, some small towns are unable to raise adequate funds from taxes for social assistance without support from higher levels of government.[10] National legislation, there-fore, created a program of categorical public assistance which is financed by the national government, the département, and the local community. Eligible for this categorical public assistance are:

1. aged, disabled, and incurable persons without old-age or disability insurance benefits;
2. needy sick persons without health insurance benefits;
3. women before and after confinement, and large families without family allowances;
4. needy nursing mothers and their infants; and
5. orphans, and abandoned and other needy children.

This program is broader than the categorical public assistance scheme in the United States which is limited to needy aged, blind, or totally and permanently disabled persons, and to dependent children living with their family or relatives. The French plan of categorical aid comprises the "medically needy" -- women before and after childbirth, families with numerous children, nursing mothers, and children in foster homes or children's institutions.

An application for categorical assistance is directed to the local bureau d'aide sociale. The applicant must have lived in the community long enough to establish residence [domicile de secours]. A national fund covers payments to applicants who

---

10. In the United States only some states carry the entire financial burden of general relief or indigent aid; the others share the cost with counties and cities or leave the responsibility to the local government unit alone.

have not resided long enough in any département. Minimum and maximum monthly payments are determined by national statutes and regulations.

Categorical assistance is given in money payments to the recipients in their own homes, but may be given on request in the form of hospitalization or placement in a home for the aged or a nursing home. Aged and disabled persons may live with foster families.

In large cities, municipal hospitals and homes for the aged or the chronically ill are administered by boards of trustees; their budget is established by the municipal council. Communities which have no institutional facilities provide care for their citizens by contract with another city or the département.

Public asylums, hospitals, and children's homes are usually financed by the département, which also supervises private charity institutions.

In Paris, however, the entire field of public welfare services is unified under the Administration générale de l'assistance publique [General Public Assistance Administration]. The director is assisted by an advisory board of ten municipal counselors. Each of the 20 arrondissements of Paris has a branch bureau d'aide sociale which differs from other local bureaus in that no representatives of private social agencies serve on its board, but only members of the conseil municipal of the arrondissement. They administer both general relief and categorical assistance, and control hospitals, asylums for the aged, infirm, and handicapped, orphanages, day-nurseries, and dispensaries in their arrondissement.

AID TO THE AGED, INFIRM, AND INCURABLE

The first type of categorical assistance in France is aid to the aged and infirm. [11] Eligible are needy French citizens of either

---

11. The percentage of the aged is very high in France. There is one person over 65 to every six in the total population, compared to one in every seven in England and Sweden, eight in the United States, and 15 in Russia. Léon Buquet, "La situation démographique," Revue d'Economie Politique, 67 (July-October, 1957), 403-405.

sex over 65 years of age or permanently disabled and unable to support themselves. Eligibility requires five years' uninterrupted residence either in the community or in the département where the application is filed. Women are entitled to old-age assistance at the age of 60 if they have reared five children to the age of 16 years.[12] Old-age assistance is paid in the form of a monthly cash allowance by the bureau d'aide sociale. Standard rates are determined by the conseil municipal but need the approval of the departmental Conseil général. The bureau d'aide sociale considers local conditions and the resources of the applicant in order to permit the old person some comfort.[13] When the aged or infirm person has no home of his own or is unable to care for himself, the bureau places him, with his consent, with a foster family or in a home for the aged. If possible, elderly married couples are given a room together. Permanently and totally disabled persons are placed in special asylums or nursing homes which provide less medical service than hospitals, but some medical supervision, custodial and nursing care.

MEDICAL ASSISTANCE [14]

For generations the three main health problems in France have been high infant mortality, tuberculosis, and venereal disease. The enactment of the Loi nationale d'assistance médicale gratuite [National Law for Free Medical Assistance] of July 15, 1893, was, therefore, considered to be one of the essential achievements in French social legislation. The protection

---

12. National Decree of July 19, 1946; no similar provision exists in the United States, although old-age insurance benefits to women may be paid at a reduced rate when they are 62 years of age or care for minor children.

13. When this assistance was set up in 1905, the age required for its benefits was 70, but it was later reduced to 65 for men and 60 for women, while old-age insurance benefits may be claimed at 60 years of age.

14. The French health insurance program is discussed in Chapter 5.

and preservation of health have remained the keynote of welfare activities in France, and numerous physicians and scientists such as Pasteur, Grancher, and Calmette have gained international fame as pioneers in public health services.

The law of 1893 provides medical care for three groups: a) the poor, b) patients in modest circumstances who are not able to pay for medical treatment and hospital expenses, and c) the medically needy who fully support themselves and their families but cannot afford to pay high medical costs during a protracted illness. The first group receives free medical care, hospital and clinical service, medicines, and appliances; the second gets free medical treatment and hospitalization, but pays for medicines, drugs, and appliances; the last category contributes to the cost of medical treatment and hospitalization within the limit of its means and pays for medicines, laboratory services, and appliances.[15]

Under this medical assistance program, the patient has a free choice of medical practitioner from his local panel, and he may consult specialists upon the referral of the general practitioner. In most communities a public hospital or dispensary provides free clinical services[16] and hospitalization for the patient upon the request of his physician.[17] Drugs and other medicines prescribed by the physician are provided by pharmacies. Midwife service is available at public expense. A list of doctors, pharmacists and midwives serving in the community under the medical assistance plan is published annually and

---

15. Severe criticism of some hospitals is raised by François Guillaume, "Le grand malaise des hôpitaux de France," Témoignage chrétien (February 7, 1958); more physicians and more efficient services of medical social workers are requested.

16. Dr. O. Lacambre, "Aspect général des vaccinations en France," Pages Documentaires, 1958, No. 1, 1337-1338.

17. The medical assistance program also pays the cost of a tuberculosis sanatorium for beneficiaries of medical care, provided the patients are admitted on recommendation of a public dispensary or a private social agency, and for members of a mutual aid society which insures against sickness of long duration.

posted on the bulletin boards of the city hall, hospitals, and post offices.

The costs of medical assistance are shared by the local community, the département, and the national government according to annually determined scales, based upon the financial conditions of the département, its special health problems, and the number of patients. The same scale of budgetary distribution

TABLE 1. COSTS OF MEDICAL ASSISTANCE IN FRANCE, 1951-1954[18] (in millions of francs)

Year	Expenses for Medical Public Assistance	Expenses for Treatment of Mental Diseases
1951	21,640	15,632
1952	28,958	22,201
1953	32,482	21,240
1954	29,738	22,940

Source: Annuaire Statistique de France (Paris: Imprimérie Nationale, 1956), pp. 50-51, Table III.

of expenditures between the local, departmental, and national government applies to the cost of hospitals and asylums for old and disabled persons. The amount the national government contributes to the medical assistance budget increases for communities which have a tax income under the average and for départements whose tax income is not sufficient to supplement local funds. The national government assumes the full cost of

18. The cost of public assistance and its relation to the gross national production is shown in Table 2, below. The changes caused by the financial stabilization measures under the De Gaulle government in 1959 and the conversion of the franc are not considered in this study. It seems difficult to predict the social and economic consequences of the devaluation of the converted franc by 17 1/2 per cent for the value of social security and public assistance payments and for standards of living and price levels in France. See Alfred Sauvy, "La Situation économique," Droit Social, 22, No. 1 (January, 1959), 10-12.

medical assistance to patients who have not resided for at least one year in any département. Patients unable to pay the full cost of medical care contribute according to their financial means. Frequently the patient's ability to pay[19] is assessed by medical social workers who evaluate his social and economic circumstances. Charges for patients in modest circumstances are made nominal to prevent long indebtedness and emotional discouragement.[20]

MATERNITY CARE AND AID TO LARGE FAMILIES

Parents and unmarried mothers who feel unable to rear a child may bring him to a particularly assigned reception center at a children's hospital in their département. However, every effort is made to persuade the mother to keep the child. The social worker offers immediate financial assistance if it is needed, and assures regular payments for the maintenance of the child for a period of at least two years. This special public aid is called secours préventif d'abandon [assistance to prevent abandonment].

For centuries in France special support has been given to families of modest means who have many children. Such assistance aux familles nombreuses [assistance to large families] is paid to needy families with more than three children under 16 years of age. If the father alone supports the children while the mother is absent, the allowance begins with the third child.

---

19. In England, the function of the "almoner," the social worker in charge of assessment of hospital patients, was established in 1895; it is applied in public as well as in private hospitals. Originally, these "lady almoners" mainly investigated the financial resources of the patient, but later they assumed broader responsibilities in contact with the patient and his family. In the United States medical social workers are frequently the intake workers and recommend to the hospital administration which charge the patient is financially able to meet.

20. Independent of this medical assistance program, a broad health insurance program protects almost the entire population of France; the latter is analyzed in Chapter 5.

If the mother alone supports the children, she receives the allowance for the second and all subsequent children. [21]

MARRIAGE AND MATERNITY PROTECTION

In order to protect the health of the newly married, a statute of December 16, 1942 requires a mandatory pre-nuptial medical examination to certify freedom from tuberculosis and syphilis. A positive result does not prevent the marriage, but it makes both parties aware of the serious consequences and their responsibilities to the unborn. The French public has favorably accepted pre-nuptial examinations, but the medical profession has raised questions as to the reliability of the examinations.

A birth premium, allocation de maternité, is granted for the birth of the first child if the mother is younger than 25 years of age,[22] or if the child is born before the parents have been married for two years. For subsequent children, the allocation is paid if the child is born less than three years after the preceding birth in the family.

France has ratified the "Maternity Care and Childbirth Convention" of the International Labor Organization.[23] After the medical confirmation of pregnancy, a woman is protected for its duration against being discharged from her job. For a period of six weeks before and six weeks after confinement, she receives maternity benefits, assistance aux femmes en couches, paid either from the social insurance funds or from the national treasury.[24] To qualify, the mother registers her pregnancy at

---

21. This categorical assistance to needy families is a supplement to the general family allowance which is paid without regard to financial need (see Chapter 5); Mme Xavier Leclainche, "Le rôle de l'Assistante publique dans la protection des mères et des enfants," Revue de l'Assistance Publique à Paris, No. 48 (July-August, 1957), pp. 397-398.

22. The allocation de maternité was introduced by a law of June 29, 1918, and has been expanded by amendments.

23. The United States has not ratified this Convention and has no grants and allowances nor maternity insurance for mothers after childbirth.

24. Until 1945 benefits were limited to eight weeks.

a prenatal health clinic and is given three gynecological examinations and receives advice on diet and personal hygiene.
While receiving maternity benefits the mother is not permitted
to work, nor may her employer let her resume work earlier
than six weeks following confinement. [25] During her pregnancy
the mother draws an allocation familiale prénatale [prenatal
family allowance] in addition to her wage or salary, the same
allowance as is paid to a mother with two young children.

At the mother's first visit to the prenatal clinic she is given
a livret de santé [health book] for free medical examinations of
the child until the end of his school attendance.

If the mother nurses her child, she is entitled to an additional
bonus, the prime d'allaitement, for a period of six months after
childbirth, and at a decreased rate for another six months if
she continues to breast-feed her child.

The first maisons maternelles [maternity homes] were opened
during World War I in a few provinces. The Family Code of
1939 requested each département to establish such a home.
Beginning at the seventh month of pregnancy, women may enter
a maternity home without regard to their marital status and
without formalities, and earlier if necessary. Every maternity
home has a social service committee and employs a trained
social worker. The mothers are instructed in home economics,
infant nursing, child hygiene, and diets. Some are permitted
to engage in industrial home work to earn extra money. [26]

Most of the mothers in maternity homes in France are domestic
servants who have no family or are no longer accepted in their
own village. The social worker encourages the mother who
wishes to keep her child, strengthens her feeling of responsibility,
and helps to overcome anxieties, guilt feelings, and apathy. [27]

---

25.   Amendment of the French Labor Code of November 2, 1945.

26.   "Le Climat de travail éducatif en maison maternelle," Informations
Sociales, Vol. 7 (1953), No. 10.

27.   Henri Aubrun, "L'aide que peut apporter aux institutions l'équipement du
service social," Les Cahiers du Musée Social, No. 516 (December, 1957), pp.
170-182.

With the young mother's permission, she contacts the family and the father to support the child. The social worker strives primarily to effect the social re-integration of the young mother into the community. She provides for her regular medical examinations and attempts to help her to find a job.

The maisons maternelles are administered either by the département or by private social agencies. Their expenses, as well as those for maternal and child care, are shared by the national government, the département, the local community, and the family allowance funds.

Private social agencies in recent years have been attempting another solution in a new type of maternity home, the hôtel maternelle, where unmarried mothers can live with their children. While the mother is working an infant nurse and, later, a kindergarten teacher care for the child; during the evening and on Sundays and holidays the mothers themselves remain with their children. The mothers pay for their upkeep and, in general, finance the maintenance of the home. It is estimated that at least 1,000 more beds in such hôtels maternelles would be needed for adequate care of all unmarried mothers and children who desire such facilities.[28]

AID TO DEPENDENT CHILDREN

Dependent children in France include orphans, half-orphans, foundlings, and abandoned, mistreated, or neglected children who receive public assistance in their own families, in foster homes, or in institutions. This categorical assistance is not limited to children living in their own homes with parents or close relatives as it is in the similar national program in the United States. The French assistance includes care in foster families and in children's homes.

---

28. "La place de la famille dans la vie de l'enfant," L'Enfance dans le Monde, Vol. 1958, No. 9.

Dependent children are divided into two main groups: those requiring only temporary aid, les enfants secourus, and those in need of permanent assistance, les enfants assistés. The first category is subdivided into three sections: a) children in economic need, b) children temporarily placed in institutions, and c) wards of the juvenile court removed from their homes.

I: Les enfants secourus [children in temporary economic need].

(a) Aid to dependent children. When parents or relatives are unable to support the children, the bureau d'aide sociale makes monthly cash payments to prevent the abandonment of children and to enable them to grow up in their own families. Assistance is given to children living with parents or older siblings, and to children living with relatives or foster families. [29]

(b) Les enfants secourus en dépôt [children under temporary institutional care]. These are children who cannot live at home because their parents or relatives are dead, or in a hospital, mental institution, or prison. They are brought to a reception center and are placed in an orphanage or other children's institution until they can return home or be placed in a foster family.

(c) Les enfants en garde or les enfants protégés [children under protection]. These are children either delinquent, seriously maladjusted, or endangered by neglect, cruelty, mistreatment, or abuse. Young vagrant boys and girls, under 21 years of age, [30] fall into this category. The juvenile court commits such children and adolescents to the bureau d'aide sociale which assumes responsibility for their care. Usually children are placed in rural foster homes with farmers or craftsmen at some distance from the residence of their parents or guardians, to

---

29. Unlike such legislation in the United States, it is not a prerequisite for this assistance in France that one parent be dead, incapacitated, or absent from home.

30. Decree-law of October 30, 1935; cf. Marcel Vismard, L'enfant sans famille (Paris: Editions sociales françaises, 1956), and Jean Rousselet, L'Adolescent cet inconnu (Paris: Flammarion, 1956).

prevent their escape or interference by the family. If their adjustment in a foster home seems doubtful, they are placed in a children's institution. Institutional placement of children is more popular and more frequently used than in the United States.

II: Les enfants assistés [children in need of permanent assistance]. The second category of dependent children in need of permanent care, les enfants assistés or pupilles de l'assistance, consists of children whose parents have been deprived of their parental rights by court decision (déchéance paternelle). The bureau d'aide sociale serves as legal guardian for these children. The parents still remain responsible for the support of the child until he is 13 years of age, but they are not permitted to know where he is placed nor to visit him. The parents may only request an annual official statement that their child is alive.[31] After three years the parents may petition for restitution de droit de puissance paternelle [restitution of parental rights]. The court may appoint a relative or another person as tuteur [guardian] for the child. A needy orphan is maintained by the bureau d'aide sociale, but the agency may delegate the guardianship to a private charity society. The children are supervised by social workers and registered public nurses; in each département a child-care committee establishes the local regulations for the protection and supervision of these children.

The expenses for the maintenance and supervision of les enfants assistés under permanent care, including the cost of personnel and administration, are borne entirely by the national government. The cost for the support of children under temporary care is shared by the national government, the département, and the ensemble des communes [federation of municipalities] which represents all local units of government. The scale of the distribution of expenses is annually

---

31. Law of July 24, 1889; see Paul Ceccaldi and H. Synvet, Le droit pénal au secours de l'enfant (Paris: Editions juridiques et techniques, 1953).

determined by an agreement between representatives of the three levels of government.

SERVICES FOR VETERANS AND WAR VICTIMS

At the end of the war nearly one million French prisoners of war and so - called slave laborers were repatriated from

TABLE 2. GROSS NATIONAL PRODUCT AND COST OF
PUBLIC ASSISTANCE IN FRANCE, 1954-1957[32]

Year	Gross National Product (in billions of francs)	Expenses for Public Assis- tance (in billions of francs)	Percentage of Gross National Product
1954	14,030	466	3.3%
1955	14,970	537	3.6%
1956	15,650	602	3.8%
1957	16,670	632	3.9%

The ratio of the entire cost of social assistance including medical assistance in relation to the gross national product in France shows only a very slight increase during these years.

Germany and East Europe to France. To accomplish their readjustment into civilian life, rehabilitation services and

32. Ministère des Finances, Statistiques et Etudes Financières (Paris), 10, No. 113 (May, 1958), 427, Table 1 and "Rapport sur les Comptes de la Nation de l'Année 1957," ibid., p. 448, Table 22.

agricultural retraining courses were established.[33] The Minis- tère des anciens combattants et victimes de la guerre [Ministry of Veterans and War Victims] determined policies and standards of rehabilitation.[34] Veterans and war victims who had been em- ployed prior to military service or deportation were reinstated in their former jobs with seniority rights.[35] When re-employment was not possible, the rehabilitation boards, in cooperation with the public employment services, found new employment for war victims and guaranteed their previous wage for six months.

When returned internees and deportees asked for separation or divorce, their legal suits were given special consideration by the court.[36]

Veterans and prisoners of war whose former occupational skills had been impaired or whose training and studies had been interrupted were given preference in the program of occupational retraining at government expense. Those who wanted to establish a business or workshop of their own, or to buy a farm, received loans from local banques populaires [nonprofit credit associations].[37]

Disabled war veterans and war victims receive free medical treatment, hospital or sanatorium care, and a military pension whose amount depends on the extent of the disablement and the

---

33. These services were first under the supervision of two national agencies, the Ministère des prisonniers de guerre [Ministry for Prisoners of War] and the Commis- sion générale des répatriés [General Commission for Repatriated Persons]. "Slave laborers" were French workers recruited by the German occupation forces to be brought in labor battalions to work in ammunition factories, military production, and agriculture in Germany, Austria, and occupied territories.

34. The Ministry has functions similar to those of the Veterans Administration in the United States.

35. Law on Re-employment of Veterans and Prisoners of War of October 15, 1940.

36. Law of March 27, 1946, on divorce and separation.

37. The Ministère des anciens combattants et victimes de la guerre guarantees these loans in full, not just a percentage of the loan as under the Veterans' legisla- tion in the United States.

loss of working capacity. Regular pensions are granted for disablement of 30 per cent of working capacity or over, but in case
of illness or unemployment all veterans receive special assistance. Widows of veterans or war victims are paid a life-long
pension at the age of 60. War orphans whose fathers or guardians
died in military service are treated as pupilles de la nation
[national wards]; the national government assumes the entire cost
of their education, apprenticeship, secondary school attendance,
and sometimes university education. When a war orphan marries
he is entitled to a marriage grant for his household and a loan
to help him buy or build his own home. [38]

An illustration of the costs of social assistance and related
programs in France which are classified as Transfers sociaux
[social transfers] from the national budget is presented by the
general budget voted by the Chamber of Deputies on February 6,
1953, in which these social transfers amounted to 7.46 per cent
of the total government budget. [39]

SOCIAL	Veterans and war victims	152.1
	Old age, family, maternity, & medical	
TRANSFERS	assistance	53.2
	Fellowships and financial aid to students	16.0
	Contribution to railroad retirement fund	13.2
IN	Contribution to miners' retirement fund	10.9
	Contribution to merchant marine insurance	9.4
BILLIONS	Increase in state annuities	8.3
	Adult education and training	4.0
	Unemployment assistance	3.1
OF	Rent subsidy to underprivileged persons	3.0
	Miscellaneous social contributions	2.7
FRANCS	Total	275.9

---

38. Law of July 27, 1917; it seems of interest that here French legislation
provided a marriage grant while Lord Beveridge's recommendation of similar aid was
not included in the British Social Security Program of 1946, because Parliament did
not consider such encouragement of the birth rate necessary.

39. Ministère des Finances, Statistiques et études financières, No. 52 (April,
1953); Warren C. Baum, The French Economy and the State (Princeton: Princeton
University Press, 1958), p. 123.

HEALTH SERVICES

HEALTH PROTECTION AND MEDICAL CARE

Although public health services are administered under the same Ministère de santé publique et de population [Ministry of Public Health and Population] as are public welfare services, they differ in their policies. Each local community has to establish a bureau d'aide sociale, but only cities with more than 20,000 inhabitants are obliged to set up a bureau d'hygiène publique [bureau of public hygiene]. In each region and département a medical director serves as the executive secretary of the local conseil d'hygiène publique [council of public hygiene] which supervises the commissions sanitaires [sanitation commissions] in the arrondissements. They control communicable diseases by enforcing quarantine and treatment of contagiously ill patients, arrange for disinfection of houses and apartments, preventive vaccination, correction of unsanitary housing conditions, safe water supply, and sewage disposal. Health education is carried on mainly by private societies, particularly by the French Red Cross and tuberculosis associations, but they are usually subsidized by annual allocations from the national treasury, the départements, and the cities.

French public health services aim at the prevention of epidemics, the control of communicable diseases, particularly tuberculosis and venereal diseases, and the protection of infants and children through the establishment of maternity and infant clinics and dispensaries.[40] Special emphasis, however, is given to the fight against alcoholism, which is one of the most serious health dangers in France. Both in urban and rural regions overcrowded and inadequate housing drive the farmer and industrial worker, the shopkeeper and craftsman, into the

---

40. Betty Bond, "Recherche sur l'efficacité des méthodes," Revue internationale d'éducation de la Santé, January, 1958.

tavern or bistro.[41] The practice of having cheap wine for lunch and dinner, strong drinks and liquors as apéritifs before and between meals has led to drinking as a social custom. The modest housing facilities of the low income groups and part of the middle class and a wide-spread general tradition of inviting only close relatives into the home make it uncommon to entertain friends and other guests at home, so that restaurants and cafes are used for parties; these, of course, encourage the consumption of wine and drinks. The treatment of alcoholics is carried out in mental hygiene clinics and sanatoriums and in public alcohol rehabilitation centers which provide withdrawing cures and psychotherapy.[42]

The registers of vital statistics are maintained in the bureau of public health of the département, not in the Ministère de santé publique et de population, as they are administered in the state departments of public health in the United States; supervision of sanitary engineering is also a departmental function. Contagious diseases such as cholera, diphtheria, and small pox must be reported to the bureau d'hygiène publique of the département.

Tuberculosis also had been a serious concern in France for a long time, since its prevalence has been augmented by the poor housing conditions discussed above. But it was only after the First World War, in 1919, that the Comité National pour la défense contre la tuberculose was founded and received public subsidies. Each arrondissement provides a dispensaire d'hygiène sociale, an out-patient division of a hospital which renders

---

41. Dr. Etienne Berthet, "Principes et techniques de l'éducation sanitaire en milieu rural," L'Hygiène par exemple, 1957, No. 3; Dr. Duchêne and Mlle Forey, "L'Alcoolisme, son aspect médico-social," Informations Sociales, 11, No. 1 (January, 1957), 204-223.

42. Dr. Jacques Laurent, "La Maladie alcoolique," Alcool ou Santé (Paris), March-April, 1958; Dr. Paumelle, "Consultation de désintoxication alcoolique et rôle du service social," Bulletin du Service social des Organismes de Sécurité sociale (Paris), February, 1957.

free preventive examination and consultation for tubercular patients, and issues free dietary food and milk. [43]

The most noted among private social agencies which administer tuberculosis dispensaries, preventoria, and sanatoria is the Oeuvre Grancher, a foundation which takes children of tubercular parents from their homes until the parents' disease has been cured and the danger of infection removed.

During the period 1931 to 1939 preceding World War II the incidence of tuberculosis had been reduced by nearly 50 per cent, but during the Occupation and the war it greatly increased again. Preventive measures and cures failed because there were insufficient nutrition, medical specialists, nurses and funds available. The spread of tuberculosis was also caused by the hardships and deprivations of the German occupation and the infections soldiers and laborers suffered in prison camps and enforced labor assignments. Since the Liberation, intensive government and private measures, increased staffs, and treatment facilities have substantially reduced the death rate from tuberculosis, as is illustrated by the following figures. [44] Mortality rates resulting from tuberculosis, per 100,000 population, were:

1900	230	1950	58
1914	213	1951	60
1918	278	1952	43
1939	121	1953	36
1941	159	1954	32
1948	74	1955	31

In Paris a special experiment has been conducted in which non-infectious tubercular patients are permitted to remain with their families while receiving closely supervised treatment from

---

43. Dr. G. Péquignot, "Les établissements de soins dans l'organisation sanitaire et sociale," Pages Documentaires, Vol. 1958, No. 5 (June-July).

44. L'Action Sanitaire et Sociale des Organismes de Sécurité Social Pendant la Période 1945-1952 (Paris, 1953), p. 10; United Nations, Report on the World Social Situation (New York, 1957), p. 31, Table 2; World Health Organization, The Killing Diseases, Past and Present, 1958, p. 4.

a logement sanatorium [health center]. Home calls are made by visiting nurses and medical social workers especially trained to work with tubercular patients. The methods of treatment of tubercular patients in France and the success in curing them are illustrated by an analysis of their placement. The number of patients in hospitals (sanatoriums and preventoriums) is decreasing, while placement in open-air centers, in families, and convalescent homes has increased slightly. The danger of tuberculosis is receding.

TABLE 3.   TREATMENT OF TUBERCULAR PATIENTS
IN FRANCE[45]

	1950	1951	1953	1954
Patients in sanatoriums	26,050	23,961	23,471	19,766
Patients in preventoriums	15,287	13,591	12,651	10,721
Patients in open air clinics	6,342	6,692	7,077	6,931
Patients in foster families	3,219	3,255	4,194	4,187
Patients in convalescent care	1,273	1,396	1,813	1,911
Total	52,171	48,895	49,206	43,516

In the treatment of tubercular patients in France, emotional and social factors are considered important for an effective cure.[46] For this reason, medical social workers give individual counseling to the patient and his family during the period of hospitalization. After the patient's release from the sanatorium or hospital he is advised by the social worker about opportunities

---

45. The number of patients includes those under social insurance and medical assistance as well as private patients, Annuaire Statistique de la France (Paris: Imprimérie Nationale, 1953), p. 45 and ibid., 1956, p. 50, Table II.

46. Etienne Berthet, "Les éléments mentaux de la tuberculose," La Semaine Médicale, August, 1952.

for vocational rehabilitation, and on any readjustment in his life and work necessitated by his illness; if necessary, financial assistance is provided through public or private agencies.

Before World War II, venereal diseases did not require notification and registration. [47] The fight against venereal diseases, especially syphilis, had been carried on by private societies, the Ligue Prophylactique and the Ligue Nationale contre le Péril Vénérien. [48] However, in recent years hospitals and clinics under public authority have assumed the major responsibility for preventive care and therapy of venereal diseases. In larger cities, dermatological clinics provide free treatment, usually at the municipal hospital. Most local welfare offices also allow needy patients to use the service of a private dermatologist for their treatment at public cost. During World War II, venereal diseases spread alarmingly as the social fabric disintegrated among hundreds of thousands of homeless, hungry refugees and under the influence of the German occupation armies. The French government was forced in 1942 to declare syphilis a notifiable disease requiring compulsory treatment — if necessary, by commitment to a hospital. After the Liberation of France, the closing of all brothels and a stricter system of regimentation of all prostitutes was ordered. [49] Though regular medical examinations of all prostitutes are now compulsory, it is impossible to require them often enough to detect all fresh contaminations. [50] One or two dermatologists in the bureau régionale

---

47. Earlier French policies in respect to prostitution are discussed in René Sand, The Advance to Social Medicine (London: Staples Press, 1952), pp. 423-426.

48. The International Abolition Federation in Paris attempts to evaluate the experience of various countries in the establishment of reception centers for promiscuous women and the methods of rehabilitation of prostitutes. "Le retour à la vie normale des victimes de la prostitution, " Revue Abolitionniste, 1957, No. 163.

49. Law of April, 1946 on the closure of brothels and the fight against promiscuity; Dr. Sicard de Plauzoles, Les maladies vénériennes (Paris: Edition Néret, 1958).

50. Dr. Georges Péquignot, "Les maladies vénériennes," Informations Sociales, 11, No. 11 (December, 1957), 1295-1302.

d'hygiène publique [regional office of public health] serve as
consultants to the departmental and local health authorities in
the fight against venereal disease. Several reception centers,
partly under the auspices of private social agencies and partly
as public institutions, assist in the rehabilitation of former
prostitutes mainly helping them to find employment, but their
number is still inadequate. In the Ministère de santé publique
et de population [National Ministry of Public Health and Popula-
tion] a confidential index of all prostitutes, Cartotèque sanitaire
et sociale [the sanitary and social registry], is maintained. A
medical social worker supervises the measures for the social
rehabilitation of the prostitutes, such as vocational training and
placement service.[51]

In 1914, American demonstrations of medical casework
practice inspired the employment of social workers for patients
suffering from venereal diseases. In 1921 this work was further
developed when an Association du service social à l'hôpital was
founded.[52] Medical social workers in hospitals, of course, are
not confined simply to helping those suffering from venereal disease; they serve all hospital patients in need of advice or counseling. In the beginning, physicians on the hospital staff were
reluctant to call on medical social workers, but they have since
gained confidence in using their services. Workers with syphilitic
patients must be graduate nurses, of whom many are also trained
in a school of social work in France.[53] They collect the social
history of the patient, inform him about the nature of his disease

51. The French experience differs from the practice in the United States where
the prohibition of brothels and red-light houses was advocated by medical and military authorities, while the efficiency of medical control of venereal disease patients
is seriously questioned. The fight against these diseases here is a function of the
American Social Hygiene Association and numerous public and private state and
local health agencies.

52. League of Nations, Committee on Social Questions, Enquiry into Measures
of Rehabilitation of Prostitutes (1938), p. 42; see also Chapter VI.

53. Dr. Touraine, "Le péril vénérien -- la lutte antivénérienne," La Prophylaxie
Sanitaire et Morale (1958), No. 8.

and the necessity for regular, continuous treatment, and they attempt to trace the source of infection. The patient is made aware of the risk to himself, his family, and others if he neglects his cure. In communicating with the patient strict regard for his privacy is maintained; letters are sent without the name of the hospital or clinic, and home calls are made only with his consent.[54]

Infected patients are brought to hospitals for compulsory treatment. Women who have been arrested three times for soliciting are registered as prostitutes and have to submit to regular medical examinations by the physician of the local police. The social worker's rehabilitation service is centered in work with girls under 21 years of age and with young women who have only recently taken up this way of living. Readjustment is approached on an individual basis, according to the personal circumstances of the patient.

SCHOOL HEALTH WORK

In 1920, regular medical examinations were initiated and trained social workers were employed under private auspices in a few schools in Paris. Several départements and municipal governments gradually introduced regular annual physical examinations. Little follow-up work, however, was done, and there was no reliable control of the children's health after the school physician were not carried out because the parents were inadequately informed and not encouraged to use clinics or to consult their family physician. After the Liberation the national government reorganized the health services for school children under a Décret de protection de santé des enfants scolaires [Decree on the Protection of the Health of School Children] of October 18, 1945.[55] Now, throughout the country, each child

54. M. Delore, "Les rélations humaines à l'hôpital," Union sociale, February, 1958.

55. Yvonne Bougé, Préparation et activités de l'assistante sociale (Paris: Bloud and Gay, 1947), p. 132.

is given a medical examination during his first year in school. Follow-up examinations are arranged once or twice a year while he is attending public school. The school medical inspector does not treat the children, but the family is informed of the results of his examinations and his recommendations by the assistante sociale scolaire [school social worker]. Since she accompanies the medical inspector on his school visits and is present at the examination, she has first-hand information for the parents of the child.[56] Regular medical examinations are free of charge for all children; examinations by medical specialists and laboratory and X-ray tests are given without cost only to children whose families are covered by the health insurance program. In some larger cities a central school clinic is operated by the bureau d'hygiène publique for the control of children's diseases found in the medical examinations of the school physician.[57] A school social worker is attached to the clinic, establishes contact with the families, and arranges for regular visits of the child to the clinic unless the family prefers treatment by their own family physician.

Several private societies are also active in the protection of the health of school children. Notable among them is the Comité national des écoles en plein air, which maintains small open-air schools for children who are susceptible to tuberculosis or respiratory diseases.[58] In these schools classes are held outdoors as the weather permits, and the children receive special physical therapy, exercises, rest, and nutrition. Preventive hygiene education is carried out by L'Hygiène par exemple, a philanthropic society which sends out mobile hygiene exhibits to

---

56. A. Nepveu, "L'orientation professionnelle et le service social scolaire," Revue Française d'Hygiène et Médecine Scolaires et Universitaires, X (1957), No. 2, 78-82.

57. Dr. M. Malbos, "Pratique de l'éducation physique et des sports et contrôle médical scolaire," Revue Française d'Hygiène et Médecine Scolaires et Universitaires, X (1957), No. 2, 110-117.

58. Albert Audiat, "Espaces verts pour collectivités: l'Ecole dans le jardin," Revue de l'Economie, May, 1958.

schools, gives demonstrations, and offers premiums to children who carefully observe hygiene suggestions. Many schools in France maintain a school kitchen in which a warm luncheon for all children and teachers is prepared with the voluntary help of the children's mothers, but there are no national supplies of food or monetary subsidies as there are in the federal school lunch program in the United States.

SERVICES FOR MENTAL PATIENTS

The Insane

Care for the insane in France is founded on the Loi sur les Aliénés of June 30, 1838, which is still in effect. Commitment to an insane asylum is possible under two procedures: a) insane persons, by reason of danger to themselves or others, may be committed by order of a cour d'assises [jury court] at the re-quest of the procureur général [district attorney] and, b) mental patients may request "voluntary placement" through relatives or friends. Commitment in this latter category requires a medical certificate, issued by a physician not related to the patient or his family, and the approval of the préfect [governor] of the département or the directeur d'hygiène publique [Director of Public Health]; in addition, to safeguard the patient against arbitrary confinement or "railroading," the district attorney must be informed.[59]

Temporary discharge from a mental hospital is possible, and special "colonies" have been founded where patients may live with their families under medical supervision and receive counseling, guidance, and material aid.[60] The patient and any

---

59. A. Mignot, "Les maladies mentales," Informations Sociales, 11, No. 11 (December, 1957), 1283-1289.

60. The first colony for family care of insane women was established at Dun-sur-Auron in 1892, and a similar colony for men at Ainay in 1900 (Charles Henderson, Modern Methods of Charity [New York: Macmillan, 1904], p. 539). Recent favorable results of family care of mental patients are reported by Dr. Henri Ey, "Le malade mental dans sa famille," Pages Documentaires, 1957, No. 5 (June-July), pp. 29-42.

responsible relatives defray the cost of maintenance if they are able to pay. Each département maintains a public insane asylum or contracts with a private sanatorium for the care of patients. The cost of institutional care for mental patients is shared by the national government, the département, and the local com - munity. Foster families have been used for mental patients in Belgium and France for a long time, and often work out very satisfactorily under the supervision of a psychiatrist and a nurse or a visiting social worker. In France, as a rule, the so-called Gheel System, or community-center system, is used. The center is staffed by psychiatrists, nurses, occupational therapists for clinical treatment, and social workers who visit the patients placed in families.[61] In the United States, Massachusetts has long experience in this type of family care, but several other states are developing similar placement practices.

At present, psychotic and seriously disturbed children and adolescents in France are placed either in mental hospitals or in separate wards of general hospitals. The placement of children in the same facility as adults is criticized by health experts, and specialized segregated institutions for psychotic children are advocated in which intensive medical treatment, therapy, and education can be given.[62]

The Mentally Defective

Morons (mentally deficient children) profit to a certain extent from training and may find employment in simple occupations. An important contribution to the correct classification of mentally deficient children was made in Paris in 1905, when Alfred Binet and Dr. Théodore Simon developed the noted psychological test bearing their names. This test enables the psychologist and

---

61. Dr. Charles Durand, "Santé mentale et technique psycho-sociale," Pages Documentaires, 1957, No. 5 (June-July), pp. 43-54.

62. Dr. Sérin, "Les internements d'enfants en asile d'aliénés," Rééducation, 1953; Dr. Thuaire and Dr. Bacconet, "Faut - il abandonner l'enfant mongolien?" Les Cahiers de l'Enfance inadaptée, March, 1957; Dr. F. Martin, "Une action médico - pédagogique en faveur des enfants épileptiques," Médecine et Hygiène, No. 382 (December, 1957), pp. 616 ff.

physician to diagnose the mental retardation of the patient and to determine his "mental age." The test is now used in many countries.

Until the beginning of this century, schools for feeble-minded children in France were private institutions which received public subsidies from national or local sources. Then, in 1909, the National Education Law[63] provided that separate public schools or classes be established for the education of retarded and feeble-minded children. The départements were to finance the special schools and classes, but financial limitations were responsible for so delaying the program that in 1939, at the outbreak of the Second World War, there were only 400 classes de perfectionnement in operation, while there were 40,000 retarded children in need of special attention.[64] After the War, the number of feeble-minded and retarded children who did not receive special training and did not attend any school was still estimated to be 25 to 30 per cent of all feeble-minded children in France,[65] but the number of classes for these children is more adequate now.

SERVICES FOR THE HANDICAPPED

Care for the Crippled

Tuberculosis of the Bones and Joints. The dominating crippling disease in France is tuberculosis of the bones and joints, and free treatment is offered in public hospitals for patients unable to pay for private hospitalization. Expenses for orthopedic treatment are met by public assistance authorities whenever the

---

63. Law of April 15, 1909.

64. At present their number is estimated at 55,000 to 60,000.

65. Georges Gastinel, "Les trois degrés," Encyclopédie Française, XV (Paris, 1939), 15-04-14; Henri and Fernand Joubrel, L'Enfance dite "Coupable" (Paris: Bloud & Gay, 1946), pp. 174-175; "La Rééducation psycho-motrice chez le débile," Sauvegarde de l'Enfance, September-October, 1957; Claude Kohler, L'Enfant arriéré dans sa famille (Paris: Centre d'activités pédagogiques, 1956).

patients or their families cannot afford to pay.[66] Segregation in sanatoria and hospitals and compulsory treatment of needy infectious patients suffering from tuberculosis are enforced by law. Hospitals on the North Sea, the Mediterranean coast, in the Pyrenees and Maritime Alps are available for convalescent care of tuberculous patients.

Non-tuberculous Cripples. Public assistance (medical and financial), surgery, and orthopedic therapy are provided for persons suffering from other crippling diseases like arthritis, poliomyelitis, and paralysis in general and university hospitals in France. Among these handicapped persons are numerous disabled veterans and crippled civilian victims of the last war.

Surgery and orthopedic treatment are provided in general and university hospitals in France. However, occupational therapy has been developed only recently through agencies such as the Centre de la Croix Faubin in Paris, which specializes in treatment and re-education of cerebral palsied children. Non-tuberculous cripples are cared for by private charities, but these agencies receive subsidies from the local or departmental public assistance authorities for this purpose.[67]

Vocational Rehabilitation. France opened a school for crippled patients at the beginning of the First World War in 1914, at Lyons. The school was later named after Marshal Joffre and became the model institution for training and rehabilitation facilities in France. War veterans and civilian war victims who have suffered amputations and are eligible for military pensions receive vocational retraining to help them become fully or partially self-supporting again.

Care for Crippled Children. There is no systematic program for locating and classifying crippled children in France as there

---

66. Dr. Michel Arthuis, "La poliomyélite," Informations Sociales, 11, No. 11 (December, 1957), 1309-1313; R. T. Neubauer, "Tuberculose et réadaption des tuberculeux," Réadoption, December, 1957.

67. G. Mathiot, "L'enseignement ménager, préparation à la vie des handicapés, moteurs et sensoriels," Les Cahiers de l'Enfance inadaptée, January, 1958.

is in the United States. Therefore, there is less certainty that crippled children will be found early and receive the necessary medical, surgical, and orthopedic treatment, or vocational training, since parents are sometimes ashamed of the child's handicap and do not ask for help in his rehabilitation.

Care for the Blind

Categorical assistance to adult blind persons in need is administered by the bureau d'aide sociale. Regulations for categorical assistance to blind and other handicapped needy persons are issued by the Ministère de santé publique [Ministry of Public Health]. Blind people apply for this categorical assistance at the local bureau d'aide sociale, but a certificate of blind status is issued under the authority of the Ministère national de santé publique et de population. [68]

In several cities private philanthropic societies find suitable positions for blind and visually-handicapped persons after they have completed training in schools for the blind. Vocational training and special placement services for the adult blind have recently been provided by the Ministère national de travail et de sécurité sociale [National Ministry of Labor and Social Security]. Payments of categorical assistance are given to the blind with the stipulation that recipients must take either apprentice placement or special vocational rehabilitation training courses, and must accept any suitable job within their physical capacities. [69] The use of a white cane in France is reserved for blind persons and the visually handicapped with less than one-tenth normal vision.

Care for the Deaf and Deaf-Mutes

The Institution nationale des sourds-muets [National Institution for Deaf-Mutes] was organized at Chamberry in 1841; it provided

---

68. The number of blind persons in France is estimated to surpass 42,000, about one blind person for every one thousand inhabitants (Informations Sociales, 12, No. 6 [June, 1958], 113), while their number in the United States is estimated at 320,000, which represents almost double this ratio.

69. Dr. Paquôt-Henry, "Le réclassement professionnel des aveugles," Bulletin Social des Industriels, 29, No. 239 (September, 1957).

academic and technical training, articulation, and lip-reading. Boys were taught agricultural work, gardening, shoemaking, and carpentry; girls were instructed in dressmaking, mending, knitting, lacemaking, laundering, home economics, and domestic work. The institution was later transferred to Paris and is now used as a training school for teachers of the deaf and deaf-mutes as well. A public school for deaf girls is located at Bordeaux, and there is a coeducational school for the deaf at Grenoble. These three schools teach both speech and sign language. Other smaller schools for the deaf use the lip-reading and sign method, and prepare their students to earn a living after the completion of their training. A private philanthropic Société pour l'instruction et protection des sourds-muets [Society for the Instruction and Protection of Deaf-Mutes] was founded in 1866, and is still active in the interest of the deaf and the hard-of-hearing. [70] A special branch of the society has been engaged in finding employment for deaf-mutes since 1897. At present, public employment services in France combine their efforts with those of private societies in placing deaf and deaf-mute adults in jobs where their vocational abilities may be used and which are not dangerous with respect to accidents.

PUBLIC HOUSING

For a long time it has been known that poor housing conditions impair the health and well-being of the population and contribute to a high infant mortality rate as well as high death rates from tuberculosis, diphtheria, and typhus. The fight against slums in large cities and against unsanitary housing conditions in urban and rural areas has been an important aspect of French social reform since the last decade of the nineteenth century. [71] In 1912, a special public housing authority for low-rent housing in

---

70. Dr. Klotz, "La réhabilitation des sourds," Revue de l'Ouïe, 1958, No. 31.

71. René Sand, L'Economie humaine (Paris: Editions Reider, 1934), pp. 94, 201-202; Pierre Lavedan, Histoire de l'urbanisme (Paris: Laurens, 1941).

the Ministère national de santé publique, the Office central des habitations à bon marché was organized. After the interruption of civilian housing construction during the First World War, several départements took an active role in this field, established provincial offices for low-rent housing, prepared new projects, purchased land and building materials, and participated in cooperative non-profit housing construction and slum-clearance. The necessity of rent control to prevent inflation after 1918 resulted in a restriction of rents to such an extent that private builders no longer saw profit in constructing apartment houses for rent.[72] Already, before the First World War in 1914, the official survey of housing facilities had revealed that France lacked 800,000 dwellings. To compensate for the increased shortage created by the standstill of building during and after the war, the Loi Loucheur of 1928 provided funds for the construction of 200,000 low-cost and 60,000 medium-cost dwelling units between 1929 and 1933. An amendment of June 28, 1930 increased the national appropriations and added larger intermediary dwellings and apartments to meet the needs of middle class families. Construction was financed in two ways: by loans from the social insurance and family allowance funds, private banks, and public savings societies, and by national, departmental, and local appropriations.[73] The least expensive houses and apartments are reserved for disabled war veterans, veterans' widows, war orphans and other "national wards" families with four or more children, municipal employees with low salaries, and families living in condemned slum areas. For each category a maximum income is prescribed; families whose incomes exceed this maximum are not eligible.[74]

---

72. Alfred Sauvy, "The Housing Problem in France," International Labor Review (March-April, 1947), p. 228.

73. Only a few of these projects are built under the auspices of the low-rent housing authorities as public works. Most of them are built by mutual-aid societies and non-profit cooperative associations, with the financial and moral support of the housing authorities.

74. Yvonne Bougé, op. cit., p. 153.

Housing projects fall into three main types. The first is
built within a city, sometimes in an area where slum buildings
have been removed; each project has space for playgrounds, and
there is usually a small garden for each family. A second type
is suburban; these projects, faubourgs-jardin, are located in
the neighborhood of larger cities, often near a park, a lake, or
a river, where the inhabitants can enjoy healthier conditions
than in the city. The third type consists of projects called cités-
jardin [garden cities]; these are constructed some distance from
urban settings, if possible in pleasant surroundings near forests,
lakes, and hills, but still with convenient transportation to the
city. [75]

Most housing projects include central heating and laundry
facilities; many have club rooms and a community center. Day
nurseries, kindergartens, a public library, and a domestic
service center are part of larger housing projects, as well as
health centers and a social service division. In other projects,
medical and social services are provided by a private social
agency which employs a staff of physicians, nurses, and social
workers.

Since the introduction of rent control the typical family budget
in France has included expenses for rental of an apartment or
mortgage payments on a house at a rate of only one-seventh of
the total budget, or 14 per cent of the family income. In 1952
families paid less than 3 per cent of their income for rent of
old houses or apartments. Even before World War II the number
of over-age, defective dwellings was estimated at two million
housing units, and at least 600,000 new houses were badly
needed. The destruction of 262,000 buildings and the severe
damage to more than one million residential quarters during
World War II by aerial bombings and fire, and the lack of construction and repair of civilian housing during this period,
created an appalling shortage. Rents are still under price

---

75. Jean Lebreton, La cité naturelle, Recherche d'un urbanisme humain (Paris:
P. Dupart, 1945).

control, but the rates are gradually being increased and rent control does not apply to new buildings. [76]

Some French housing experts are convinced that housing needs cannot be met merely by a moderate increase in rent, because it does not provide sufficient incentive for private capital to build for profit. For 40 years legislation has maintained rent controls and has held rents at a low level. The present high cost of living makes it difficult enough for low-income groups to maintain a household, and their situation would be aggravated by a substantial increase of the rents; nevertheless, a gradual equalization seems necessary.

For an alleviation of the severe housing shortage in urban areas the following proposals have been made: first, to allocate to the most deserving applicants any apartment or house that has become vacant through the death or departure of the owner; second, to introduce the consideration of the family income into the determination of the amount of rent; and third, to create a "housing allowance" according to the size of the family, financed from general taxation like the family allowances. Such changes in housing policies would lead to a fairer distribution of available houses and apartments and would especially benefit the younger generation, which suffers most under the present lack of housing. [77]

A step toward alleviating the housing shortage was achieved by the Loi des habitations publiques [Public Housing Law] of August 12, 1947, which provides loans at an annual interest of only one to two per cent to associations and societies engaged in the construction or conversion of low-cost housing. Loans are repayable within 65 years for new construction and within

---

76. Alfred Sauvy, op. cit., pp. 229-231; Georges Desmottes, "Les logements à la portée des budgets familiaux," Informations Sociales, 12, No. 1 (January, 1958), 62-72.

77. Dominique Ceccaldi, "Données financières d'une politique familiale du logement," Informations Sociales, 7, No. 15 (1-15 August, 1953), 888-901; Maurice Langlet, "Fonctionnement et activité des organismes d'H. L. M.," ibid., pp. 902-913; Henri Vergolle, "Activité des Offices Publics d'H. L. M. et future développement de leur action, " ibid., pp. 914-923.

30 years for improvement or conversion of houses. The loans are determined by the size of the building and the number of family dwelling units. [78]

In 1953, the Loi des Habitations à Loyer Modéré, a statute on low-rent housing, brought a change in the stalemate of construction of dwellings. It enacted a housing construction tax of one per cent of the payroll to be paid by employers. This tax is used for the construction of dwellings for families with numerous children and for families with modest incomes. These families receive housing allowances which enable them either to rent such apartments or houses, or to purchase a new house or a flat in a larger apartment building by installment payments at low interest. Municipal governments, family allowance funds, and employers' associations offer supplementary loans to individuals and to mutual aid and cooperative societies to encourage the building of new housing projects and redevelopment of slum regions. [79] In Paris and other départements comités de propagande et d'action contre le taudis [committees of publicity and action against slums] are organized which inform the population of the possibilities of obtaining construction loans from the public housing authorities. Special loans for housing improvements are also available which may be paid back in three years at a reduced rate of interest of one per cent. Home improvement loans may be used for the purchase of vacuum cleaners, washing machines, and other household equipment. [80]

Housing allowances and loans from public housing authorities are further supplemented by mutual-aid associations and cooperative societies which assist in the construction of cooperative buildings for rent or for sale to their members. Some housing cooperatives in France, e.g., the "Baticoop Society," purchase

---

78. "Cheap Housing in France," International Labour Review, LVI, No. 4 (October, 1947), 484; Pierre Chombart de Lauve, La vie quotidienne des familles ouvrières (Paris: Centre Nationale de la recherche scientifique, 1956), pp. 7-9.

79. Dr. R. F. Hazemann, "Taudis anciens et taudis neufs," Logement, March, 1958.

80. Robert Garric, op. cit., pp. 16-18.

land and build housing projects at considerable savings for their members. Other housing cooperatives have been organized by large industrial firms through agreements between management and workers who consent to a regular monthly or weekly deduction of a subscription rate from their pay check which entitles them to obtain an apartment in a housing project financed by the employer and the workers' contributions. [81]

The combined efforts of legislative and administrative government measures and activities of voluntary groups seem to have broken the apathy of owners of rental property who were unwilling to spend money for repairs and improvements before the legislation of 1953. The long-lasting inflation had prevented banks and loan associations from granting credit at reasonable interest for construction and repair. Since 1953, housing loans have been tied to the gold standard so that more credit has become available for new construction under favorable conditions and with low interest, and thus the housing program has expanded.

The industrial expansion of France has caused a further complication to the housing shortage in addition to the lack of adequate new construction and repair as workers move from rural regions into urban industrial centers and large cities to find employment. [82] From 1945 until 1956 about 600,000 dwelling units were built, of which 100,000 were constructed under the auspices of the public housing authorities, but less than 20 per cent of these were rental units; thus many thousands of applicants, particularly young couples of modest means, [83] had very little chance to rent a house or apartment. Industrial firms use the one per cent salary tax for the building of new housing units,

81. Maurice Langlet, Le Logement et l'aménagement de la cité (Paris: Comités interprofessionnels du Logement, 1957).

82. Jacques Parisot, "Effets de l'industrialisation," Réponse Française, VIIIe Conférence Internationale de Service Sociale (Munich, 1956), pp. 18-20, 33-42 .

83. Ibid., p. 39; Georges Malignac, "Le Logement des 'faibles'," Population (Paris), April-May, 1957; Isabel de Hurtado, "Problèmes sociaux créés par les nouvelles formules de l'habitat moderne," Les Cahiers du Musée Social, 1958, No. 4 (July-August), pp. 112-118.

but prefer to rent them only to their own workers and employees, so that other applicants cannot obtain housing. A rural or suburban house with a garden offers advantages only for families which have sufficient incomes to meet the cost of equipment, maintenance, and regular amortization. Owning a housing unit in a large apartment house seems less desirable for a worker's family if the bread-winner receives a low wage and has not even a regular income. The management of such a block of flats is complicated, and it is difficult for persons not trained in business to share in the administration of an apartment block.[84]

Before the legislation of 1953, new houses were practically reserved for the small number of wealthy persons who could afford to invest large sums of money to build private residences or pay the very high rents for new houses. The mass of the working population, however, having no adequate old housing, was left in substandard dwellings, cheap hotels, or overcrowded living conditions with relatives or friends.[85]

With the support of the new housing tax and housing allowances, new construction has made the housing situation more satisfactory. The number of new or reconstructed dwellings for rent or home ownership is illustrated by the following figures:

Dwellings Completed in France in Selected Years[86]

1954	162,000
1955	233,467
1957	273,700
1958 (January-September)	132,100

With a gradual further decrease of rent control and a continuation of this progress in housing construction, it may be

---

84. A. Bahuaud, "La gestion de l'équipment social et ses problèmes financières," Informations Sociales, 12, No. 1 (January, 1958), 144-154.

85. E. Jay Howenstine, "Appraising the Role of Housing in Economic Development," International Labour Review, 75, No. 1 (January, 1957), 22.

86. Annuaire Statistique de la France, 1956, p. 225, Table XVII; p. 226, Table XXI; United Nations, Economic Bulletin for Europe, 10 (1958), No. 3, 21, Table 12.

hoped that France will eventually overcome her severe housing problem. [87] There still remain severe shortages in housing facilities, and the continuous growth of industrialization requires careful planning for the expansion of industries. French experts favor the development of new middle-sized industrial cities not too near larger urban regions, but still not too far from cities with their educational and cultural facilities. [88] They feel that small new industrial towns should be built with sufficient open spaces for playgrounds and for sport fields for youths and adults. City planning should provide, with the support of the new industries, hospitals, schools, community centers, day nurseries, kindergartens, health centers and social services, churches, and a movie theater and play-house which may be used for operas and concerts as well.

SOCIAL WORK IN THE FIELD OF CORRECTION

Although French delegates participated in the early international movements for prison reform, [89] it was only after the Second World War that a thorough reform of France's penal institutions and correctional social services was initiated. In the eighteenth century when prisons were heavily overcrowded, attempts were made to transport convicts to the colony of French Guiana, but several experiments failed. [90] In 1854 a national

---

87. A. Bordessoule and P. Guillemain, Les collectivités locales et les problèmes de l'urbanisme et du logement (Paris: Sirey, 1956), Chapters 2 and 5.

88. Jacques Parisot, op. cit., pp. 40-42; André Cotto, "Conséquences de l'industrialisation sur le logement familial," La Vie et Nous, September, 1956.

89. For example, in the Penitentiary Congress in Frankfurt/Main, 1846 and in Brussels, 1847; the International Congress of Charities, Corrections and Philanthropy in Paris, 1855, in Brussels, 1856, in Paris, 1878, 1889, and 1900; the International Penal and Prison Congress in London, 1872, Stockholm, 1878, St. Petersburg, 1890, and Paris, 1895; the International Congress on the Protection of Convicts and Children in Moral Danger in Antwerp, 1890; and the International Congress for the Protection of Discharged Prisoners in Paris, 1900.

90. Arthur Griffiths, Secrets of the Prison House (London, 1894), I, 171 ff., 184, 197-210.

statute ordered felons sentenced for a second time to be deported to travaux forcés [hard labor] in French Guiana or New Caledonia in the South Pacific. Deportation was intended for les incorrigibles, hardened habitual criminals considered dangerous on French soil. In fact, however, prison authorities, faced by impossibly overcrowed penal institutions, deported even first offenders sentenced for crimes from larceny to murder. [91] The prisoners lived on the mainland of Guiana near Cayenne and on the Safety Islands (called "Devil's Island" by the convicts). They were housed in blockhouses, tents, and army barracks that were overcrowed, dirty, and without adequate ventilation. For the slightest infraction of rules prisoners were severely punished, beaten, and confined to dark isolation cells. During the first three years of the penal colony, 33 per cent of the 6,915 deported convicts died, and the mortality rate later increased to 63 per cent. [92] Of every thousand deported criminals less than 10 per cent survived five years of confinement. Also, after serving the term of their sentence, the statute forced the convicts to remain for an equal period in the penal colony at Cayenne as libérés [liberated convicts]. They were then even worse off than the inmates, because they had to support themselves without any jobs available under the miserable economic conditions in the colony. In vain many tried to earn a few francs a day to save money for their return to France, since the government made no provision for return passage. Working in tropical jungles among the snakes and mosquitoes, many died from fever and dysentery, and only a few succeeded in escaping without being killed by the sharks on the coast or dying in the marshes and the quicksand. [93]

---

91. The French deportation system followed the earlier example of England, which had deported convicts in large numbers, beginning in 1619 to North America and from 1791 to 1829 to Australia.

92. A. Griffiths, op. cit., I, 184-187.

93. Best known among the successful fugitives was René Belbenoit, whose story was published by Mrs. Blair Niles in Condemned to Devil's Island (Jonathan Cape,

Several attempts by the governors of the Guiana colony to improve sanitary and living conditions on Devil's Island were sabotaged by the administrative staff and the prison guards, who did not want to lose the profits they were making from graft and exploitation of the prisoners.

In 1931, a social worker of the Paris Salvation Army, Charles Péan, after several futile attempts, received permission from the French Ministry of Justice to observe conditions in the penal colony. He lived for six months with the prisoners in their barracks on Devil's Island and in jungle camps. He became ill with tropical fever, but when he returned to Paris he described his observations of the suffering of the convicts in lectures and articles, and aroused severe public criticism of the desperate conditions in the penal colony. With three other Salvation Army workers, he returned to Guiana in 1933 and opened a Salvation Army shelter for liberated convicts. The guards and administrators tried everything to thwart their work, but Charles Péan succeeded in organizing a banana plantation and workshops for the rehabilitation of the prisoners. After the war, in 1956, Péan was sent back as commissioner of St. Laurent, one of the islands of the Guiana colony; since this time Devil's Island has not been used as a penal colony.

A thorough reform of the entire French prison program became necessary after the Liberation in 1945. Before the war the number of offenders in French prisons had been less than 20,000. After the Liberation a large number of "collaborators" were sentenced to prison -- 29,000 of them were in penal institutions on January 1, 1946, but after the government adopted the policy in 1952 that only those who had caused the death of Frenchmen or others should be classified as collaborators, the number of prisoners in this category decreased sharply. Thus on January 1, 1954 there were only 900 such prisoners, and on January 1,

---

1928); Belbenoit published his horrifying experiences in the penal colony under the title Dry Guillotine (New York: Dutton, 1938) and Hell on Trial (New York: Dutton, 1940). See also Harry Elmer Barnes and Negley K. Teeters, New Horizons in Criminology (New York: Prentice-Hall, Inc., 1946), pp. 447-451.

1958 only 30 were still incarcerated.[94] The number of prisoners in French penal institutions reflected the government policy. From the prewar 20,000 the figure rose to 67,000 in 1946, and decreased gradually to 23,000 in 1954.[95] Two other categories of prisoners, unknown in French prisons before World War II, were 3,200 of the hard-labor convicts previously deported to penal colonies, and 1,600 of the habitual offenders who also would have been deported until 1939. In spite of this special burden to the penal program, the total prison population has decreased below the prewar period because of a general reduction in the number of felonies and major crimes.

The number of convicts in penal institutions in France has remained fairly stable in recent years, as the following figures show:[96]

TABLE 4. CONVICTS IN PENAL INSTITUTIONS	
	Number of Prisoners
January 1, 1955	20,086
January 1, 1956	19,540
January 1, 1957	17,696
January 1, 1958	17,619

At the end of the war most prisons were in poor condition as the result of the lack of proper maintenance or repair during war and occupation; the prison personnel were mainly untrained and largely unfit for working toward a rehabilitation of the prisoners.

---

94. "Chronique Pénitentiaire," Revue de Science Criminelle et de Droit Pénale Comparé, 13, No. 4 (October-December, 1958), 880.

95. Charles Germain, "Postwar Prison Reform in France," The Annals, 298 (May, 1954), 139 ff.

96. Compiled from "Chronique Pénitentiaire," Revue de Science Criminelle et de Droit Pénale Comparé, 11, No. 2 (April-June, 1956), 569 and 13, No. 4 (October-December, 1958), 880.

Postwar reform included the establishment of a social and medico-psychological service in penal institutions, transfer of the control of the execution of punishment and of the transfer of prisoners to judges, and the assignment of decisions on parole to a special board under the Ministry of Justice.[97] There is only a beginning of consideration of the social and personal circumstances of the individual offender in criminal courts in France. Depending upon the gravity of the crime, the offender is either sentenced to prison [emprisonnement correctionnel], to solitary confinement [réclusion], or to penitentiary confinement at hard labor [travaux forcés]. Actually, the differences between these types of confinement are no longer very distinct; in some penal institutions the administration determines the treatment the prisoner shall receive on the basis of his personality and behavior.

France maintains five penitentiaries, each for from 500 to 900 adult prisoners, in which treatment consists mainly of labor and discipline. Six reformatories use vocational training and a program of re-education for young adults and first offenders. An observation period is followed by several progressive stages of treatment leading, after placement in a transition home, to the parole of the offender.

For young offenders there are a prison for boys (with a controlled-freedom hostel as an annex) and another for girls, where the youngsters are not mixed with adult prisoners. An apprentice-training institution for prisoners between 25 and 35 who show manual aptitude, and two open reformatories of minimum security character, without high walls, and permitting work in the surrounding communities, make more individualized treatment possible. For habitual offenders there are three observation clinics and five penal institutions for their treatment. In all prisons and reformatories vocational training is provided for prisoners who can profit from technical training whereby

---

97. Charles Germain, "La réforme des institutions pénitentiaires en France," Revue pénale Suisse, 1953, pp. 277-320.

trade certificates may be obtained that do not indicate the prison background. [98]

For convicts suffering from mental disabilities, penal institutions of hospital type provide neurological and psychiatric treatment. Mentally ill (psychotic) offenders are not detained in penitentiaries, however; they are committed to mental hospitals.

There are no special statutory provisions for the jurisdiction of crimes committed by young persons between the ages of 18 and 21, such as there are in some states in the United States and in Germany in the Juvenile Court Law. [99] There are no legal directions for the criminal court to consider the lack of maturity and insight nor the emotional imbalance of these young offenders, nor are there provisions for social investigation, observation of the behavior of the offender, nor for any special methods of rehabilitation and social adjustment for this particular age group. Legislation in the juvenile court law of 1912 and its amendments for children and adolescents under 18 years of age leads to a special treatment of this younger group, but the older adolescents are left to the same treatment as the fully adult offenders. The measures for children and young delinquents such as suspension of sentence [sursis] and probation ordered by the judge do not apply to offenders older than 18. Like the adults, they are sentenced to fines, imprisonment, and hard labor. [100]

New experiments have been conducted in two institutions of reformatory type, one for young men between 18 and 25 at

----

98. Charles Germain, Le traitement des recidivistes en France (Melun: Imprimerie administrative, 1953).

99. The German statute of 1953, Section 106 authorizes the judge to substitute for life imprisonment commitment to the penitentiary from 10 to 15 years, and for other hard labor, prison terms for the same period. He is also authorized to set aside security incarceration and loss of civil rights for the offender under 21 years of age.

100. Louis Joseph. "Die kriminalrechtliche Behandlung von jungen Rechtbrechern (uber 18 Jahre) in Frankreich," in H. Mannheim, Die kriminalrechtliche Behandlung von jungen Rechtsbrechern (1958), pp. 27 - 29; Paul Charlier, "Action publique et probation," Revue de Science Criminelle et de Droit Penal Compare, XIII, No. 3 (July-September, 1958), 575-586.

Oermingen, and another for women 18 to 30 years of age at Doullens. They are called prison-école [prison school] and are oriented toward therapy and adjustment. After a clinical examination and classification by the director, the counselor, the judge of the sentencing court, the psychiatrist, the medical consultant, the priest or minister, and the social worker, the team works out a therapy plan. The subsequent treatment does not exceed 18 months and is carried out under the direction of one counselor in small groups selected according to character traits, attitudes, and type of vocational training. A variety of workshops for technical training permit the young men and women to obtain a certificate which facilitates skilled employment after their release. For inmates who have no suitable family home, a temporary shelter provides a period of adjustment for the return to community life.

The visiting of prisoners and their families and professional probation services are still a recent development in France.[101] One of the pioneers of such prison service was Henry Van Etten, the head of the Paris Quaker Centre, who started prison visiting during the First World War with a few volunteers of the Société des Amis. Later this Quaker service, following the example of Elizabeth Fry in England, spread to all parts of France, covering 21 penitentiaries, reformatories, and prison camps. Other social agencies engaged in prison social work are L'Entr'Aide sociale aux prisonniers; L'Oeuvre de la visite des détenus dans les prisons, which also administers a detention home for juvenile delinquents at Asnières near Paris; La Fédération Française des Charités de Saint-Vincent-de-Paul, providing services to 11 women's prisons with vocational guidance and placement facilities; La Société de Patronage des prisonniers libérés Protestants; and L'Oeuvre Protestante des prisons de femmes.

The essential function of the social worker in penal institutions is to assure the convict that his family, relatives, friends, and community have not lost interest in him or his future fate. They

---

101. Céline Lhotte, "Un An de service social dans les prisons de Droit Commun," Pages Sociales, No. 16 (March, 1946), pp. 22 ff.

help the prisoner to maintain or establish contact with his family and friends, and to prepare his reception and job possibilities after his release from prison. The social worker encourages him to resolve upon a change in his way of life after he is released, and attempts to orient him toward making the best of his imprisonment.[102] He discusses with him, particularly if he is a young offender, the possibilities for occupational training. Industrial workshops in penal institutions and craft instruction are usually conducted by social agencies engaged in prison work, with the support of the prison administration. Social agencies also provide medical care and nutrition for prisoners whose health requires special diets. Sometimes the social worker succeeds in reuniting families which had been separated before the prisoner committed the crime for which he is imprisoned. In securing a job for prisoners whose parole or release is planned, the social worker uses the help of employment services and other social agencies in the community. The establishment of contact with the family and the securing of a place to live and suitable employment often determine the decision of the prison administration and the parole board when considering whether a prisoner should be paroled.[103] The requests of the prisoners in interviews with the prison social worker are concerned as frequently with the fate of the family and the chance of getting a job after discharge as with financial, medical, or moral aid for themselves.[104] It is an indication of the growing official interest in prison social work that since 1945 a social worker has served as instructor on the faculty of the training institutes for prison personnel held regularly under the auspices

---

102. C. De Buyst, "Le Rôle de l'assistant social au cours du traitement des certaines catégories de délinquants," Service social dans le Monde, July, 1957.

103. Geneviève de Bonne, "Une réalisation du service social des prisons," Pages Sociales, No. 16 (March, 1946), pp. 24-25; Jean Chazal, J. Granier, D. Szabo, and J. Vernet, "Inculpés et délinquants," Revue de l'Action populaire, February, 1958.

104. Céline Lhotte, op. cit., p. 24.

of the Direction Générale de l'Administration Pénale [Central Prison Administration] of the Ministère de la Justice. In 1954, 164 trained social workers were employed in the larger penal institutions of France, 94 serving full - time, 70 part-time, although 36 smaller prisons did not yet have a social worker on their staff. [105]

Parole services are carried out under the supervision of the Comité d'aide aux prisonniers libérés [Discharged Prisoners' Aid Committee], of which the presiding judge of the criminal court is the ex-officio chairman. Its members serve as volunteers and supervise the behavior and employment of the parolee. When home conditions are not suitable, the Committee makes arrangements with local social agencies which provide shelter for discharged prisoners. Before his full sentence has been served, a convict may be placed in a hostel (transition home), which gives him an incentive toward normal adjustment in the community.

Since 1891 the criminal court has had the authority to suspend the sentence for juvenile delinquents, and probation services have been used if the court rules that a young offender shall not be committed to a penal institution, but shall remain under the supervision of a representative of the court. A suspended sentence includes the provision that the juvenile offender may earn a court decision that his sentence is considered void if he behaves well and does not commit a new crime within five years. The principle of suspension of sentence combined with an order for probation which is so frequently used for juvenile and adult offenders in Great Britain and the United States has not been established for the adult criminal. Suspension of sentence and probation are still limited to juvenile delinquents in France. [106]

---

105. Charles Germain, op. cit., p. 148.

106. Sociologists, criminologists, and social workers are, however, concerned to provide preventive measures as well. See S. de Plauzoles, "Prophylaxie du Crime," La Prophylaxie Sanitaire et Morale, Nos. 11 and 12 (1957), No. 5 (1958).

SELECTED BIBLIOGRAPHY

Ancel, Marc. La Défense sociale nouvelle. Paris: Editions Cujas, 1954.

Armand - Délille, Paul F. Le Service social dans les collectivités contemporaines. Paris: Librairie Delagrace, 1929.

Berthet, André. Le Problème de l'assistance et le rôle social des Bureaux de Bienfaisance. Paris: L'Effort, 1934.

Bordessoule, A. and P. Guillemain. Les Collectivités locales et les problèmes de l'urbanisme et du logement. Paris: Sirey, 1956.

Campagnole, Edouard. L'Assistance obligatoire aux vieillards, aux infirmes et aux incurables. Paris: Berger-Levrault, 1924.

Ceccaldi, D. "Aspects Sociaux du logement," Informations Sociales, 12, No. 1 (January, 1958), 2-160.

De Bonne, Geneviève. "Une Réalisation du service social des prisons ," Pages Sociales, No. 16 (March, 1946), pp. 24-27.

"Economic Rehabilitation of Prisoners of War in France," International Labour Review, LII, No. 4 (October, 1943), 434-446.

Fernald, Walter E. "The History of the Treatment of the Feeble-minded," Proceedings of the National Conference of Charities and Corrections. Boston: Geo. H. Ellis, 1893, pp. 203-221.

Foulard-Piganiol, Mme C. I. Le Nouveau régime de l'interdiction de séjour. Paris: Editions Montchristien, 1957.

Gastinel, Georges. "Les Trois dégrès," Encyclopédie Française, XV, 1939, 15-04113-16.

Gérando, Baron de. De la Bienfaisance publique. Paris: Jules Renouard, 1839.

Germain, Charles. Le traitement des récidivistes en France. Melun: Imprimérie administrative, 1953.
_____. "Postwar Prison Reform in France," The Annals of the American Academy of Political and Social Science, 293 (May, 1954), 139-151.

Graille, Emile. Services Publics d'assistance (2nd edition). Paris: Recueil Sirey, 1947.

Hautier, Jean. "Les Oeuvres dans les prisons," Pages Sociales, No. 16 (March, 1946), pp. 20-22.

Hazemann, R. F., and Henri Sellier. "La Santé publique et la collectivité: hygiène et le service social," Third International Conference of Social Work, London, 1936 (Proceedings), London: The Play House, 1938. Pp. 323-350.

Howenstine, E. Jay. "Appraising the Role of Housing in Economic Development," International Labour Review, 75, No. 1 (January, 1957), 21-33.

Iliovici, Jean et al. Service Social: situation présente et perspectives d'avenir. Paris: Droit Social, 1949.

Imbert, Jean. "La Réforme hospitalière," Droit Social, 21, Nos. 9-10 (September-October, 1958), 496-505.

International Labour Office. International Survey of Social Services, Geneva: 1936. I, 219-311.
_____. Housing Policy in Europe, Cheap Home Building, Studies and Reports, Series G (Housing and Welfare), Geneva: 1930. No. 3, pp. 197-234.

Joseph, Louis. "Die kriminalrechtliche Behandlung von jungen Rechts-brechern (über 18 Jahre) in Frankreich," in H. Mannheim, Die kriminalrechtliche Behandlung von jungen Rechtsbrechern. Frank-furt a. M.: A. Metzner, 1958. Pp. 27-36.

Kohler, Dr. Claude. L'Enfant arriéré dans sa famille. Paris: Centre d'activités pédagogiques, 1956.

Lacombe, S. "L'Action Sociale des caisses de vieillesse du régime général," Droit Social, 21, No. 5 (May, 1958), 305-311.

Lhotte, Céline. "Un An de service social dans les prisons de Droit Commun," Pages Sociales, No. 16 (March, 1946), pp. 22-24.

Neret, J. Les Enfants et les adolescents inadaptés. Paris: Editions sociales françaises, 1954.

Pillu, Jean. L'Administration générale de l'assistance publique à Paris. Paris: Recueil Sirey, 1934.

Rauzy, A. La Réforme des lois d'assistance. Paris: Recueil Sirey, 1954.

Rochaix, Maurice. Essai sur l'évolution des questions hospitalières de la fin de l'ancien régime à nos jours. Dijon: Presse universi-taire, 1957.

Sand, René. L'Economie humaine par la médecine sociale. Paris: Editions Rieder, 1934.

_____. Le Service social à travers le monde. Paris: Armand Celin, 1931.

_____. "Les Tendences Nouvelles du Service Social," Third International Conference of Social Work, London, 1936 (Proceedings). London: The Play House, 1938. Pp. 217-220.

Sauvy, Alfred. "The Housing Problem in France," International Labour Review, LV, Nos. 3-4 (March-April, 1947), 227-246.

Savatier, René et al. Traité de droit médical. Paris: Librairies techniques, 1956.

Smith, Anna Kalet. "France Provides Health Service to Mothers and Children," The Child, 12, No. 1 (July, 1947), 10-11, 14.

Verbizier, J. de. La Crise de réadaption sociale. Bordeaux: Drouillard, 1954.

Vexliard, Alexander. Introduction à la sociologie du vagabondage. Paris: Marcel Rivière, 1956.

Wells, Carlotta. "Social Work in France," The Social Service Review, I, No. 4 (December, 1927), 537-556.

CHAPTER **3** CHILD WELFARE
IN
FRANCE

SERVICES FOR CHILDREN AND YOUTH

For a long time the persistence of a high infant mortality and of a declining birth rate have created serious national problems in France which greatly influenced her social policies. A comparison of the population trends of several selected countries during the period following the First World War illustrates the seriousness of those demographic trends at that time for France. For a long period the increase of population in France was much smaller than that of her neighbor countries, particularly Germany and Italy. Up to the Second World War, France and Belgium had the lowest proportion of population of children under 15 years of age and the highest proportion of old people in Europe. Because of these demographic conditions, child welfare policies in France emphasized maternity and infant care, financial aid to large families, and a variety of health services of preventive and curative nature which were essential for the protection of maternal and infant health. Particularly important was the development of the first system of family allowances, [1] and the strong national and local support of mutual aid societies.

----

1. See Chapter 5 below; also J. F. Gravier, "Expansion démographique et expansion économique," Pages Documentaires, 1958, No. 4 (April-May), 241-250.

Another aspect of child care was the establishment of maternity and child health centers, infant nurseries, and day care facilities for young children. In these services France was a pioneer among the European nations, and her methods have since been widely adopted in other countries. In contrast to those health services and economic measures for the well-being of families and children, other social, psychiatric, and educational services were accepted much later in France because the people wanted to preserve the individual freedom of the family and did not like government interference.

The hardships of war and occupation during the Second World War led to a large number of prenatal illnesses, spontaneous abortions, undernourishment of infants, and deformities caused by malnutrition. Therefore, after the war the restoration of child health was considered an urgent task by public and private social agencies in France. After World War II the birth rate first increased substantially, and reached its peak in 1947, but has since somewhat declined as shown in Table 5 below, on page 85. It has remained stable during recent years.

This excess of births over deaths in the first years after World War II was particularly significant, since it was the first reverse of a declining birth rate for a long period and the highest increase in recorded French history.[2] It was partly due to the return of hundreds of thousands of prisoners of war, and partly to the restoration of normal family life. However, economic reasons played an important role in the increase. The large number of marriages and new-born children was made possible by the labor shortage and the resulting full employment which the country enjoyed after the war, particularly with the aid of Marshall funds granted by the United States for the restoration of industry. Dudley Kirk convincingly argues that the increase of the birth rate was also supported by a basic change in French ideology resulting from the experiences of the war, occupation, and the resistance movement. Instead of clinging

---

2. Dudley Kirk, "Population Trends in Modern France," in E. Earle, Modern France (Princeton: Princeton University Press, 1951), p. 322.

to the classic French individualism which placed the highest importance on the well-being of the individual, the new generation showed an inclination to recognize the value of the group and the nation. For this reason social planning, social legislation, and social security with special measures favoring children were demanded in the programs of the resistance and enacted during the years following the war.[3] This program differs widely from the earlier values of classical individualism so characteristic of France.

CARE FOR MOTHERS AND YOUNG CHILDREN

Among the social institutions for prenatal protection and infant care in France, the dispensaries and consultation centers play an important role. Formerly they were administered mainly by private charity societies, but more recently they have become part of the public health services. Those centers organize milk distribution stations which offer free milk, cereals, medical examination, and expert advice to expectant and nursing mothers. In lying-in hospitals and maternity homes unmarried mothers and other women who cannot afford to pay for hospitalization receive free care. Maternity and infant dispensaries which were earlier subsidized by cities and départements are now frequently part of the public health services under municipal government, but many private dispensaries under religious or non-sectarian auspices are still in operation. Families of small means receive a cradle and a layette for the baby and financial support if they are not eligible for maternity allowances because of lack of residence or citizenship.[4]

No official legal permission for birth control exists in France. Abortion and advertising of contraceptives are not allowed. But it is generally known that abortion is widely practiced, and that

---

3. See Chapter 5, infra.

4. J. Cordet, "Action sociale et service social en France," Pages Documentaires, 1955, No. 5, pp. 40-42.

prosecution of the physicians and patients is extremely rare. In fact, birth control is extensively applied and contraceptives are freely available in drug stores and comfort stations. [5]

Despite widespread popular opinion, illegitimate births in France are not very numerous compared with those in other countries. Among 55 nations whose illegitimate birth rate is analyzed in the United Nations Demographic Yearbook for 1959, France is 28th in rate of illegitimacy -- her children born out of wedlock constitute 7 per cent of the total live births, as compared with 78 per cent in Panama (which has the highest rate of the countries analyzed), 4 per cent in the United States, 3 per cent in Switzerland, and 8 per cent in the Federal Republic of Germany. [6]

At the beginning of the nineteenth century, infant mortality in France (the death rate of children who died before their first birthday), amounted to 17.6 per cent and, at the beginning of this century, was still nearly 15 per cent. Child care and maternity services between the two world wars had reduced this figure to 6.6 per cent, but during World War II infant mortality rose again in several of the occupied regions of France to 22 per cent as a result of a number of factors: general malnutrition, and mothers who were not only overworked but under the psychological pressure of fears for the fate of their husbands as prisoners of war or fighters with the Maquis. [7] After the war, as mentioned above, the birth rate rose for the first time following its long static period, and increased for several years, but declined again slightly after 1948 as shown in Table 5, below.

5. International Labour Review, May, 1943, p. 665; and May - June, 1946, p. 426; H. Duchêne, "Les Conflits conjugaus," Informations Sociales, 12, No. 6 (June, 1958), 87.

6. Demographic Yearbook, 1959 (New York: United Nations, 11th issue, 1959), p. 16, Table 8.

7. International Labour Review, May, 1943, p. 665; and May-June, 1946, p. 426; E. Bourgeois - Pichat, "Evolution de la population française en XVIIIe siècle," Population, No. 2, 1952.

TABLE 5

LIVE BIRTH, DEATH, AND INFANT MORTALITY RATES IN FRANCE IN SELECTED YEARS*

Years	Live Birth Rate[a]	Death Rate[a]	Excess of Birth Rate[a]	Infant Mortality[b]
1911-1913	19.0	18.1	0.9	- - - -
1921-1925	19.4	17.2	2.2	- - - -
1926-1930	18.2	16.8	1.4	- - - -
1930-1932	17.6	15.9	1.7	77.0
1935-1937	15.0	15.3	-0.3	66.4
1946	20.8	13.4	7.4	73.8
1947	21.3	13.1	8.2	67.0
1948	21.0	12.4	8.6	51.9
1949	20.9	13.7	7.2	55.8
1950	20.5	12.6	7.9	47.2
1951	19.7	13.3	6.4	45.6
1952	19.2	12.2	7.0	40.8
1953	18.9	12.9	6.0	37.5
1954	18.8	12.0	6.8	36.6
1955	18.5	12.1	6.4	34.2
1956	18.4	12.4	6.0	31.6
1957	18.4	12.0	6.4	29.2
1958	18.1	11.1	7.0	27.1

[a] per 1,000 inhabitants
[b] under 1 year, per 1,000 live births

*Sources: Louis Henry, "La situation démographique en France en 1951," Informations Sociales, 1951, No. 24, p. 1605; Annuaire Statistique: 58 (Paris, 1951), p. 365, Table V, 2; 65 (Paris, 1959), p. 13, Table I, and p. 26, Tables XVI and XVII, and p. 28, Table XIX. Demographic Year-book, 1957 (New York: United Nations, 9th issue, 1957), pp. 167, 171, 173, 409, 410-411, 417, 425; 1959 (11th issue, 1959), pp. 4, 8, 10, 12, 16, 359.

Midwifery plays a more important role in France than in the United States, particularly in rural areas where few doctors are in residence and only a midwife is available. Midwife practice is under government regulation and requires a state license, which is issued after the completion of a training course of at least two years in an approved midwifery school. There is no further regular supervision of the practice of the midwives, who deliver about 50,000 babies annually without the assistance of a physician. [8]

Maternity and infant care is supervised by the inspectors of public health, primarily in the départements. The director of maternity and child care is a pediatrician and usually has on his staff a deputy pediatrician and social workers. Statutory provisions require that a prenatal clinic must be established for every 20,000 people and a child-care clinic for every 8,000 persons. Both are to be equipped with laboratories for the diagnosis of tuberculosis and the treatment of venereal diseases, and serve at the same time for examination and treatment of preschool children. Social workers of child health clinics regularly visit children placed in boarding homes and those whose parents have been convicted for begging or drunkenness. Parents who place their children for more than one week in another family have to notify the mayor's office. The Division de santé publique of the département provides free the vaccinations which are required for admission of children to day nurseries, kindergartens, schools, and vacation camps, and furnishes dental examinations and correction to preschool children.

Private and public children's agencies and child health centers had begun casework and counseling of young mothers by 1920. After World War II rural and urban family-life associations developed systematic family and housekeeper services and formed a national federation. [9] It is affiliated with the Union Nationale Interfédérale des Oeuvres Privées Sanitaires et Sociales [National Confederated Union for Private Health and Social Services]

---

8. L'Hygiène Sociale, No. 1122 (January 25, 1934), p. 2379; "Familles ouvrières et action familiale," Action Familiale, January, 1959.

9. M. Girard, "L'Action sanitaire et sociale propre aux groupes locaux," Résponse Française, VIIᵉ Conférence Internationale de Service Social (Toronto, 1954), pp. 9-15.

These associations recruit young girls from villages and train them as housekeepers in three training institutes which organize three-month courses for 25 to 30 girls for service mainly in rural communities. Before her examination the housekeeper spends two three-month periods in practical field work: the first in a maternity home, hospital, or infant home; the second in an office of a caisse d'allocations familiales [family allowance fund] or a social agency. Upon passing the examination she receives a license as a "rural family worker" from the Ministère de santé publique et de population.

There are about 4, 500 housekeepers employed in France under the auspices of private mutual-aid and family-life associations. [10] The rural family worker helps in families after the confinement of the mother, but families which employ a domestic servant are not entitled to request an additional rural family aide. The housekeeper runs the household, takes care of the convalescent mother, sick members of the family, and the children, but may refuse other heavy work. She operates under the supervision of a local committee which selects the families to which she is assigned and determines the period for which she will remain in each family. The committee is also responsible for providing a small apartment for her and for raising part of her salary. Grants-in-aid for this service are contributed by the Ministère nationale de santé publique, the family allowance funds, farm cooperatives, and other rural associations. Families able to pay for the housekeeper service are requested to do so by the local committee. By 1954, 76 départements had organized provincial organizations for rural family aides.

Day nurseries and kindergartens must be directed by a trained day-nursery teacher. Many day-care institutions provide a hot lunch for children and have facilities for outdoor games in gardens or playgrounds. In larger cities, supervised free public playgrounds are available for children of preschool age. [11]

---

10. Jacques Parisot, Réponse Française, VIIIᵉ Conférence International de Service Social (Munich, 1956), pp. 14, 15, 136.

11. Fr. Léandri, "La Socialisation de l'enfant par l'école maternelle, " L'Ecole nouvelle, No. 58 (January-February, 1958).

In order to coordinate the efforts of public and private agencies for young children, a <u>Conseil</u> <u>Supérieur</u> <u>de</u> <u>la</u> <u>protection</u> <u>de</u> <u>l'enfance</u> [Superior Council of Child Welfare] was organized in the <u>Ministère</u> <u>nationale</u> <u>de</u> <u>santé</u> <u>publique</u> <u>et</u> <u>de</u> <u>population</u> by a decree of January 8, 1947. The members of the council are appointed by the <u>Ministère</u> <u>de</u> <u>santé</u> <u>publique</u> and include public health officers, distinguished pediatricians, and a social worker. The Council advises the <u>Ministère</u> on social services for infants and preschool children, investigates problems in the field of child health, and serves as liaison between the public and private organizations engaged in activities for the welfare and health of young children.

CHILDREN IN INSTITUTIONS AND FOSTER CARE

For many centuries orphanages and children's institutions have been common in France. Infant asylums which receive children under three years of age are allowed to operate only after an inspection by the <u>directeur</u> <u>de</u> <u>la</u> <u>division</u> <u>d'hygiène</u> <u>publique</u> [departmental director of public health] and upon receipt of a formal license. They must provide for regular medical supervision of the children by a pediatrician, and their staff must comply with the regulations for professional training and conduct. The superintendent of the asylum must be a registered nurse, a licensed social worker, or a midwife who has competence in the management of a children's institution. Children over three must be placed in separate children's homes. The number of children living in asylums and orphanages is estimated at 200,000,[12] but only in recent years has some effort been directed toward more effective supervision as well as toward in-service training of personnel.

The large number of children placed in orphanages and other children's homes will surprise American readers. It is explained by the long-standing French tradition of using children's homes

---

12. <u>International Child Welfare Review</u> (Geneva), 1 (1947), 25-26; Françoise Liévois, "L'équipment français pour la jeunesse inadaptée," <u>Educateurs</u>, 1955, No. 56, 10-15.

in preference to foster-family care, even when there are no specific physical handicaps or emotional disturbances to be considered, although we might have expected the high respect for family life in France to create a preference for foster-family care. Only recently have social agencies increased their efforts to find foster family homes in cities and urban areas. French social legislation has not favored family placement either, nor the keeping of children in their own families as much as our Social Security Act, our state laws, and child care practice do. Some foster homes for children, as well as institutions, have been used since the thirteenth century in France, but the number of children living in foster families has always been small compared with those in orphanages and children's asylums, and also small compared with the large proportion of children placed in foster families in the United States. Foster parents must send the children to school regularly, and if they take good care of them, they are given special cash premiums. When children reach the age of 14, they are usually employed by some farmer or are apprenticed to an artisan, unless the foster parents want to keep the child free of charge.

The most important legislation for the protection of foster children in France is the Loi Roussel, the Loi de la protection de jeunes enfants [Law on Protection of Young Children] of December 23, 1894. It introduced the regular inspection and medical supervision, at government expense, of children placed in foster families. [13] Foster homes are supervised by the medical officer of the arrondissement and his staff, and by the local municipal authority; in small communities, by the mayor; and in larger cities, by the public health officer and the public health nurse. Each child is examined by a pediatrician before his placement in a foster home is approved. [14] Regular follow-up

13. Nettie McGill, Infant Welfare Work in Europe (U. S. Children's Bureau Publication No. 76, 1921), p. 81; Guy Nevron, L'enfant vagabond (Paris: Presses Universitaires, 1952), pp. 8-10.

14. Etienne Berthet, "La prévention des accidents de l'enfant," Revue de l'infirmière et de l'Assistante Sociale, 1958, No. 10.

medical examinations, and home calls by public health nurses or licensed social workers are required.

The bureaux d'aide sociale place in foster homes children whose parents are unable to care for them because of death, hospitalization, desertion or imprisonment. Brothers and sisters are frequently placed in the same family, or at least in the same community, in order to preserve their family ties.

Maladjusted, difficult, or delinquent children are placed, as a rule, in children's institutions or training schools. Juvenile courts in France use either probation, foster-family placement, or commitment to an institution.[15] The following groups of children might be placed in foster homes: 1) young children who cannot remain with their own family; 2) children who return from a children's institution, but who cannot live in their own homes because the parents are in a hospital or tuberculosis sanatarium; and 3) older children, in need of protection, who are not suited for institutional placement.

It is recognized as desirable in France that children be observed in a reception center by a psychiatrist, psychologist, and social worker before a decision on the most suitable placement is made, but there is a shortage of such centers.

Some correctional institutions place children in a youth hostel or transition home for an intermediate period before their final release; this method is used, however, mainly for delinquent children.

For exceptionally gifted children, the bureau d'aide sociale selects foster families who live near secondary or high schools which the children can attend, or sends the children at public expense to a boarding school offering higher education.

Foster homes are selected by both public and private social agencies. Before a placement is made, these agencies make a social investigation to determine the hygienic conditions of the

---

15. There are exceptions, particularly in Paris and a few metropolitan areas, where juvenile courts attempt foster-family placement with the aid of private children's agencies. Paul Lutz and M. Gain, International Child Welfare Review, IV (1950), No. 3, 110-119; "La place de la famille dans la vie de l'enfant," L'Enfance dans le Monde, 1959, No. 9.

home, the character and educational competence of the foster parents, and their ability to give the child affection and a feeling of security. After the investigation is completed, a contract is drawn up between the child placing agency and the foster parents; it contains a statement of the monthly board to be paid and defines the parents' duties. The amount of board varies in the different départements according to the average income and the prices of food and rent. For children placed by the public assistance authorities, minimum monthly board payments are classified in the annual national budget. Board is paid until the child completes elementary school. When a child has been with the same foster family for ten years and has attended school regularly, a premium from public funds may be granted to the foster parents and to the child's teacher. If the child is physically or mentally unable to work when he reaches the age of 14, or if he shows superior intellectual abilities, the Conseil général [General Council] of the département may grant an extension of the board payments for a continuation of study. In addition to the monthly board, child placing agencies provide clothing and school supplies.

Although private social agencies supervise their foster homes,[16] legal responsibility for the supervision of foster families rests upon the directeurs des divisions d'assistance publique et d'hygiène publique [directors of public assistance and public health]. To aid them in this work they have a staff of medical officers, social workers, and public health nurses. The directeur de la division d'assistance publique [director of the division of public assistance] serves ex officio as the public guardian for foster children placed by public assistance agencies and is authorized to remove a child from a foster home when necessary.[17] He reports such measures to the prefect (governor) immediately. He also submits to the prefect a regular annual

16. Paul Lutz and M. Gain, International Child Welfare Review, loc. cit., p. 113.

17. Lucile Tinayre-Grenaudier, "Droit de garde et droit de visite sur les enfants mineurs," Informations Sociales, 12, No. 3 (March, 1958), 151-156.

report on the care and supervision of all foster children in the département.

Crèches [day nurseries]have been used primarily for children from low-income families in France for a long time, to permit widowed, deserted, or unmarried mothers to earn a living and to keep their children. Since World War II, the rising cost of living combined with low salaries in industry, and the increasing number of young couples who marry before obtaining positions which enable the husband alone to support the family, have caused a heavy demand for more day nurseries and an overcrowding of the existing institutions. Some French educators prefer to have mothers stay at home with their young children, but because of economic conditions there is little chance that mothers will give up their jobs.[18] The physical and sanitary conditions of day nurseries have been improved since World War II, but the personnel of day nurseries is still inadequate, and the impossibility of assigning one nurse to the continuous care of each child often prevents that healthy mental development which results from personal attachment and a feeling of security.

Authorities rule that children in day nurseries be divided into three groups: babies under ten months, infants from ten to 18 months, and older children between 18 months and three years. Trained infant nurses are employed for each group. Play materials, toys for the children's physical and emotional development, and a garden or lawn for outdoor play must be available. Parent education is an integral part of the day nursery; wherever possible it is desirable to have a reading room for the parents equipped with books and pamphlets on the education of the young child, to show films and hold regular discussions on child development.[19] For children between the ages of three and six, jardins d'enfant [kindergartens] continue

---

18. "Le Problème des Creches," Informations Sociales, 8, No. 1í (December, 1954), 1287-1289.

19. G. Viatte, Y. Lagriée, F. Russo, and Dr. Le Moal, Progrès et incertitude de l'Education Nouvelle (Paris: Universitaires de France, 1954); Fr. Léandri, op. cit., pp. 7-9.

the educational function which the day nursery performs for the younger child.

ILLEGITIMATE CHILDREN

In contrast to English law, either parent may acknowledge the child as his before the civil court, and the child then receives the name of this parent. If the other parent later acknowledges the child also, no change of family name is permissible except by formal adoption. If both natural parents acknowledge the child simultaneously before the court, the father's name is given to the child, even if he is not married to the mother. The formal acknowledgement secures general inheritance for the child, but does not establish a legal relationship between the illegitimate child and other relatives of either the father or the mother, in contrast to other countries such as Austria, Denmark, Germany, and Norway, where the child is only related to the mother and to the mother's family. A child may file a formal filiation suit in civil court against a father who is unwilling to recognize him.

During the child's minority, the mother is authorized to file the suit on his behalf. In general, the lawsuit of a child for the establishment of paternity against the father is allowed in cases of conception through rape or abduction, in case of seduction by means of guile, promise of betrothal or marriage, or in case of notorious cohabitation. Paternity also may be established by the court when the father treats the child as his offspring, [20] or if a written document proves the father's paternity beyond reasonable doubt. The father is primarily responsible, the mother only secondarily, for the maintenance of the child until he becomes self-supporting. When the father is a minor, he may still acknowledge the child without the legal consent of his parents; a married woman can do so without the consent of her husband.

A child born out of wedlock becomes legitimate through the subsequent marriage of his parents only if he has been previously

---

20. "Possession d'état d'enfant naturel". Similar legal provisions exist in several adoption laws in the United States but require the consent of the natural mother of the child for the adoption.

recognized, but has then the full status of a legitimate child with all family and inheritance rights. However, if the mother alone recognizes the child, she assumes full parental rights.[21]

If an illegitimate child is acknowledged neither by his mother nor his father, the civil court may appoint a custodian for the administration of his property.

No general public guardianship for illegitimate children exists in France. The property of an acknowledged child is administered by his father or mother. The court may appoint a guardien substitut [surrogate guardian] to supervise this property management if particular reasons indicate that such a control is necessary. The religious education of the acknowledged child is determined by the parent. Any child born in France may claim the nationality of either his mother or his father in order to obtain French citizenship.[22] For dependent illegitimate children the court may establish the guardianship of the bureau d'aide sociale which assumes the responsibility for the maintenance of the child, or make the governing board of the children's institution in which he is placed his guardian.

Contrary to public opinion in the United States and some European countries, as indicated above, illegitimacy is not very high in France. The actual figures for the years 1956 and 1957 are:[23]

Year	Legitimate Births	Illegitimate Births	Total	Percentage of Illegitimate Births
1956	752, 218	50, 889	803, 107	6.3
1957	762, 447	50, 142	812, 589	6.1

---

21. This principle complies with the ideal of strict individual rights of the family. In the Scandinavian and central European countries the institution of public guardianship, on the other hand, protects illegitimate children by law, and serves at the same time as a legal counsel to the mother, who often needs such assistance in the interest of the child. The French legislation resembles several state laws in the United States where the mother is legal guardian for her child.

22. League of Nations, Advisory Committee on Social Questions, Study on the Legal Position of the Illegitimate Child (Geneva: 1939), pp. 11, 19, 23-26, 85-86.

23. Etudes Statistiques (Ministère des Finances), Supplement No. 4 (October-December, 1957), pp. 5-6; and No. 4 (October-December, 1958), pp. 4-5.

These figures indicate a decrease in both the total number and
the percentage of illegitimate births in recent years, while the
total number of live births showed a slight increase. The French
rate of illegitimate births in these years (6.3 and 6.1 per cent
of the total) is higher than the 1957 average of 4.4 per cent in
the United States, but is lower than the 10 per cent figure of
Denmark and Norway.

ADOPTION

Although adoption was used in Roman law, it was not practiced
in France before the Revolution of 1789 because the influential
landed gentry, like those in England, opposed the disposition
of landed estates outside the genuine, natural family by inheritance to children not related by blood to the aristocracy. Under
Napoleon the civil code introduced adoption as a court procedure
which gave the adopted child basically the status of a natural child
in the family of his adoptive parents.

As a legal process, adoption establishes the relationship of
parent and child between persons who are not necessarily related
by blood. Its legal foundations in France are articles 343 to 370
of the Code Civil which were amended by a Decree of December
25, 1958 that introduced important changes and new principles
for adoption. [24]

The creation of a parent-child relationship by adoption must
be properly motivated, seriously meant, and must be in the
interest of the child. The adopting couple or individual must be
at least 15 years older than the adopted child, unless the child
is the natural offspring of the spouse of the adoptant (stepfather
or stepmother). The adoptant must be 40 years of age, but if a
married couple adopts a child, one of them may be only 30 years
of age, provided they have been married for eight years and
have no living child of their own at the time of the petition for
adoption. If the wife of an adopting couple proves by medical

---

24. Michel Soulé et al., "L'Adoption. Plan et perspectives," Informations
Sociales, 12, No. 11 (December, 1958), 1-134; and Lucile Tinayre-Grenaudier,
"Modification du régime de l'adoption et de la légitimation adoptive, " ibid.,
pp. 168-170.

certificate that she is unable to give birth to a child, the couple
may petition for adoption without regard to their age or to the
length of time they have been married. [25] Adoption laws in the
United States differ from those of the French; they usually permit
the adoption of a child by married parents having a living child
or children, and they do not require a minimum age for the
adopting parents or individual beyond legal majority, 21 years, and
a certain difference in age with the adopted child. In fact, young
couples are preferred by adoption agencies in the United States
because their age usually corresponds to that of the natural
mother or parents of the child. In France a child who is severely
neglected by his parents or endangered in his health, his moral
development, or his education may be adopted on authorization
of the court through an appointed guardian who is entitled to
conclude the adoption contract with adopting parents. The law
permits readoption after the death of one or both adoptive
parents. The child may be either legitimate or illegitimate; if his
parents are known, their formal consent before the court is
necessary. For the adoption of a child born out of wedlock either
the mother or the natural father who has first acknowledged the
child must consent to the adoption. Orphans and abandoned
children may be adopted with the consent of their guardian or of
a custodian appointed by the court. [26]

The French adoption law distinguishes two types of adoption:
the adoption ordinaire and the légitimation adoptive. Both types
of adoption are granted by court decree after legal examination
of the justification of the petition, the necessary consent, and
exploration whether the adoption is in the child's interest. As
a rule, the court requires a social investigation by a public or
private social agency before the judges of the court make a
decision of the petition. If a child under the care of the bureau

---

25. Previously the legal requirements were that a couple had to be married for
ten years and childless at the time of adoption; even if a child had died, they
would be ineligible.

26. Michel Soulé, Bernard Meyer, and Solange Weyl, "La Sélection des
enfants adoptifs," Informations Sociales, 12, No. 11 (December, 1958), 29-30.

d'aide sociale is considered for adoption, the consent must be given by the Conseil de famille des pupilles of the département. Formerly an announcement of the court's adoption decree had to be published in the local newspapers; this provision was abolished by the Decree of December 25, 1958 because such publicity might lead to discrimination against the adopted child, and had been known to lead to blackmail attempts against the adoptive parents. If one or both adoptive parents should die while the child is under age, a conseil de famille [family council] consisting of one to three relatives or friends is appointed by the court to look after the child's interests.

Through the adoption decree the child receives the legal status of a natural child in the family of the adoptive parents or parent. Under the adoption ordinaire the child retains his rights and his family obligations toward his mother or his natural parents unless the court excludes them by decree. He acquires the status of son or daughter of the adopting parents with the right to add their family name to his old one or to carry the new family name. The adoptive parents assume all legal obligations for his support, maintenance, and education. The child acquires inheritance rights toward the adoptive parents, but not toward their relatives. The adoption contract must be signed by both parties, the natural parents or their substitute and the adoptive parents or the individual adoptant, before a justice of the peace or a notary public. The adoption decree of the court cannot be repealed as long as the child is under 13 years of age except by decision of the court in the child's interest. A child older than 13 but under 21 years of age may ask the court to appoint a custodian to petition for a repeal of the adoption decree.

The second form of adoption, légitimation adoptive, may be chosen only by a married couple for the adoption of an orphaned or abandoned child under seven years of age.[27] The adopted child gains by légitimation adoptive the full legal status of a

---

27. In Paris and the Département de la Seine the number of this second type of adoption during recent years has exceeded that of ordinary adoptions. See Mme Vézien, "L'Adoption des pupilles du service de l'aide sociale à l'enfance de la Seine," Informations Sociales, 12, No. 11 (December, 1958), 7-8.

legitimate child of the adoptive parents. All ties to his natural parents are severed, but he assumes the obligation of supporting his new grandparents, provided they have formally agreed to the adoption, should they later be in need of financial support. No revocation or annulment of the légitimation adoptive is possible.

As in most countries, the majority of adopted children in France are born out of wedlock. The social worker investigating the petition for adoption requires particular skills and responsibility. The unmarried mother is often under severe emotional and economic stress before the birth of the infant, and is inclined to agree to suggestions about adoption submitted by midwives, doctors, nurses in maternity wards, and lawyers which she may later deeply regret. There is no legal requirement in France that the unmarried mother or the parents of a child consult a social agency before placing a child for adoption in another family. There is no legal guardianship for an illegitimate child as in Germany, Switzerland, and Austria. Unmarried women and parents planning to relinquish their child for adoption are in need of sympathetic, understanding counsel and guidance so that the solution which is best for the child may be secured. [28] After the child is placed for adoption, the social worker visits the adoptive family and the child for a certain period until the final court decree is granted, and assists in the adjustment of adoptive parents and child. Social workers recommend that the fact of the adoption be revealed to the child as soon as he is able to comprehend its meaning. [29] For counseling in adoption, therefore, French experts strongly advocate the cooperation of a team consisting of a child psychiatrist, a psychologist, and social workers to perform the difficult task of preparing the suggestions for the decision of the court on adoptions. [30]

------

28. Michel Soulé, Janine Noel, and Françoise Bouchard, "La Sélection des parents adoptifs," Informations Sociales, 12, No. 11 (December, 1958), 58-68.

29. Ibid., pp. 96-97.

30. Ibid., pp. 118-123.

CHILD LABOR

The Code de travail et de prévoyance sociale [Code of Labor and Social Welfare] of November 26, 1912, codified previous child labor legislation and is still in effect. Children may not work in industry unless they have completed elementary school, and have a health certificate. Later amendments raised the general age of protection to 15 years. In the interest of the arts, special permits may be granted by the departmental authority to children for theatrical and musical performances and for movie productions. Employment in public entertainment is not permitted for children under 12. Girls under 18 cannot be employed as waitresses in inns, restaurants, and shops selling alcohol.

On the other hand, children may be employed without restrictions in agricultural work as long as they comply with the compulsory school attendance law; their working hours here are the same as for adults. In orphanages, children's homes, schools for retarded and handicapped children, and industrial training schools, children under 12 may not work more than three hours a day, and the work must be of educational value for the children.

APPRENTICESHIP AND VOCATIONAL TRAINING

For centuries apprenticeship has been used in France for the boarding out and vocational training of dependent children through charitable agencies and public authorities. Apprenticeship contracts were regulated by the statutes of craft guilds and by local customs. Orphanages and child care agencies arranged for craftsmen to accept the wards of the institutions for occupational training. In 1935, a Division d'éducation technique [Division of Vocational Training] was organized in the Ministère nationale de l'éducation publique [National Ministry of Public Education]. In its annual budget, funds for special awards and scholarships to encourage apprentice training are available to children between 13 and 15 years. Such grants are used to develop apprentice training for the construction and repair of rural machinery and equipment in agricultural craft shops. In order to be eligible for such awards, the apprentice has to pledge that he will remain for five years in a rural community of the département in which he receives his vocational training. Technical continuation schools add general and theoretical knowledge to the practical skill learned on the job. In general, the French experience of apprentice training with individual craftsmen has not been too satisfactory because modern industry requires more diversified technical skills. In each département a special Commission d'apprentissage et de l'éducation professionnelle [Commission on Apprenticeship and Occupational Training] approves apprenticeship contracts.[31]

Apprentices and workers under 18 years of age have paid vacations of two days for each month they have worked with the firm or employer, but not exceeding 30 days annually. For minors between the ages of 18 and 21, the paid vacation is one and one-half days for each month worked up to 22 days per year.[32]

Vocational guidance has aroused great interest among teachers and social scientists. Local vocational guidance centers are supported and supervised by the Ministère Nationale de l'éducation publique. As a rule, a vocational guidance center is directed by a counselor, one or more assistants, a medical or psychiatric advisor, and a social worker. If the center has no social worker on its staff, it maintains contact with local and departmental social agencies.[33] Although no rigid methods are prescribed, the practice of vocational guidance is fairly uniform. A substantial set of psycho-technical tests with an objective marking system determines the young candidate's intelligence, aptitudes, and flexibility. Interviews with the applicant and his family supplement the testing. Medical examination and school records are used for the final recommendation of the vocational guidance counselor to the youth and his parents. Research in this area is conducted in the Institut national de travail et d'information

---

31. International Labor Office, Problems of Vocational Guidance (Studies and Reports, Series J, No. 4, 1935), pp. 12-13, 29-31, 156, and 174.

32. Law on Paid Vacations for Young Workers of August 19, 1946.

33. C. Bénassy - Chauffard, "Vocational Guidance in France," International Labour Review, 60, No. 4 (October, 1949), 390 ff., 398.

professionnelle [National Labor and Vocational Guidance Institute]
in Paris.

SOCIAL GROUP WORK AND RECREATION

Leisure time activities of children in France have been developed under the auspices of schools, religious agencies, mutual
aid societies, youth organizations, neighborhood centers, and
the settlement houses. Sports, playground activities, hiking,
swimming, rowing, tennis, and other games are carried on
under supervision of teachers or volunteers. But sports do not
play as important a role in France as in the United States and
the Anglo-Saxon countries. Athletics and physical training of
children are, as a rule, given less time and attention than the
academic curriculum in the school programs.

Colonies de vacance [vacation camps] are an essential
recreational element for children. [34] There are summer camps
by the sea, in the mountains, or in the countryside. Most summer
camps were not built for that purpose. Old mansions, former
hotels, and even medieval castles are utilized for vacation
camps, and are sometimes more picturesque than suitable for
children's recreation and lack sanitary facilities. Some camps
are managed by unskilled individuals; others, by teachers who
want this job primarily as a source of additional earnings. But
there are other camps properly administered by public or
private child welfare agencies, schools, mutual aid societies, and
family allowance agencies, which conduct the camps without
profit for the recreation and health of the children. Non-profit
camps also receive a large number of children whose parents
cannot afford to take them to a summer resort, at the suggestion
of the school physician. Camps under private management
accept children whose parents are able to pay the required fees.

Youth hostels were introduced in 1932 by Marc Sangier, one
of the pioneers of the Catholic youth movement. They are

---

34. Dr. Delamarre et al., "Les Vacances des enfants d'âge scolaire," Informations Sociales, 12, No. 7 (July, 1958), 2-92.

equipped with simple facilities for overnight stays or for a few days' vacation for adolescents interested in hiking trips, swim - ming, and mountain climbing. Beginning in 1933, the trade -union movement and mutual aid societies founded separate youth hostels. The mutual aid and family societies formed a national association, the Ligue Française des auberges de jeunesse [French League of Youth Hostels], while the Centre laïque des auberges de jeunesse [Lay Center of Youth Hostels] was founded and supported by teachers' associations, trade unions, and cooperatives. There is at present a network of youth hostels spreading over most regions of France which permits young people to hike or bicycle and to find healthy overnight accomodations on vacation trips without having to pay for expensive hotels and restaurants.

Youth organizations, first founded in 1925 in France, include Boy Scouts, Girl Guides, the "Young Catholic Action," Protestant youth groups, various Catholic and Jewish religious societies, and groups formed by mutual aid associations, trade unions, and various political parties. The establishment of these organiza - tions was retarded because the curriculum of the secondary schools in France requires a considerable amount of daily home work, so that little time is left for leisure activities. It was not until the decade before World War II that educators and social workers became more interested in organized youth activities and recognized their value for physical training and mental health. Young people were encouraged in group activities; school gymnasiums and class rooms, halls in neighborhood centers, and club rooms were made available for sports and recreation; and the government began to support their programs. The Second World War brought most of these activities to a standstill, but since the liberation of France the support of leisure-time activities of youth groups has been resumed and expanded. 35

In order to coordinate the activities of public and private organizations in the area of recreation, sports, and social group

---

35. R. Caillois, Les jeux et les hommes (Paris: Sirey, 1958); "Croissance et développement de l'enfant normal," Pages Documentaires, 1958, No. 6 (August-September).

work on a national level, the Haut Comité de la jeunesse [National
Youth Committee] was founded by a decree of June 23, 1955 under
the Ministère nationale de l'éducation publique. It is composed
of 30 members, including representatives of all national minis
tries which deal with youth problems, the presidents of the
Fédération nationale des sociétés familiales [National Federation
of Family Associations] and of the Fédération d'éducation
nationale [National Education Federation], representatives of
sport and youth organizations, and of the major political parties
This committee is supported by an advisory commission, the
Commission de la jeunesse, which has its headquarters at the
Ministère nationale de l'éducation publique in Paris.

SURESNES: AN EXPERIMENT IN CHILD WELFARE SERVICES

An interesting demonstration of a modern program of services
for children as well as adolescents, developed on the initiative of
Mayor Henri Sellier, exists at Surèsnes-sur-Seine, an industrial
city of 60,000 inhabitants about 25 miles west of Paris.[36] The
characteristic elements of this comprehensive system of
municipal social services are child and maternity clinics, modern
schools, special facilities for weak and handicapped children,
playgrounds, pools, low-rent housing projects, and child welfare
and public health services. New residential areas have been
constructed in a pleasant "green belt" surrounding the business
district, factories, and industrial plants. The school units are
situated so that they are readily accessible to the residents of
each city district. The schools include day nurseries, crèches,
kindergartens, elementary, secondary, and high schools, and
continuation schools. In each elementary school a child health
center with a medical, nursing, and social casework staff gives
maternity and infant consultation. The center also serves as
a clinic for young children who are not in attendance at the

---

36. Henri Sellier's pioneer role in the area of public housing projects has been
discussed in Chapter 2. He also served as a member of the Conseil Général of the
Département de la Seine, as a senator, and from 1935 to 1938 as the head of the
Ministère de santé publique et d'assistance publique.

school crèche or day nursery, and offers regular free medical examinations of children from kindergarten through high school, follow-up home visits, and casework services. Regular com - bined staff conferences of the school faculty with the physicians, nurses, and social workers of the child health center secure the full sharing of professional knowledge on health, mental, and social conditions in each family whose children are under the care of the center. [37]

Of particular interest among the social institutions of Surèsnes is the Ecole en plein air pour les enfants en danger [Open-Air School for Children Susceptible to Diseases]. It receives children susceptible to respiratory illness and those who are pre-tubercular or orthopedically impaired. Located on a hillside park, it consists of cottages constructed primarily of glass and steel, with solid brick walls toward the hill. The south walls of each cottage are built entirely of ultra-violet plate glass so that the children may get the full benefit of the sun's rays. The glass walls may be lowered into the ground by a simple electric device, so that the main hall of each cottage, serving as class and play room, is open to the air during clear weather. Most cottages have a swimming pool on the grounds, and swimming exercises are used to strengthen the limbs of crippled children. School lunches are served on the lawn near the cottage; the furniture is made of light aluminum so that the children may conveniently move it to the lawn. The entire project is constructed without a single stairway so that crippled children who use crutches or wheel chairs move easily to their classrooms, the health center, and the clinical laboratory. The school accommodates 300 children between the ages of two and 14 years, selected by the school medical inspectors. The expenses of this experimental school are shared by the city of Surèsnes, the Département of the Seine, the Ministère de santé publique, and the social insurance and family allowance funds. The faculty of the school is carefully

---

37. Louis Boulonnois, "La Municipalité en service social. L'oeuvre municipale de M. Henri Sellier à Surèsnes," La Revue d'Hygiène et de Médecine Sociales, May-June, 1937.

selected from teachers who are especially interested and experienced in working with handicapped children. The schedule of classes provides ample rest periods, and the medical super-vision and regular examinations of the children are intensive. A medical social worker attached to the school maintains contact with the parents and public and private social agencies concerned with the children attending the school. [38]

JUVENILE DELINQUENCY

Until the Code Pénal of Napoleon was enacted in 1810, delinquent children had been treated just like adult criminals. The Code ruled that children under 12 were not responsible for criminal action; if the public prosecutor sought punishment for children between 12 and 16, he had to prove that they had maturity and insight into their offenses. Children under 16 might not be committed to a prison with adults -- it was a law much in advance of its time. Not until 1850, however, did the practice of correction of juvenile offenders provide separate institutions for their commitment. Amendments of 1889 and 1898 gave the criminal court a choice between referring a juvenile offender to the care of the public assistance authority or committing him to a colonie pénale [penal colony], e.g., a rural reformatory school. Children referred to the public assistance authority were to be placed in foster homes, orphanages, or correctional schools. The law permitted the release of a juvenile offender in case of good behavior before the termination of his sentence, but parole was rarely used because the correctional institutions had no trained or skilled personnel, and no parole supervision was available except from a few volunteers who offered their services to some courts. Toward the end of the nineteenth century, public opinion was aroused against incarcerating children in jails and prisons, particularly if they had committed only minor offenses (which were mainly begging and vagrancy). Under the guidance

---

38. For the general aspects of school social work in France and Belgium, cf. S. De Coster, Aspects sociologiques et psychologiques de service social scolaire (Brussels: Institut d'études sociales, 1958).

of Henri Rollet, a young lawyer active in charitable organizations, the Société pour la protection de l'enfance, a private child
protective service, was founded in Paris in 1887. It concerned
itself mainly with the protection of mistreated and neglected
children who were apprehended by the police. Similar societies
were organized in Lyons, Bordeaux, Toulon, Marseilles, and
Montpelier. A survey made by the Paris society in 1890 showed
that of 2,102 children under 16 years old committed to jails and
prisons during that year, 855 were merely vagrants, and had not
been sentenced for any "crime" except poverty.

The first Loi pour la protection des enfants maltraités [Law
for the Protection of Mistreated Children] of July 24, 1889, was
a direct fruit of the activities of Henri Rollet and the Société. An
amendment to the Code Pénal of April 12, 1906 provided for the
commitment of juvenile offenders up to the age of 18 to reform
schools instead of general prisons.   Following the repeated
suggestions of Henri Rollet and several other justices, juvenile
courts were created in France by the Loi pour les tribunaux des
enfants et adolescents et pour la probation [Law for Courts for
Children and Adolescents, and Probation] of July 22, 1912. After
the liberation of France, an executive order of the Ministère de
la Justice [Ministry of Justice] of February 2, 1945 revised the
jurisdiction, methods, and procedures of the juvenile courts, and
replaced the juvenile court law of 1912.[39]

PRINCIPLES AND PROCEDURES OF THE JUVENILE COURT

There are three basic principles underlying the present method
of dealing with juvenile offenders in France: young persons under
18 are not legally responsible for criminal actions; judges of the
juvenile court must use a simplified procedure; and readjustment
of the juvenile delinquent is the main objective of the court's

---

39. Henri and Fernand Joubrel, L'Enfance dite "coupable" (Paris, 1946), p. 64.
In contrast to this concept, the British Juvenile Court deals with children between
eight and 17 years, and has jurisdiction over correction as well as civil protection
and adoption.

action. [40] Under the legislation of 1945, children and adolescents up to 18 are no longer treated as criminals, but are only subject to "methods of protection, assistance, supervision, education or readjustment."[41] Only particularly dangerous and difficult juvenile offenders may still be sentenced to prison terms, but their punishment must be less severe than that for an adult offender. For delinquents between 16 and 18, the juvenile court may refuse to concede extenuating circumstances if the character of the offense and the attitude of the young offender seem to make a severe punishment necessary. Such a prison sentence for a juvenile delinquent may be suspended, but since it is recorded in the criminal registry, it may prevent civil service or other employment in the later life of the young offender.

As in many other countries, juvenile gangs present a serious problem in present-day France. The asocial behavior of these adolescents, predominantly boys, is usually caused by a lack of attachment to the family, lack of understanding, love, and education at home, and lack of authority and discipline. The boys attempt to find a substitute for these in the street gang which shares their feeling of frustration and deprivation and offers companionship, mutual trust, and protection, combined with an attitude of rebellion and protest against adult authority and law. [42] Delinquent acts are committed in revenge for the good things of life which the youngsters feel are withheld from them.

Another cause of juvenile delinquency has been the desire of boys and girls to go to the movies, for which they try to get the

---

40. Ibid. pp. 96-107.

41. Adolescents between 16 and 18 are now under the exclusive jurisdiction of the juvenile court and are no longer brought before the criminal court, while in the United States the jurisdiction of the juvenile court, especially for serious felonies, varies among the states and often permits trial for serious offenses of juveniles before the criminal court.

42. Jean Chazal, "Les bandes asociales d'enfants et leur réintégration dans les cadres," L'Enfance vagabonde (Paris: UNESCO, 1950), pp. 49, 51; "Les perspectives et les tendances actuelles de l'inadaption des jeunes sur le plan judiciare et sur le plan de la rééducation," Les Cahiers du Musée Social, 1958, No. 5-6 (November-December), 147-160.

money by petty theft. The influence on these children of gangster movies which describe the planning of hold-ups and killings in great detail and glorify crime, it is felt, has increased offenses by young persons in Paris.[43] Some children who went five or six times a week to exciting adventure movies were so well instructed in burglaries and hold-ups that they carried them into real life. The influence of such films weakens the resistance of children to suggestions by members of juvenile gangs or to other temptations to become accomplices in theft or burglary.

The court, to determine the most effective treatment of the young delinquent, must have a profound knowledge of his personality. For this purpose a social investigation, a medical report, and a report on the observation of the juvenile offender are required. If a person between 13 and 18 violates the law, the district attorney refers the report to the judge of the juvenile court. The judge then requires a social investigation from a centre d'observation [observation center], child-guidance clinic (whenever such an institution exists), a service de sauvegarde de l'enfant [child protective agency], or a social worker. The staff of an observation center is composed of a psychiatrist, a psychologist, social workers, and a special observateur de comportement [counselor]. The children remain in the center no longer than six months, usually less, until diagnosis permits classification and suggestions for a plan of treatment for their readjustment. One specialized clinic in Paris, the Centre d'orientation éducative, serves only children who have been brought before a juvenile court on the complaint of their own parents. If no agency functions in this area, the commissaire de police [police commissioner] is required to investigate.[44] A

---

43. M. Bourdelles, "Notes sur le cinéma et la délinquance Juvenile," Rééducation, 1948, No. 8, 25 ff; and Jean Chazal, Etudes de criminologie juvenile (Paris, 1952), pp. 85-89.

44. There is no doubt that an investigation by the commissaire de police in most instances may not be a "social" investigation. J. Pariente - Calvet et al., "L'Intervention de la jurisdiction des mineurs à l'égard de l'enfant en danger moral," Revue de Science Criminelle et de Droit Pénal Comparé, XIII, No. 4 (October-December, 1958), 805-840.

physician is asked to make a medical examination and report. Maladjusted, pre-delinquent, and delinquent children are treated in observation centers, child guidance clinics (frequently organized as cliniques externes d'orientation [out-patient departments of hospitals], and in dispensaires d'hygiène mentale [mental hygiene clinics]. Standards of the clinics are developed by a private national association comparable to the Child Welfare League of America, the Union nationale des associations régionales de sauvegarde de l'enfance; the association publishes a periodical, Sauvegarde, and organizes annual conferences for the exchange of experiences in child guidance practice. In addition to the clinics, several internats médico-pédagogiques [residential institutions] render in-patient treatment. However, the judge who interprets the reports and proposals submitted to him has the power to decide on the future of the young offender.

The requirements that the judge of the juvenile court must have special competence and qualifications for his office and that his appointment be made for a period of three years are important features of French legislation. Knowledge and understanding of child behavior, especially of the treatment of difficult and problem children, demands a thorough psychological training and a technical skill beyond common knowledge. The judge of the juvenile court is appointed by the Ministère de la Justice [Minister of Justice] and cannot be assigned to another duty without his consent. He may be reappointed for the same period. Although no special theoretical academic preparation of the juvenile court judges is required beyond the law degrees, annual institutes for these jurists are held at Vaucresson near Paris.[45] Internships for students in the legal curriculum and for lawyers interested in juvenile delinquency have been suggested. The remuneration of juvenile court judges is higher than

---

45. The juvenile court in Paris, to which more than one-half of all young delinquents in the whole of France are referred, has a presiding judge and a vice-president. Their tenure of office is not limited, so that the "children's judges" in Paris may remain in office until they resign. Decrees of December, 1958 rule that children's judges are selected upon consideration of their special interest and competence in youth behavior problems.

that of other justices, so that outstanding justices are attracted to this specialization wherein they have equal chances for promotion and prestige with their colleagues in the civil and criminal courts. [46] The prestige and standing of the juvenile court judges in France is the most favorable on the European continent.

Since 1951 départemental tribunaux pour enfants have been established to facilitate the specialization of juvenile court judges familiar with social and family problems, child and adolescent psychology, and child protective agencies. The judge of a departmental juvenile court is well trained in socio-psychological, psycho-pathological, and pedagogic questions. He should have experience in the study of child and adolescent personalities. Beyond this academic background, he needs long experience to combine the maintenance of the court's authority with a full understanding of the child's behavior, and be able to interpret the court's rules to child and parent in ordinary language. [47]

Arrests of juvenile offenders, their incarceration in adult prisons, and interrogations under a formal trial procedure are avoided, if possible. The judge investigates the legal case and decides what shall be done for the young offender. [48] Educational measures which the judge orders (e.g., forbidding visits to bars and dance halls) are still entered in the judicial record, but the record is filed in a secret court register, [49] so that the young offender is not classified as a criminal.

---

46. Joubrel, op. cit., pp. 100-101; Decree of December 22, 1958 (No. 58/1287).

47. The French juvenile court's experience resembles that in juvenile courts in our country. The author had an opportunity to discuss these problems with former Presiding Judge Jean Chazal of the Tribunal pour enfants of the Département of the Seine, in Paris.

48. Previously each case of a juvenile offender was investigated by a juge d'instruction [examining magistrate] before it was submitted to the juvenile court, and the trial was prolonged by this procedure. Now, the juge d'instruction is asked for an investigation only in difficult cases when the judge of the juvenile court considers himself unable to complete the investigation.

49. André Klotz, "New Methods of Dealing with Juvenile Delinquents in France," in Margery Fry, et. al., Lawless Youth (London: G. Allen & Unwin, 1947), pp. 188-191.

Before pronouncing sentence, the judge requires an investiga - tion by a social worker, and often also a medical and psychiatric examination of the offender. In smaller cities, however, where experienced psychiatrists are not available, the psychiatrist sometimes makes no significant suggestions for the adjustment of the adolescent. The court operates in two forms: minor offenses are decided by the judge alone; if a serious crime is involved, the court consists of the judge and two lay assesseurs [assessors], and is called Le Tribunal pour enfants. 50 The trial is not public, and no audience is admitted except the parents of the young offender, the witnesses, and the social worker or probation officer. No publication of the proceedings is permitted on the radio or in the press, books, or movies. Sentence is pronounced in open court, but newspapers may mention the juvenile offender only by his initials.

The goal of the juvenile court is the readjustment of the young offender, not his punishment. For children under 13 no criminal punishment, but only educational measures, may be ordered. They are: 1) return to the care of parents or guardian, or placement with a foster family; 2) commitment to a private child-care institution; 3) commitment to a private school; 4) assignment to the public assistance authority when no other support for the child is possible; 5) commitment to a training school or an institut médico-pédagogique [psychiatric clinic with residential facilities]; and, 6) probation. For children over 13 the court may order these measures, or order commitment to a public institution of occupational training, an institution d'éduca - tion surveillée [reformatory school], or an institution d'éducation corrective [correctional school]. The judge of the juvenile court

---

50. Until 1945 the court was composed of three professional jurists. Lay assessors had been suggested after successful experience in the Scandinavian coun - tries, Germany, and Switzerland. Jean Chazal, Etudes de criminologie juvenile (Paris, 1952), p. 83.

51. An average of 17 to 25 per cent of all young offenders brought to juvenile courts are released to their parents without adequate supervision. J. Neret, Les enfants et les adolescents inadaptés (Paris: Editions sociales françaises, 1954), pp. 15 ff.

maintains jurisdiction over the young offender under probation or released under liberté surveillée [parole after commitment to an institution], and he may revise all measures according to the needs of the young offender.

Appeal against the decision of the juvenile court is carried to a special youth chamber of the Cour d'appel [Court of Appeals] to which a Conseiller pour la protection de l'enfance [Counselor for the Protection of Children] is appointed, but the juvenile court may order the immediate execution of its decision (for instance, placement in a correctional school) even if such a decision is appealed. If the parents ask for the return of the child and their petition is denied, it may not be renewed before one year has elapsed.

In the Tribunal pour les adolescents [Court for Adolescents] a member of the Tribunal supérieur [Superior Court] is the presiding judge, and two other judges serve as members -- if possible these are judges from the district juvenile court. Critical considerations of citizens' groups in France indicate that the system is still too judicial, and that more educational and social emphasis is necessary. Experts recommend that more women judges be assigned to the children's courts, and that the participation of social workers in the adjustment of delinquent children be strengthened. [52]

CORRECTION OF DISOBEDIENT CHILDREN

The Napoleonic Code Civil provided la correction paternelle, special court measures for unmanageable, difficult children who menaced or attacked their parents. Parents unable to handle such children could file a petition with the civil court to ask for

52. André Klotz and Paul Samana, "The Treatment of Juvenile Offenders in France," in Margery Fry, Lawless Youth, pp. 185-188; Alfred Brauner, Les Enfants Ont Vécus La Guerre (Paris: Editions sociales françaises, 1946); Maurice Dubois, Enfance coupable, enfance malheureuse (Paris: Louvain, 1947); and T. C. N. Gibbens, "Les problèmes posés par le traitement psychiatrique des délinquants," Revue de Science Criminelle et de Droit Pénal Comparé, XIII, No. 3 (July-September, 1958), 575-586.

TABLE 6: STATISTICS OF JUVENILE DELINQUENCY
IN FRANCE 1912-1958*

Year	Number	Year	Number	Year	Number
1912	13,670	1931	11,598	1943	34,127
1919	21,095	1932	10,034	1944	23,384
1920	18,569	1933	8,972	1945	17,578
1921	16,241	1934	10,434	1949	22,761
1922	11,915	1935	11,035	1950	19,239
1923	11,443	1936	10,879	1951	14,971
1924	12,671	1937	11,817	1952	14,624
1925	12,932	1938	13,310	1953	14,070
1926	14,185	1939	12,165	1954	13,504
1927	14,407	1940	16,937	1955	13,975[a]
1928	12,825	1941	32,327	1956	14,778
1929	11,882	1942	34,781	1957	16,366
1930	12,234			1958	12,886

[a] Convictions of juvenile offenders by the juvenile courts for the period 1955-1958 have not been published; the data given for these years represent all young persons placed by the courts in correctional institutions of public or private nature in France. They include some children and adolescents who have been committed to these schools without having committed an offense; however, they do not include young persons who have been convicted of delinquency but have not been committed to a correctional institution.

*Data derived from official statistics quoted in Joubrel, op. cit., pp. 9-10, Annuaire Statistique, 1952, p. 90; Annuaire Statistique, 1956, pp. 78, 92-94; Ministère de la Justice, Rapport Annuel, 1955, pp. 7-9 and letters to the author with statistics of May 30, 1959 and June 22, 1959.

help in the discipline of the child. On the court's order, the child was apprehended by the police. At the court hearing the father, or in his absence the mother, could request the court to have a child under 16 confined to jail for no longer than one month, and adolescents over 16 for up to six months. In 1935, an amendment of the Civil Code abolished the child's arrest, but still permitted him to be confined in prison. Child welfare workers and the association of juvenile court judges

criticized this institution as outdated and in conflict with modern
ideas of education. In 1945, commitment of a disobedient, unmanageable child was limited to those situations in which the
presiding judge of the juvenile court authorized this measure. If
requested by either parent, a social investigation by a child
welfare agency or a probation officer is submitted before the
court makes a decision. The judge may place the child in a
foster home, a children's home, or an orphanage until he is
considered ready to return home. [53]

PROBATION SERVICES

Liberté surveillée [probation] was first introduced in France
in 1906, after Justice Edouard Julheit had visited the Cook County
Juvenile Court in Chicago. Until recently, however, the functions of the French probation officer differed from those in the
United States and England. [54] With a few exceptions the probation
officers were volunteers -- mainly society ladies, retired army
officers, a few businessmen. Their good will and philanthropic
but paternalistic approach, however, did not provide an understanding of the young offender's social and economic needs, his
attitude, nor the means of achieving his adjustment. They
supervised many children, sometimes over 100, without training
or competence for such an assignment. It is not surprising that
the results of probation were not encouraging, nor that it did not
live up to the expectations its pioneers in France had held for it.
There has been some improvement since the juvenile courts began
to select the délégués à la liberté surveillée from nomination
lists of experienced persons presented by child protective
agencies, particularly the local comité pour la protection des
mineurs delinquants [committee for the protection of delinquent
minors]. In Paris, Lille, Marseilles, Lyons, and other large

---

53. Decree-Order of September 1, 1945.

54. Henri Rollet, "The Probation System in France," in Sheldon Glueck,
Probation and Criminal Justice (New York: Macmillan, 1933), p. 296; Joubrel,
op. cit., p. 124.

cities the volunteers have federations and organize lectures, dis-cussions, and training institutions under the guidance of judges, psychiatrists, and public welfare officials. [55]

Professional probation practice started in France in 1923 when a private social agency in Paris, Service social de l'enfance en danger moral (now called Service social de l'enfance) began to assist the juvenile court. The court assigned to this agency the children of parents deprived of parental rights for abuse, severe neglect, or mistreatment, children under 13 years of age involved in crime, and other delinquent children who were left with their families but who needed careful supervision. In 1929 La Sauve-garde de l'adolescence, another agency for juvenile delinquents, was founded in Paris. It maintains a detention home and conducts social investigations of the families of adolescents detained before court trial. A third agency, L'Aide morale de la jeunesse, is licensed for probation services for girls. In these agencies the social investigation by trained social workers is followed by a medical and a psychiatric examination[56] which give the juvenile court material on which to base its decision.

Following the example of Paris, other cities founded similar social agencies under the name of Service social de sauvegarde de l'enfance et de l'adolescence [Social Service for the Protection of Children and Adolescents]. [57] The judges of the juvenile court usually assign the task of probation to these agencies, which employ trained social workers whenever difficult cases make skilful investigation and supervision necessary. Since 1945 the

---

55. The juvenile court law of 1912 did not mention trained social workers, but the decree of 1945 includes provisions for the employment of licensed social workers as probation officers.

56. Elisabeth Huguenin, Les Tribunaux pour Enfants (Paris and Neuchatel: Delachaux & Niestle, 1935), pp. 32 33; Jean Chazal, L'Enfance délinquante (Paris: Presses Universitaires, 1953).

57. Another agency in Paris, Les Marraines sociales [The Social Godmothers] was engaged in serving juvenile delinquent girls, particularly vagrants and prostitutes who had been arrested and could not return to their homes, but it ceased to function in 1943.

juvenile courts have appointed a number (in general at least one for each court, and in Paris six) of délégués permanents à la liberté surveillée [full-time probation officers] to their staffs.[58] The probation officers must be competent to work with juvenile delinquents and neglected children, having either an academic degree, a license as a social worker, or substantial experience in social work. They perform individual work with difficult adolescents, supervise volunteers in probation service, and suggest the replacement of unqualified volunteers.

Nationwide federations of child protective agencies providing probation services are the Association amicale des délégués à la liberté surveillée, the Service social de l'enfance, and the Union des patronages. In the practice of the courts, volunteers engaged in a profession or otherwise gainfully employed shall not supervise more than two or three children, so that they can devote enough time and interest to each.[59] If the parents interfere with the work of the probation officer, they may be fined or have their family allowance cancelled. The probation officer reports to the Tribunal pour enfants [Juvenile Court] regularly, as a rule every three months, on the adjustment and behavior of the children under his supervision. He has to inform the judge whenever the child evidences misconduct, becomes morally endangered, or attempts to evade supervision. Parents and guardians have to notify the probation officer if the child becomes seriously ill, or if he leaves his place or remains absent without permission.

INSTITUTIONS FOR JUVENILE DELINQUENTS AND PAROLE

Correctional education for maladjusted or delinquent children in France has its legal foundations in the law of August 5, 1850, with its amendments, and the Loi d'assistance à l'enfance of April 15, 1943. There are two legal classifications for these

---

58. There are six juvenile court sections in Paris, each serving a regional sector of the Capital.

59. Decree of July 1, 1945, Article XI.

:hildren: difficiles [difficult] and vicieux [incorrigible]. Both nay be committed to an institution by either the Tribunal pour enfants or the civil court. The majority of the institutions for he readjustment of children are private schools and reforma-.ories (whose endowments and financial resources are usually .imited).[60] Most institutions are therefore dependent upon public subsidies granted by the local or departmental government, or occasionally by the national treasury. However, sources of income are often insufficient for proper equipment and especially for the employment of well-qualified personnel.

There are four types of correctional institutions:

1. Centres d'observation [detention homes and observation centers],

2. Etablissements de rééducation agréé [training schools],

3. Colonies correctionnelles [correctional schools], and

4. Maisons d'éducation surveillée [reformatory schools].

n some adult prisons and jails a separate ward is still used for he detention of juvenile offenders, but they are usually taken to other institutions maintained by private child protective agencies and patronages [neighborhood centers]. Only a few have an observation center staffed for psychiatric consultation, such as the Foyer de Soulins at Brunoy near Paris. Some private social agencies specialize in the placement of boys or girls in rural communities, but farm families often do not understand the problems of urban youth, and a large proportion of the children run away. One of the best known child protective agencies in Paris, called the Patronage Rollet in memory of Judge Henri

---

60. The reformatory school at Mattrey, established as early as 1839 by Judge Frédéric Auguste Demetz, was the first to develop care for young offenders in small separate groups, called the "family system"; it was observed by American visitors, and became the inspiration for the "cottage system" in American reformatories and children's institutions. Its development and methods are described in Teeters-Reinemann, The Challenge of Delinquency (Englewood Cliffs, N. J.: Prentice-Hall, 1950), pp. 61-64.

Rollet, maintains two children's colonies in the départements of
Lot and Lot-et-Cher, each of which has a centre communal de
jeunesse [community youth center] with clubrooms and recreational facilities under trained supervision. Here the youngsters
no longer feel isolated as they do on the farm, but are part of a
peer group with a similar background, feel more secure, and
are able to adjust to the rural community. [61]

Although the 51 industrial training schools in France are
under governmental supervision, only three are public institutions. These training schools are used for the treatment of
difficult and maladjusted children who cannot remain in their
own homes and are not suited to foster-family life, and of
juvenile delinquents who, after a psychiatric examination, are
recommended for commitment to a training school. [62] One of the
serious difficulties in France is the lack of proper specialization
of facilities in most training schools, which accept all age
groups and types of children and adolescents without consideration
of the climatic, academic, and vocational facilities the school
has to offer. The time and emphasis given to the children's
physical education and recreation are often insufficient. Rarely
are there enough specialized observation clinics or medical
treatment for children suffering from nervous disturbances
based upon endocrinological or syphilitic causes. Physiotherapy,
social casework, and a more systematic medical and psychiatric
observation and treatment are needed. [63]

Colonies correctionnelles [correctional schools] are used for
the adjustment of juvenile delinquents sentenced by the children's

---

61. Joubrel, op. cit., pp. 129-131.

62. Until 1945 the supervision of these schools was under the jurisdiction of the
Administration nationale des prisons [National Prison Administration]. At present
a special division in the Ministère de la Justice is in charge and emphasizes the
educational aspects of the schools.

63. More details are given by Joubrel, op. cit., pp. 188-189. The same
fundamental deficiencies are found also in the correctional and reformatory schools.
See T. C. N. Gibbens, "Les problèmes posés par le traitement psychiatrique des
délinquants," op. cit., pp. 579-581.

court for serious crimes to more than two years of confinement, and for severely maladjusted adolescents, the so-called pupilles vicieux, who are so insubordinate that they cannot be kept in a regular training school.   Colonies correctionnelles are also used for the re-education of problem boys and delinquent adolescents in the 18 to 21 age group.

Maisons de l'éducation surveillée [reformatory schools] care for children or minors committed by the Tribunal pour enfants or the civil court. 64 The court in France orders a definite period of confinement, but it may later permit an earlier release on parole if the school report justifies such action.   Parole is granted if the adolescent's progress indicates that he may return to his home or be placed in a foster family.   If no parole is suggested, the adolescent may remain in the reformatory school until he reaches the age of 21.   A minor who is paroled from the reformatory school by order of the court remains under the supervision of a special parole committee, the comité de secours et patronage, organized by the board of the school. 65 A few public and private schools use a hostel as a transitory arrangement so that the youngsters may adjust more easily to community life after their release.

There are 130 maisons de l'éducation surveillée [reformatory schools] in France, of which only six schools for boys and two for girls are public institutions. The public reformatory schools are organized according to age groups and training facilities. One of them is reserved for first offenders; another is for boys suffering from tuberculosis.   The schools are equipped with industrial workshops; one trains boys in maritime science and

---

64. The commitment to the reformatory school may be ordered by the civil court on the petition of the parents or guardian for unmanageable, disobedient children.

65. The supervision of paroled adolescents was a charge of the public assistance authorities until 1930, but they had no parole staff and their inspectors were so burdened by other duties that they could not devote sufficient interest to this assignment.   The parole committees of the schools use volunteers, as a rule, but there is a trend to employ a trained worker or to cooperate with a child welfare agency with trained staff whenever possible.

fishery techniques. Each public reformatory school has a board on which the deputy prefect of the département serves as chairman.

Among private reformatory schools, there are twice as many institutions for girls as for boys. During the last war many of these schools lost their financial support when the devaluation of the franc affected their endowments, bequests, and investments. Subsidies are provided through state appropriations for each child whose parents cannot pay his expenses, but these public allocations are not sufficient for all the necessary improvements, sanitary facilities, medical supervision, and employment of trained personnel.

There is still a tendency to commit to the public reformatory schools only the most difficult youngsters, and to send the rest to private institutions with which the court is familiar. The development of public control over private reformatory schools has led to some improvements, particularly in boys' schools, but substantial reforms are still needed in the schools for girls. In the last decade, with increased government subsidies, [66] the facilities for vocational instruction and training have been improved, and teachers and social workers are now employed.

Some reformatory schools still have iron-barred windows and high gray walls, which give a prison-like appearance. In a few boys' schools the gardiens [guards] have changed little but their name; they are now called moniteurs [monitors]. Criticism of the brutal treatment of the young inmates of the bagnes d'enfants [children's penitentiaries] has led to reform measures by special legislation. [67] The most important change is that

---

66. The subsidies are now granted by one government agency in charge of the control, while until 1946 several government units granted subsidies (Joubrel, op. cit., pp. 202-203).

67. For example, the laws of August 13, 1936 (on the reform of the school at Saint-Maurice) and of July 12, 1937 (on the reform of the reformatory at Saint-Hilaire). The dangerous aspects of correctional institutions are not overlooked in France; see Michel Lemay, "Le contagion psychique en internat," Rééducation, 12, No. 98-99 (April-May, 1958), 3-17.

untrained attendants have been replaced by teachers and licensed social workers. In many schools the children now are classified according to their adjustment needs, and the cottage system is slowly replacing the large dormitories.

Social workers in France complain that in rural départements detention homes and observation centers are still lacking, and that there are insufficient well-staffed institutions for the education of various categories of children. Even where psychiatric classification and diagnosis are available, facilities for effective treatment of the children fall short. The personnel in most religious reformatory schools have no formal educational and social work training, and too few give sufficient attention to the personal needs of adolescent boys and girls.

In a few institutions, particularly the Ecole Théophile-Roussel at Montesson near Paris, experiments are conducted in the use of industrial machinery for the main types of vocational and agricultural training, and in a full program of recreational activities. Each child has an attractive room; there are comfortable living and dining rooms and a well-equipped library. This school also serves as a training center for educators and social workers in the field of correctional education. Experts in correctional work, physicians, neuro-psychiatrists, and psychologists are on the faculty of this training institute. The period of specialized training is six months, and the academic and clinical courses are combined with an internship at the school. There are similar institutes at Nantes and Rennes.[68]

In all public correctional schools, vocational training is mandatory. Emphasis is placed on realistic vocational training for boys in industrial or trade skills, auto mechanics, and laboratory work, and for girls in home economics, dietary skills, and textile work, according to the aptitude of the youngsters. The trade training is intended to equip the young people to find skilled or semi-skilled work after their return to the family or community, to give them a feeling of self-confidence and facilitate a change in their attitude toward society. Vocational training is

---

68. Joubrel, op. cit., pp. 135-136.

thus an important, integral part of the whole education program in the correctional institution. On the basis of vocational advancement, a program of parole has been developed to allow youngsters who cannot return to their own families to be placed in trade or industrial work in cities or villages near the institution, under the supervision of a parole officer. [69]

The personnel problem has still not been solved. Many correctional colonies and reformatory schools are located far from large cities and their educational and cultural facilities. The simple living conditions, the demanding, responsible work with difficult adolescents, and the very modest salaries have not attracted the appropriate kind and necessary number of devoted professional workers.

The most hopeful aspect in the treatment of juvenile delinquents is the establishment of public <u>centres</u> d'accueil d'observation [reception and observation centers] under the auspices of the departmental authorities to which the <u>juge</u> d'enfants may refer a juvenile offender. These centers, comparable to residential child guidance clinics in England and the United States, are connected with general or psychiatric hospitals, or with schools or children's institutions. Under a team of psychiatrist, physician, social worker, and psychologist, each child receives a thorough medical and psychiatric examination when his case history is taken. [70] A social investigation of his family and home supplements material on social and economic conditions. After the child completes his personality and aptitude tests, has been placed for a certain period in a work shop of the observation center, and has been also observed in play and recreation, the staff of the center recommends measures of treatment for the youngster.

---

69. Paul Lutz, <u>op. cit.</u>, p. 15; Jean Chazal, <u>L'Enfance Délinquante</u> (Paris: Presses Universitaires, 1953), p. 90.

70. <u>Centres d'accueil et d'observation,</u> organized since 1942, but developed on a broader basis since 1945, and regulated by a decree of the <u>Ministère de la Justice</u> of July 20, 1950. See also M. Chaurand, "Satisfaction des besoins de l'enfant en Centre d'observation," <u>Sauvegarde de l'Enfance,</u> 1953, No. 1, Suppl.

National centres psycho pédagogiques [child guidance clinics] have been organized by the education and public health ministries in Paris, Lyons, and Marseilles. Children with severe adjustment difficulties, neurotic and delinquent tendencies, emotional imbalance, and sexual problems are referred to them. [71]

A clinical type of treatment for certain difficult and delinquent children is attempted in Paris, Brive, Béziers, and Lyons. Such youngsters are left with their families, but come to a clinic for regular psychotherapy or group therapy. The clinics cooperate with vocational guidance and placement services, and include special orientation of and cooperation with the families of the children. [72]

---

71. Joubrel, op. cit., pp. 216-217; Rééducation, 1947, No. 2, 22 ff; Sauvegarde de l'Enfance, 1951, Nos. 9 and 10.

72. H. Michard, L'observation en milieu ouvert (Vaucresson: Centre de formation et d'études de l'éducation surveillée, 1957).

SELECTED BIBLIOGRAPHY

Banu, G. Hygiène Sociale de l'Enfance. 2 Vols. Paris: Masson, 1930-1933.

Bar, P. L'Hygiène Sociale. Paris, 1934.

Bécart, Etienne. Organisation et fonctionnement des colonies des vacances. Paris: Edition Jeunesse au plein air, 1955.

Bénassy-Chauffard. C. L. "Vocational Guidance in France, "International Labour Review, 60, No. 4 (October, 1949), 391-408.

Beno, N., H. Bersot, and Lucien Bovet. Les enfants nerveux, leur dépistage et leur traitement par les services médico-pédagogiques. Neuchâtel and Paris, 1947.

Boulonnois, Louis. "La Municipalité en Service: L'oeuvre municipale de M. Henri Sellier à Surêsnes, " La Revue d'Hygiène et de Médecine Sociales, May-June, 1937.

Bourrat, Dechaume, et al. L'enfance irrégulière, psychologie clinique. Paris: Presses Universitaires, 1946.

Cannat, P. La prison-école. Paris, 1955.

Chassot, Maurice. Les conséquences pénales et civiles de l'infraction commise par un mineur. Dijon: Darantière, 1943.

Chauderlot, Gaston. De la protection légale des enfants et des adolescents. Paris: V. Giard & E. Brière, 1911.

Chazal, Jean. Les enfants devant leurs juges. Paris: Presses Universitaires, 1946.

————. L'Enfance Délinquante. Paris: Presses Universitaires, 1953.

————. "Les bandes asociales d'enfants et leur réintégration dans les cadres," L'Enfance vagabonde. Paris: UNESCO, 1950.

————. "Mésures de rééducation et peines devant les tribunaux pour enfants," Revue de Science criminelle et de droit pénal comparé, No. 4 (1953), pp. 621 ff.

Debesse, M. La crise d'originalité juvénile. 3rd ed. Paris, 1948.

————. "Psychologie du problème moral chez l'adolescent," L'Ecole des Parents (Paris), December, 1952.

De Casabianca, Pierre. Guide des tribunaux pour enfants. Paris: Office Central des Oeuvres de Bienfaisance, 1934.

————. Recueil de la législation relative à l'enfance malheureuse ou traduite en justice, promulgé de 1934-1941. Paris: Office Central des Oeuvres de Bienfaisance, 1941.

Dubois, Maurice. Enfance coupable, enfance malheureuse. Paris: Louvain, 1947.

Etten, Henry van. "L'éducateur de Foyer de semi-liberté," Rééducation (Paris), Nos. 55 and 56, 1954.

Favre, Henri. La Maison d'éducation surveillée d'Eysses. Toulouse: E. Privat, 1933.

François-Unger, Claude. L'adolescent inadapté. Paris: Presses Universitaires, 1957.

Frey, E. L'avenir des mineurs délinquants. Paris, 1947.

Guex, G. La névrose d'abandon. Paris, 1950.

Heuyer, G. "Délinquance juvénile et alcoolisme," Rééducation (Paris), No. 53, 1954.

————. "Psychopathologie de l'Enfance Victime de la Guerre, " Sauvegarde, 2, No. 17 (January, 1948), 3-46.

Huguenin, Elisabeth. Les tribunaux pour enfants. Paris et Neuchâtel: Delachaux & Niestle, 1935.

International Labour Office. Children and Young Persons under Labor Law (Studies and Reports, Series I [Employment of Women and Children], No. 3). Geneva, 1935.

————. Problems of Vocational Guidance (Studies and Reports, Series J, No. 4), 1935.

Joubrel, Henri. "L'éducateur de jeunes socialement inadaptés, " Educateurs (Paris), No. 56, 1955.

————. La Pierre au Cou. Paris: Bloud & Gay, 1953.

Joubrel, Henri and Fernand. L'Enfance dite "Coupable". Paris: Bloud & Gay, 1946.

Keller, Franklin and Morris S. Viteless. Vocational Guidance Throughout the World. New York: W. W. Norton, 1937. Chapter V, pp. 158-199.

Lafon, R. Psycho-pédagogie médico-sociale. Paris, 1950.

Launey, Clément and Michel Soulé. L'Adoption. Paris: Editions Sociales Françaises, 1954.

League of Nations. The Placing of Children in Families. Geneva, 1938. II, 94-109.

————. (Child Welfare Committee). Auxiliary Services of Juvenile Courts. (Series IV, 1, Social.) Geneva, 1931.

————. (Child Welfare Committee). Enquiry into the Question of Children in Moral and Social Dangers. Geneva, 1934.

————. (Child Welfare Committee). Organization of Juvenile Courts and the Results Attained Hitherto. (Series IV, Social.) Geneva, 1931.

Léonard, Madeleine. La Protection de l'Enfance Malheureuse. Paris: A. Pédone, 1938.

Liévois, Françoise. La Délinquance Juvénile. Paris: Presses Universitaires, 1946.

————. "L'Equipement français pour la jeunesse inadaptée, " Educateurs (Paris), No. 56, 1955.

Lox, Fl. Jeunes filles en liberté. Paris: Les Cahiers de L'Enfance May, 1958.

Mazo, Geneviève. Le centre d'observation et la Loi du 27 Juillet 1942 rélative à l'enfance délinquante. Paris: H. von Etten, 1944.

Nevron, Guy. L'Enfant vagabond. Paris: Presses Universitaires, 1952.

Parker, D. Puissance et responsabilité du film. Paris, 1945.

Rollet, Henri. "The Probation System in France, " in Sheldon Glueck, Probation and Criminal Justice. New York: Macmillan, 1933. Pp. 296-304.

Save the Children Fund. Children in Bondage, A Survey of Child Life in Occupied Countries of Europe and Finland. London, 1942.

Schindfessel, J. Organisation et fonctionnement d'un centre psycho-médico-social. Liège: Centre d'études, January-February, 1958.

Sérin, Suzanne. "L'Internement d'enfants dans les Asiles d'Aliénés, " Rééducation, 8, No. 53 (January-February, 1954), 3-8.

Siméon, J. La protection judiciaire de l'enfance délinquante ou en danger en France. Paris: Edition de l'Epargne, 1958.

Trivas, J. "Etudes sur quelques facteurs d'inadaption juvénile, " Sauvegarde de l'Enfance, Vol. 1954, Nos. 6 and 7.

Voirin, M. "La collaboration de l'éducateur et du psychiatre en observation, " Rééducation, Vol. 1954, Nos. 60 and 61.

4

THE PRIVATE
SOCIAL
AGENCIES

FUNCTIONS OF RELIGIOUS AND NON-SECTARIAN
SOCIAL AGENCIES

Until the Revolution, private charities, most of them under the auspices of the Catholic Church, provided the bulk of charitable services in hospitals, asylums, orphanages, and other institutions in France. Since that period, a more distinct separation has developed between the fields of public and private welfare work in France than in the Anglo-Saxon countries. The public assist-ance agencies have taken the main responsibility for the financial support of the various needy groups of the population, but they are primarily concerned with the legal and administrative aspects of their services. The public welfare activities are strictly directed by laws and regulations; comparatively less attention is paid to the personal needs of the individual. Private social agencies, on the other hand, are often poorly organized and are continuously struggling to raise funds for their services from collections, donations, and subsidies because of the lack of adequate endowments, regular contributions, or other types of financial support. However, they are free of strict regulation of their activities, are able to experiment, and are flexible in their methods. Both religious and non-sectarian welfare agencies maintain numerous charitable institutions, such as homes for the aged and for different types of handicapped adults and children, a large number of hospitals and asylums, summer recreation camps, children's institutions, and convalescent homes. Many private social agencies are subsidized by local, departmental, or national government agencies. Some private social agencies still continue to provide material aid to certain groups of the population. The homeless find relief in the shelters of the Salvation Army; soup kitchens are maintained in a few cities with free meals for anyone during the winter. The number of private social agencies in the large cities is substantial. In Paris about 10, 000 agencies are still listed in the official directory of charity organizations, Le Paris charitable, but many of these engage in rather limited activities. The majority of private agencies are sponsored by religious groups, about 90 per cent of them Catholic. The number of non-sectarian agencies is less impressive, and they devote their efforts to health services, child protection, and work for the handicapped. The anti-clerical policy of the state at the end of the nineteenth century made relations difficult between public and private religious welfare organizations, but the policy has since changed to one of coopera-tion in the interest of the clients.

Coordination of the various private agencies and, more recently, of the public welfare services constitutes one of the difficult problems in the field of social work. An attempt to coordinate the activities of the numerous Catholic charities operating without common plan and with much duplication of effort was made in 1833 by Frédéric Ozanam when he founded the Société de Saint Vincent - de - Paul. He organized parish conferences in Paris and in other French cities which established principles similar to those of the London Charity Organization Society in 1869, and led to more effective cooperation among all participating organizations. But it was only in 1892 that a central information service, the Office central de la bienfaisance, was set up in Paris.

NEIGHBORHOOD CENTERS AND SETTLEMENT HOUSES

Family and child welfare work is carried on by private as well as public agencies. In group work, the patronages [neighborhood centers] play an important part in the lives of children and adolescents. The first concept of a settlement house was initiated by Fourier (1772-1837), who conceived the idea of founding a small "ideal community" designed to promote cooperation among the different social classes. A realization of this idea was an experiment by Godin, who was a disciple of Fourier. In 1859, at Guise, he established a consumer's cooperative in a factory which served not only the firm's employees but the entire community. Balzac, in "The Brotherhood of Consolation," describes a community center which closely resembles the settlement houses in England, founded 20 years later in London when Edward Denison opened his "labor school," followed in 1884 by Samuel Barnett's founding of Toynbee Hall.[1]

The number of résidences sociales [settlement houses] in France is not large compared with that in the United States.[2] But the settlement houses are an important factor in French social welfare and cultural activities, and are often the center of medical and social services in a district. "L'Oeuvre sociale de Popincourt," the first settlement house in France, was founded in Paris in 1899 by Mlle Gahery, and another was established in 1903 by Mme Le Fer de la Motte. In 1919, after the First World War, Mlle Marie-Jean Bassot and Mlle Girault established a settlement house in one of the worst slum regions of Paris. Their example was followed in several other cities and led to a federation of settlement houses in 1921. The federation now has 150 settlement houses in France as members, and there are, in addition, rural community centers organized by the agricultural cooperative societies.[3]

---

1. Robert A. Woods, "The Settlement's Foothold of Opportunity," in Lorene M. Pacey, Readings in the Development of Settlement Work (New York: Association Press, 1950), p. 155.

2. The terms maison sociale or centre social, as well as résidence sociale, are used for settlement houses; there are about 260 settlement houses in the United States.

3. Mlle de Gourlet, "La Maison Sociale," Pages Sociales, No. 16 (March, 1946), pp. 3-6; S. Chalvet, "Social Settlements in France," (Paris: Centre d'Infor-

As defined by the French federation, the centre social is an organization which, with the cooperation of the citizens of the neighborhood, attempts to solve special problems of the population of a ward or geographical area. The centre offers educational, social, and health facilities for its neighborhood. A social worker who is responsible to the directors of the centre has frequent office hours in which he is available to the public; he often resides at the centre.[4] Experience indicates that a settlement house is able to serve a population of 1,000 to 20,000 inhabitants, of whom from 500 to 8,000 may use the services of the agency directly. The average is 1,000 families with 3,000 individuals.[5]

The services of the settlement houses include, as a rule, a kindergarten, day-care center for school-age children, library with reading room, consultation center for mothers, vocational training courses, and adult discussion and study groups. The settlement houses are usually financed by social agencies, church groups, industrial plants, family allowance funds, and self-help cooperatives; some are supported by private philanthropists. The emphasis of their activities varies: some stress child-care activities, vocational training of adolescents, and preparation for trade or industrial work; others, health education and cultural activities for adults. A few settlement houses in France organize and operate family colonies de vacances near their children's vacation camps. The family cottages are reserved for parents of children who are at that time in the children's camp. People of various occupations and religious

---

mation Documentaires, 1936); and Mlle J. Moze, "Les Centres Sociaux de France," The Building of Human Relationships in Our Times (Utrecht, Holland: International Federation of Settlements, 1952), pp. 53-59.

4. J. Moze, op. cit., pp. 55-56; Mlle Théry, "Insertion de l'action sociale dans les centres résidentiels," Pages Documentaires, 1958, No. 4 (April-May), 283-290.

5. J. Moze, op. cit., 56-57; J. M. Arnion, "Les centres sociaux," Droit Social, 22, No. 1 (January, 1959), 13-16.

and political beliefs live together, become friends, and enjoy the beauty of the mountains or the countryside.

In rural communities there are about 20 centres socials, and about 75 community centers without residential facilities are conducted by the agricultural cooperative society. These centers provide recreational activities, a day nursery, a small library, playgrounds, and lectures and movies. They also distribute free literature on rural economic and health questions and render consultation services for mothers and babies. [6]

THE RED CROSS

Among the private social agencies the Croix-rouge français [French Red Cross] occupies a prominent position. After the Liberation of France in 1945, the Red Cross was completely reorganized. Since it enjoys the privileges of an "organization of public utility," all its property and affairs are exempt from taxation. The activities of the Croix-rouge français include ambulance transportation, nursing service for wounded and sick members of the armed forces, first-aid training, parcel and correspondence service to prisoners of war, auxiliary services to the armed forces and war veterans, and emergency activities in natural disasters, such as floods and forest fires. [7]

MEDICAL SOCIAL WORK

In the field of health services, private organizations first organized visiting-nurse activities when Dr. A. Calmette advised

---

6. Mlle Th. Moutillard, "Service Social Rural Bonnetable," Pages Sociales, No. 16, March, 1946, pp. 7-8.

7. National decree of April 27, 1945 on the reorganization of the Red Cross; the program of the French Red Cross resembles that of the American National Red Cross, but does not have a specialized family service division like the "Home Service Division" in the United States.

that effective treatment of tuberculosis in the hospitals required home visiting and follow-up care. Dr. T. Granier advanced the theory that not only did tubercular patients need social service in addition to medical treatment, but that their families had to be included in the rehabilitation process as well. For this reason he employed trained visiting nurses (the forerunners of the modern medical social worker) in his hospital, and introduced regular supervision of the patients' families. This method led to the establishment of clinical dispensaries outside the hospitals -- to ensure free medical examinations and X-ray tests -- in an effort to combat this disease. [8]

The first medical social workers in hospitals were employed in Paris in 1914, when Professor M. Marfan engaged a trained social worker for the Hôpital d'enfants [Children's Hospital]. In 1922, a Fédération des services sociaux à l'hôpital [Federation of Hospital Social Services] was founded and assumed respon- sibility for professional training and the provision of current information for medical social workers. [9] The activities of social workers in hospitals include case-work with the patients, contact and counseling with the families, and cooperation with other agencies which might assist the patient and his family after his release from the hospital. The main task of the medical social worker is the interpretation of the doctor's information about the illness and its treatment to the patient and his family. Several private agencies provide nursing care and social service to paralyzed, cardiac, cancer, and rheumatic patients. Particularly active is the Société des rheumatiques paralysés [Society for Paralyzed Rheumatics], which conducts occupational retraining courses in watch-making, fine mechanics, and the manufacture of jewelry. It is supported by the Entr'Aide Française, the national

---

8. League of Nations, European Conference on Rural Life, August, 1939, Publication No. 22, p. 21; M. Maroselli, Annuaire médical de l'hospitalisation française (Paris: Edi-Publi France, 1958).

9. The Fédération has six divisions: maternity, children, syphilis, tuberculo- sis, general medicine, and surgery. Dr. Jean Imbert, "La réforme hospitalière," Droit Social, 21, No. 9-10 (September-October, 1958), 496-505.

coordinating agency, and with this subsidy it is able to employ a number of trained medical social workers in addition to its craft instructors and volunteers for counseling work with the families of patients.[10]

CATHOLIC CHARITABLE SOCIETIES

Among the large number of Catholic charitable societies in France, Les Soeurs de Charité [Sisters of Charity] and Les Filles de Charité [Daughters of Charity] are the most renowned. Everywhere in France one meets these women in their long blue-grey gowns and their white "cornettes" which look like the wings of a bird. The activities of most Catholic charities are organized within the church parish.[11] They often maintain a maison de la charité [house of charity] which includes an infant nursery, a kindergarten, a residential orphanage, a parochial school, and a continuation school for older girls with instruction in domestic work and home economics. Sometimes a dormitory for working girls is also a part of the charity house. Some of the larger institutions of this type are equipped with an ouvroir [workshop] where unemployed girls and women of the neighborhood can earn a living by sewing, dressmaking, and repair work.

FAMILY ASSOCIATIONS

An important role in the area of community development in France is played by the mutuelles familiales and mutuelles coopératives [family associations and mutual-aid societies]. Family associations were founded about the turn of this century, when Abbé Viollet organized "Le Moulin Vert" in Paris in 1902, a Catholic family association based on the principle

---

10. Yvonne Bougé, Préparation et activités de l'assistante sociale (Paris: Bloud & Gay, 1947), pp. 240-242.

11. Special services for the aged are frequently provided; see Pierre Médard, "Les oeuvres Catholiques d'aide aux personnes agées," Les Cahiers du Musée Social, 1957, No. 4 (September), 106-118.

that families should not count on charity or public support but
should help themselves. Another organization of similar nature
is the Union familiale des pères méritoires [Family Union of
Deserving Fathers], established in 1904 in Artas (Isère),
consisting of families with four or more children. Family
associations are formed by people of the same religious faith, by
members of the various political parties, by families living in
the same neighborhood, by members of the same profession or
occupation, or by families whose breadwinners belong to the
same trade union. The function of these family associations and
mutual-aid societies is cultural and educational as well as social
and economic. They are concerned with the improvement of the
economic, health, and social conditions of their members, and the
maintenance of their self-respect, status, and moral well-being;
they also represent their interests before local, provincial, and
national governments.[12] Some family associations conduct
research and social surveys, and engage in social action in order
to obtain suitable legislation. Frequently family associations
cooperate with trade union groups and other cooperative
societies in order to achieve these goals.

In 1945, a Union nationale des sociétés familiales [National
Union of Family Associations] was established by government
decree, and the number of local associations has increased from
850 in 1945 to more than 12,000.[13] Certain aspects of the work
of the associations are similar to the British Citizens' Advice
Bureaus in which people receive proper counsel and information,
but other activities include features of consumers' cooperatives
(providing favorable prices and discounts for food, coal, clothing,
hairdressing, drugs, and spectacles for their members). Some
associations manage small cooperative shops selling at nominal
prices perishable food ordered a week in advance; others
administer attractive, modest summer vacation camps in the

---

12. M. Mazé, "La Communeauté locale et le progrès général," Reponse
Française, Conférence Internationale de Service Social (Toronto, 1954), pp. 5-9.

13. French Committee for Social Service and Social Work, French Report for
the 7th International Conference of Social Work (1954), p. 7.

country or the mountains for their members, with special day-care provisions for small children. Family associations and mutual-aid societies are also organized in public housing projects where the members participate in courses in child care, home management, and dressmaking. The development of family allowances in the modern social security program has received effective support from the initiative and pressure of many family associations. [14]

SOCIAL SERVICE WORK AMONG SEAMEN

A special agency for work among sailors, merchant seamen, and fishermen was founded by M. de Thézac in 1900, under the title Le Service social maritime. The agency maintains shelters for seamen in many ports at nominal prices, and provides technical training courses to improve their skill and make their employment easier and more regular. The centers also provide recreation facilities and arrange for free medical examinations and treatment. The Sécrétariat social maritime employs trained social workers for counseling and casework services to the seamen; it is combined with the Union nationale maritime, maintained by the association of shipowners and overseas shipping companies. The personnel on the vessels of the French Navy are served by a separate voluntary social agency, the Service social central de la Marine [Central Social Service of the Navy], which is concerned with material and personal aid to families of navy personnel who serve overseas, or who are sick or missing. This organization offers counseling, casework service, recreational facilities and summer camps for the families and children of navy men. [15]

---

14. A. Joseph Brayshaw, "Family Associations in France," Social Service, 28, No. 1 (June-August, 1954), 24-28 and Chapter 5, infra.

15. Yvonne Bougé, op. cit., pp. 204-210.

PROBLEMS OF COMMUNITY ORGANIZATION

The lack of coordination and cooperation among the activities of the private and public social agencies has led to numerous attempts to achieve some solution of this administrative and functional problem. In Paris, private social agencies founded the Office central des oeuvres de bienfaisance [Central Office of Welfare Agencies], the Comité d'entente [Committee of Coordination], the Groupement des unions d'oeuvres d'assistance et d'aide sociale [Alliance of Associations of Relief and Social Work Agencies], and the Permanence d'entr'aide sociale [Permanent Social Coordination Service]. The objective of these agencies was to establish a method of cooperation among the welfare activities of private and public agencies, comparable to the function which the Council of Social Agencies or the Community Welfare Council perform in the United States. The Cromwell Foundation supported this development by employing 29 trained social workers for this specific goal of coordination, one for each of the city halls of the 29 boroughs of Paris and eight surrounding suburban communities. These workers served as interviewers and liaison officers, rendered information, and referred clients to the public assistance authorities or to the private agency best equipped to help them in their individual needs.

Beyond the local level, other efforts were made to achieve some coordination of the activities of health services and social agencies. By a decree of May 12, 1951, the Ministère de santé publique established another agency, the Groupement d'action des services sociaux [Coordination of Social Services Activities]. It was organized as a semi-private agency, vested with important public and voluntary functions, and replaced the Permanence d'entr'aide sociale in coordinating the activities of public and private relief and health services and in expanding their facilities on a national level. One of its functions was the raising of funds to supplement the financial support appropriated from taxes by all governmental levels for the operation of social services.

In each arrondissement [district] a competent social worker was appointed as the field representative of the Groupement

d'action des services sociaux. This délégué technique[16] was
selected from the staffs of the private and public agencies of
the district and was formally acknowledged by the prefect
(governor) of the département. He was officially introduced
to all public authorities of the district, accumulated a complete
file of all families residing in the district, and prepared a
roster of public and private health and welfare facilities. His
main activity was to serve as an information center for the
public and for the social agencies about available community
resources.[17] Usually executives or supervisors were selected
for this work. In larger districts, the délégué technique
was entitled to employ one or more social workers under his
direction. In order to achieve better coordination among the
agencies in the district, staff conferences were held according
to local needs, sometimes monthly, sometimes more often.[18]
Later this coordinating function was transferred to another
semi-official organization, L'Entr'Aide française, financed
by the Ministère de santé publique, which has the objective
of coordinating and subsidizing private welfare and health
agencies.[19] In all départements the Entr'Aide française
cooperated with the government in establishing reception
centers for the returning veterans, deportees, and political
refugees. Its summer vacation camps provided recreation and
new strength to millions of undernourished and war-exhausted
children.

---

16. The social worker may be male or female -- the use of the masculine
ending is purely grammatical; women represent the vast majority of social workers
in France, actually.

17. The functions of this délégué technique are comparable to those of the
Citizens' Advice Bureau in England, developed during the Second World War, or to
the information offered in a Community Welfare Council in the United States.

18. Yvonne Bougé, op. cit., pp. 254-255.

19. The Entr'Aide française is also the successor to the Secours National
[National Relief] established as the central semi-public relief organization during
the war. Apolline de Gourlet, Cinquante Ans de Service Social (Paris: Editions
Sociales Françaises, 1947).

After a transition period, in 1947, the Entr'Aide française reformed its program. It is now devoted to making arrangements for emergency relief whenever necessary. Its second function is to provide individual aid and assistance to those for whom no other social services are available. The agency employs 600 trained social workers as field representatives, and receives assistance from public and private funds. The third function of the Entr'Aide remains the most essential one: to serve as a coordinating agency among the private social agencies. It does not interfere with the autonomy and independence of any charitable sectarian or humanitarian organization, but provides for an exchange of experience, serves as a planning body for the development of general welfare and health measures, and represents the interests of private social agencies in relation to public authorities. The Entr'Aide française also has representatives in foreign countries, ambassadeurs de service social [ambassadors of social work] of France, who cooperate with relief activities of former French citizens and cultural groups such as the Alliance française, and in the exchange of French students and social workers. The fourth activity of the Entr'Aide française is to develop research and experimentation in the field of social work which neither public nor private social agencies have initiated, such as a program of after-care for patients released from sanatoria, the expansion of social services in penal institutions, the organization of services for merchant seamen and their families abroad, and recreational and cultural programs. In this broad variety of social services the Entr'Aide française serves as a coordinating center, combining the forces of private social agencies and the public welfare authorities. It is equipped to act as a social planning body on the national and departmental levels. [20]

---

20. Robert Garric, "L'Entr'Aide Française du Temps de Paix," Pages Sociales, No. 29 (September, 1947), pp. 1-2. In the field of group work and recreation, special agencies of coordination had been founded in the 1920's under the leadership of Albert Thomas, later director of the International Labor Office. These 120 regional leisure-time committees under a central board in Paris were supported by civic societies, schools, and the consumer cooperatives; they are now merged with the activities of the Entr'Aide française.

COORDINATED FAMILY SERVICE

Individual social work to help families and children in health, emotional, and economic difficulties had been carried on in France until the First World War primarily by private social agencies, mostly under religious auspices. Their traditional development led to a situation in which workers of various organizations -- child and family welfare societies, hospitals, clinics, maternity homes, settlement houses, old-age homes, and orphanages -- frequently took care of the same family. Later local bureaux d'aide sociale [municipal departments of public welfare] as well as family allowance funds, social insurance agencies, and local public health offices also provided social services to the same families. These services included home visits, family counseling, and sometimes material assistance in cash and in kind. This variety of welfare activities led, particularly in large cities, to a chaotic situation. Social workers of various agencies were busy giving economic aid and other services to the same family, while, on the other hand, people in serious financial and personal need were not assisted by any organization because their suffering remained unknown. The lack of a social service exchange except in Paris (such as those in England or the United States), with a complete confidential register of clients of social agencies, was another reason for the frequent duplication of effort and waste of energy and funds which were criticized by social workers and the public alike.

After the Second World War, social problems were intensified by the death of many soldiers and members of the Maquis, the absence of prisoners of war and deportés, a severe housing shortage, lack of food and clothing, and wide-spread unemployment. A reform of the methods of social work with families was urgently needed. A new attempt to coordinate the various family services was initiated in Paris. In 1948, the Conseil général [General Council] of the Département of the Seine (which consists of the capital, Paris, and the surrounding communities) enacted a statute, the Règlement intérieure du service départemental de coordination des services sociaux, in order to integrate the social services of all organizations within the region.[21] The territory of the département is divided into a hundred units, each comprising one of the 80 communities of the département and of the 20 arrondissements [boroughs] of the capital. In these districts all private and public social agencies which employ family-service workers voluntarily joined to coordinate their home visits and family welfare work under a combined staff of trained social workers.[22]

Each arrondissement is subdivided into a number of sections (usually between 17 and 19) on the basis of the location of the local resources such as hospitals, dispensaries, clinics, children's institutions, old-age homes, and settlement houses. Each section is assigned to a social worker of the combined staff that is composed of all trained social workers engaged in family social work in the district. These social workers remain staff members of the agency which employs them, but they form a combined social welfare department for family services in the district. The government of the arrondissement provides a headquarters for the unified family service, usually in the City Hall, and places at its disposal an office with the necessary technical equipment, reception room, clerical help, interviewing facilities, records, files, and telephones.

Social workers are assigned to the united family service by their various agencies; they must be graduates of a recognized school of social work and must have a state license.[23] The entire staff of family social workers of the arrondissement

---

21. See: Préfecture de la Seine, Direction des Affaires Sociales, The Coordination of Social Services in the Department of Seine (Paris: Lucien Maréchal, 1951), pp. 15-20; and the author's "Coordination of Family Welfare Services in France," Social Service Review, 27, No. 1 (March, 1953), 62-66.

22. The establishment of a coordinated family service unit is not mandatory; but, based upon the favorable experience in Paris, a national law of August 4, 1950 provides that each department is to establish a coordinating committee and is authorized to create a combined unified family service whose structure, organization, and finance are determined by statute.

23. See Chapter 6, infra.

elects as its director an assistante sociale déléguée à la coordination [supervisor of coordination] for a period of three years. A licensed social worker who has been active in social service for at least two years is eligible for this position. In practice the supervisor (most are women) is between 28 and 57 years of age. The election of the assistante sociale déléguée à la coordination is performed by secret ballot, and an election committee under the chairmanship of the maire [mayor] of the arrondissement supervises the election.

The assistante sociale déléguée [supervisor of coordination] remains a member of the staff of the social agency with which she has been connected, but she is also responsible to a Comité de coordination de service social aux familles [Committee on Family Service Coordination] set up in the district. Election regulations require that she be chosen on the basis of outstanding professional ability and moral stature. She advises social agencies and other organizations regarding problems of family living, serves as chairman of the entire staff of the unit through individual and general conferences, and arranges for staff meetings and in - service training courses. Her main task is to coordinate the work of all members of the family service unit, making them familiar with all community facilities such as public and private social agencies, hospitals, dispensaries, well-baby clinics, mental hygiene and child guidance centers, schools, educational and recreational opportunities, summer vacation camps, and playgrounds. Every month she holds a staff con-ference, not only for her own staff but also for other social workers in the district. In the operation of the headquarters she supervises the secretary and other clerical help of the coordination service. In densely populated districts in Paris, one or two other full - time social workers are engaged as her assistants by the bureau d'aide sociale. They keep regular office hours at the coordination center, giving information and advice about community resources, interviewing new clients and referring them to the private or public social agency best equipped to provide the services required. Frequently, both the assistante sociale déléguée and her assistants carry a small case load in their district in order to remain familiar with the clients and the

current local problems of family service work. A central index
of all families under the care of any of the public or private
social agencies in the district is set up and administered by the
assistante sociale déléguée or her staff. She informs social
agencies which have given previous service to a family whenever
their clients reapply for aid. Thus, the new coordinating system
now provides facilities similar to those of a social service
exchange in Great Britain and the United States. Confidential
information is limited to authorized social agencies and is not
available to the public.

    This method of coordination does not force an individual family
to accept the social worker assigned to its section. Statutes and
regulations provide explicitly that a family is entitled to select
another social agency or an individual social worker in the district
to give them casework service instead of the regular section
social worker. This provision allows a family that wants to be
under the care of a denominational social agency to obtain its
services. In practice only an insignificant number of families
have expressed the desire to be served by a social worker other
than the one regularly assigned to their section of the district. In
general, the families under the care of the coordinated service
have been well satisfied with the social worker in charge of the
neighborhood.

    In each département a special bureau for the coordination of
the social services has been established. It is responsible for
organizing cooperation among all public, semi-public, and private
social agencies with the goal of distributing their activities in
the best interest of the population. This departmental bureau
exercises a certain general supervision over the activities of all
social agencies and settles conflicts and differences of opinion
between them. The bureau issues general rules in the interest of
effective cooperation among public and private social agencies. It
works under the direction of the Conseil de surveillance, a board
appointed by the Conseil général of the département. The board is
composed of representatives from the public assistance and social
insurance agencies, the family allowance administration, private
charities, the social workers' organization, and the Association
médicale regionale [Regional Medical Association]; it includes the

medical consultant of the <u>Direction</u> <u>de</u> <u>sécurité</u> <u>sociale</u> [Social Security Division], the directors of the public assistance, public health, and social security authorities, those of the population and social affairs divisions of the département and, in Paris, one <u>maire</u> of an arrondissement elected by the mayors' association. The prefect (governor) of the département is ex officio president of the board.

The <u>Conseil</u> <u>de</u> <u>surveillance</u> studies social problems in its territory, determines which reports shall be submitted to the <u>Conseil</u> <u>général</u> [the legislature], issues information to private charities and public welfare authorities, arranges for the subdivision of districts, and issues regulations for the coordination service. It is authorized to decide conflicts that may arise among the cooperating organizations with regard to the coordination of the family social service, meets at least every three months, and is assisted by an advisory technical commission.

How does the work of the coordinated family welfare service operate in practice? A public or private social agency which has seen an applicant or client in its office and desires a social investigation, further information, or discussion with the family in their home, refers the case to the coordinated family service of the district. The request is assigned to the social worker who is in charge of the local section in which the family resides, and because each social worker serves only a specific territory, it is easy for him to make home visits in the same neighborhood and to devote more time to interviews and counseling, since he is not obliged to travel around in distant parts of the city or the rural district. [24] The coordination prevents the duplication of effort resulting from several workers dealing with the same family, and strengthens the personal contact and confidence between the social worker and the family members. The social worker discusses their needs with all the members of the family although public assistance, family allowance and social insurance benefits, medical and psychiatric services, and vacation camps

---

24. This is more time-consuming in France since few social workers have cars; the majority depend upon a bicycle or have to walk, even in rural districts.

for children are provided by a variety of social agencies. This family social worker is concerned with his clients' economic, legal, social and health problems, and maintains a continuous personal contact with the families in his district. In case of difficult technical questions the worker will ask the advice of the assistante sociale déléguée [coordination supervisor], or will refer the client to the offices of the particular agency in charge of the appropriate services.

Of course, the family welfare service is not able to take care of all problems, and a number of specialized agencies have therefore been exempted from the principle of family service coordination. The exempted services are tuberculosis care, service for cancer and venereal disease, school social work connected with psychiatric-medical clinics, and probation and parole work with juvenile delinquents and adult offenders. Social workers of agencies charged with these services, however, are invited by the assistante sociale déléguée to the regular monthly staff meetings of the district and, when needed, special case conferences are arranged between the family social worker and the specialized social workers. Practice has shown that social investigation and information (including questions of health, en-vironmental influences, and social and economic adjustment) are obtained more precisely and more speedily than before the social service coordination system was instituted.

As a rule, therapy in psychiatric, cancer, and venereal disease clinics, as well as in the medico-psychiatric centers of the conseil d'instruction publique [board of education], and probation work are initiated through the coordinated family service unit. The section worker of the family service agency informs the specialized service of the need, introduces his colleague from the latter agency to the client, and establishes within the family a feeling of confidence in the specialized agency. In some districts outside of Paris where the need for specialized service is rare, some of the family social workers assume the function of the specialist if their training is sufficient and the general case load permits.

Health protection and the medical needs of the family receive special emphasis in social work education and in the orientation of family social service in France. In general, the family social worker is present during the office hours of the child-care and prenatal clinics, and during the medical consultations for school children and their parents at the settlement houses; the family worker cooperates closely with social and medical institutions. The concern with protecting the population against illness and death explains the insistence on medical aspects everywhere in the French social service system. Recently, however, economic, social, and educational aspects have received increasing consideration. The development of the coordinated family service encourages a greater independence of the social worker in the district and makes him less subordinate to the physician and administrator.

The coordinated family service system in France became necessary because of the differences in urgent social needs among the population. Particularly important were the housing shortage and family disorganization resulting from the war and the Occupation. The coordination of family welfare work eliminates costly duplication of effort among private and public social agencies and greatly improves the standards of aid. In spite of some original scepticism among administrators and social workers as to the successful cooperation of the representatives of the family welfare unit's varied private and governmental agencies, the first 12 years of practice have been encouraging. The structures of the coordination committees in the districts and the supervisory committee in the département may seem complicated to the foreign observer, but in practice the work has been carried out with enthusiasm and devotion by social workers and social agencies.

THE ROLE OF VOLUNTARY SOCIAL AGENCIES

The characteristic features of private social agencies in France are similar to those in the United States and Great Britain: they are flexible in the development of their programs, which are not restricted by statutes and tax appropriations; they are able to take speedy action when required and to engage in new social experiments and planning which public organizations cannot easily undertake. The main programs of private agencies developed during the nineteenth century in connection with the social and economic changes caused by the industrialization of France, which was slower than that of the United States, Great Britain, and Germany. The essential social services under private auspices of both religious and non-sectarian agencies have been mentioned in Chapters 2 and 3. These agencies were not only pioneers in charity and aid to children and adults, to sick and handicapped persons, but they are still of importance today in supplementing the health and welfare services of public authorities and in attempting new ventures in the field of social work and social reform. [25]

However, the sectarian and philanthropic social agencies are only a part of the voluntary activities in France designed to assist in the improvement of health and welfare. Mutual-aid associations and family-life societies (as self-help organizations of members of the working and middle classes), family coopera- tives, industrial cooperative societies, and housing cooperatives participate in preventive and curative health measures. They support families in economic need and assist in family protection and related social services, thus supplementing the work of professional private social agencies. Since their financial resources are based upon contributions of their members, they usually have only limited funds to carry out their objectives. But they are influential in conducting health education for members and their families and in providing help to young mothers and infants. There are in France more than nine million members of these mutual-aid and family-life associations, engaged in a great variety of activities and services that extend from health centers and economic aid in cases of emergency to recreation, adult education, and cultural programs. [26]

25. Jacques Parisot, "Responsabilités de la bienfaisance privée," Réponse Française, VIIIe Conférence Internationale de Service Social, Munich, 1956, pp. 133-135.

26. J. Parisot, ibid., p. 139; see also pp. 133-135, supra.

Voluntary social agencies in France maintain 850 children's homes -- now no longer called orphelinat or asile d'enfants [orphanage] -- and care for 80,000 children. They administer 10,000 vacation camps, primarily during the summer, for both children and their families. The majority of infant nurseries, day nurseries, and kindergartens are established by private welfare organizations, which are in charge of most institutions for mal-adjusted and difficult children and adolescents as well, and of psycho-therapeutic clinics. They administer maternity homes, family guidance centers, parole committees, 150 correctional schools, many institutions for mental defectives, 800 homes for the aged, 250 settlement houses and community centers, 600 convalescent and nursing homes, and 200 youth hostels. [27]

Their services also include residential homes for young work-ing women and young industrial workers, and training workshops with placement services for retarded young people. Among new experiments of the private agencies are special centres d'accueil pour les enfants pré-scolaires [day homes for preschool chil-dren]. These are organized in cooperation with a child health center for school children, so that the medical, psychological, and social work staff of the center can extend their services to the preschool group; mothers are allowed to leave their children here for observation and education supervision for several hours or for the whole day. Voluntary agencies organize abris de réception transitoire [transition hostels] where persons released from penal institutions can find shelter until they obtain work and are resettled in the community; they also administer institutions for the homeless. They provide reception centers and residential homes for North Africans and other colonial French nationals who have difficulty finding dwellings for their families at modest rents. For the aged, some private organizations establish holiday camps, recreation and cultural centers, and home-care services to enable them to live in their own homes with some nursing and household help.

---

27. J. Parisot, Ibid., pp. 133-136.

The private social agencies in France are united in a central federation, L'Union nationale interfédérale des oeuvres privées sanitaires et sociales [National Union of Voluntary Health and Social Organizations], with headquarters in Paris.[28] The Union assists in the coordination of private and public social welfare programs with other measures of protective labor legislation, social security, and health preservation. It keeps private social agencies informed of current social legislation and of pending changes, of experiments in methods and of new programs of health education and social welfare. It supports its members in obtaining financial support from industry, foundations, and government sources, represents them before parliament and public authorities in the various ministries, and interprets the problems and achievements of the voluntary agencies to local, provincial, and national legislatures and to the public at large. The Union serves as a bridge between the public author-ities and the entire group of voluntary social organizations and agencies in France in the interest of the people whom both groups serve. It may thus be compared to the National Welfare Assembly in the United States, and it plays an important role in the coordination of public and private efforts for improvement of the health and welfare of the French population.

SELECTED BIBLIOGRAPHY

Armand-Delille, Paul Félix. "Le service social et la collectivité," Report of the Third International Conference on Social Work. London: Le Play House Press, 1938. Pp. 45-52.

Arnion, F. J. - M. "La coordination des services sociaux," Droit Social, No. XXXIV (February, 1949), pp. 28-31.

_____. "Principes et définition du centre social," Informations Sociales, 11, No. 7 (July, 1957), 683-696.

Boylan, Marguerite T. They Shall Live Again: the Story of the National Catholic War Council Overseas After World War I. New York: Cosmopolitan Science and Art Service Company, 1945.

28. Ibid., pp. 137-138.

Cabot, Richard C. Essais de médecine sociale. Paris: Georges Cres and Company, 1919.

Caillois, R. Les jeux et les hommes. Paris, 1958.

Calvet, Henri. La société française contemporaine. Paris: F. Nathan, 1956.

Chalvet, S. Social Settlements in France. Paris: Centre d'Informations Documentaires, 1936.

Chevalley, E., and Marcelle Trillat. "Le service social d'aide aux émigrants," Droit Social, No. XXXIV (February, 1949), pp. 22-24.

Chombart de Lauve, P. La vie quotidienne des familles ouvrières. Paris: Centre nationale de la recherche scientifique, 1956.

Cloupet, M. "Service social et structure sociale," Informations Sociales, 11, No. 1 (January, 1957), 195-198.

"Coordination des services sociaux," Informations Sociales, 11, No. 7 (July, 1957), 784-788; No. 8 (September, 1957), pp. 926-928; No. 9 (October, 1957), pp. 1071-1077.

David, Myriam, Jacqueline Ancelin, and Geneviève Appel. "Les colonies maternelles in France," Informations Sociales, 11, No. 7 (July, 1957), 811-893.

Defert, Pierre. "Aspects critiques du tourisme social," Informations Sociales, 11, No. 2 (February, 1957), 231-283.

De Gourlet, Apolline. "La maison sociale," Pages Sociales, No. 16 (March, 1946), pp. 3-6.

Delamarre, Dr. and Mlle Eyrigoux. "Vacances -- nécessité d'ordre médical et social," Informations Sociales, 12, No. 7 (July, 1958), 4-8.

Dreyfuss, Madeleine and Colette Laconte. "Vacances en famille," Informations Sociales, 12, No. 7 (July, 1958), 23-30.

Droz, Juliette. Histoire des cinq dernières années. Paris: Fédération des Centres Sociaux, 1945.

Dubois, Raoul. "La littérature pour la jeunesse," Vers l'Education Nouvelle, October-November, 1956.

Emorine, Andrée, and Jacques Lamoure. Histoire des auberges de jeunesse en France. Paris: Ligue française des Auberges de la Jeunesse, 1955.

Escarpit, Robert et al. "Littérature et grand public, " Informations Sociales, 11, No. 1 (January, 1957), 2-138.

Friedlander, Walter A. "Co-ordination of Family Welfare Services in France, " Social Service Review, XXVII, No. 1 (March, 1953), 62-66.

Fritsch, Y. "Le service social polyvalent, " Droit Social, No. XXXIV (1949), pp. 15-16.

Garric, Robert. "L'Entr'Aide française du temps de paix, " Pages Sociales, No. 29 (September, 1947), pp. 1-2.

Getti, J. "Centres sociaux et centres de voisinage, " Familles dans le Monde, September, 1956.

Goutos, M.-P. "L'esprit médico-sociale moderne," Familles dans le Monde, June, 1956.

Jacquin, François. Les cadres de l'industrie et du commerce en France. Paris: Armand Colin, 1955.

Jousselin, Jean. Présence de la jeunesse. Toulouse: Ed. Privat, 1956.

League of Nations. European Conferences on Rural Life (Publication No. 22). Geneva: August, 1939.

Lebel, Roland. "Répercussions des initiatives officielles sur les institutions privées dans le domaine de l'action sociale, " Informations Sociales, 5, No. 3 (February, 1951), 159-176.

Lemay, Michel. "Le contagion psychique en internat," Rééducation, April-May, 1958.

Marchand, Jacques. "Le placement familiale de vacances, " Informations Sociales, 12, No. 7 (July, 1958), 48-53.

Martin, Yves. "Le niveau de vie des familles suivant le nombre des enfants, " Population (Paris), No. 3 (July - September, 1956), pp. 407 ff.

Moinet, M. and Mme Rossi. "La coordination des services sociaux," Informations Sociales, 12, No. 5 (May, 1958), 143-148.

Parisot, Jacques et al. Le Comité Français de service social. Historique de son action, 1927-1941. Nancy: Berger-Levrault, 1947.

_____. "Résponsabilités de la bienfaisance privée, " Réponse Française, VIIIe Conférence Internationale de Service Social (Munich, 1956), pp. 133-150.

Rain, Mlle et al. "Les centres sociaux," Informations Sociales, 11, No. 7 (July, 1957), 675-757.

Raude, Eugène and Gilbert Prouteau. Le message de Léo Lagrange. Paris: La Compagnie du Livre, 1954.

Reboulleau, Guy. "La maison familiale de vacances," Informations Sociales, 12, No. 7 (July, 1958), 31-35.

Réverdy, Ch. J. "La place du service social dans l'ensemble de l'action sociale," Informations Sociales, 5, No. 3 (February, 1951), 144-158.

Rochard, Poky. "Les mouvements de jeunes," Informations Sociales, 12, No. 6 (June, 1958), 100-112.

Sorin, Louise. "La colonie de vacances," Informations Sociales, 12, No. 7 (July, 1958), 44-47.

Spitzer, E. "Résidences sociales," Droit Social, XXXIV (1949), 12-14.

Virton, P. "La protection sociale en France," Revue de l'Action Populaire (Paris), March, 1957.

Vismard, Marcel. L'enfant sans famille. Paris: Editions Sociales Françaises, 1956.

Vimond, Claude. "La prévision de l'emploi," L'Education Nationale, November 22, 1956.

Ziolkowsky, Jean. Les enfants de sable. Blainville-sur-Mer: L'amitié pour le livre, 1957.

CHAPTER **5** SOCIAL SECURITY
IN
FRANCE

BASIC CONCEPTS OF SOCIAL SECURITY

France and Belgium were the pioneers in the development of a
system of family allowances, and their example has been followed
by most other nations. France was more reluctant, however, to
recognize the need for a system of compulsory social insurance
programs such as the one Germany instituted in the 1880's. Even
the British National Insurance Act of 1911 did not convince the
French of the validity of a compulsory social insurance system
they still considered "un-French." It was only the acquisition of
Alsace-Lorraine by France in 1919, following the First World
War, that made the enactment of social insurance legislation
imperative, since the populations of these two provinces did not
want to give up the social insurance program that had operated
under German rule, and the other provinces could not be denied
the same privileges. The parliament debated a social insurance
bill from 1921 to 1928, enacted the first law in 1928 and a comprehensive program in 1930 -- which did not, however, include
unemployment insurance or workmen's compensation, for which
voluntary systems were in operation. [1]

---

1. Loi des assurances sociales [Law on Social Insurance] of April 5, 1928,
amended April 30, 1930; see André Rouat and Paul Durand, Sécurité Sociale
(Paris: Dalloz, 1958), Chapter 1.

The program is divided into two schemes, one for industrial, domestic, and commercial workers, and the other for agricultural and forestry workers. Social insurance began to operate in 1930 and proved its value in combination with family allowances in providing for basic economic security during the Second World War and the Occupation. In 1943 workmen's compensation was incorporated into the unified compulsory system. The government attempted to expand social security to relieve the working masses from the danger of future poverty. It wanted to create genuine enthusiasm for the economic and moral reconstruction of the country.

Professor André Siegfried has explained that the French character reveals two contradictory propensities: a very practical common sense with an immediate concern for material interests and, on the other hand, a great idealism, universalism, and humanism with intellectual brilliance. The Frenchman is an intellectual idealist, but his skepticism often makes him unfit for action.[2] He has a deep desire for intellectual, social, and economic independence in his private life. From this stems his urgent wish to be economically self-sufficient, to save from his work just enough to be able to retire as early as possible to a house in the country or a comfortable apartment in the city. This desire for social and economic security could be satisfied for about 100 years after the Napoleonic Wars (from 1815 to the 1920's) by the typical Frenchman with some thrift. He could acquire a small business, some property, a little house or cottage in the country, and certain small investments for himself and his wife in their old age. But after World War II the losses of the war, inflation, and the depreciation of the franc almost eliminated this type of security. This is the main psychological reason why the mass of the French people -- not only the members of the working class -- have accepted the concept that social legislation must provide the social security which can no longer be obtained by individual initiative and thrift.

---

2. André Siegfried, "Approaches to an Understanding of Modern France," in Edward M. Earle, Modern France (Princeton: Princeton University Press, 1951), pp. 6-7.

Social insurance in France is based on the Loi de la sécurité
sociale [Law on Social Security] of May 22, 1946 and a series
of amendments embodied in the Code de la sécurité sociale of
December 10, 1956. Its basic concept is that social security
shall protect the entire population -- not only wage-earners and
their families as envisaged by the previous legislation, but also
employers, farmers, and self-employed persons.[3] The new
French legislation applies the principle developed by Lord
William Beveridge, that a unified system of social insurance
under flexible rules and with a widened scope of benefits should
guarantee economic security for the entire people and remedy
inequities in the distribution of income. While the main objective
of the British approach was the prevention of unemployment
and the guarantee of a minimum income, the French program
attaches primary importance to family allowance benefits and
income maintenance through social insurance payments, health
protection, and medical care insurance. Other important
features of the system are determined by the demographic
conditions of France.[4] More than in other European countries,
social security payments and family allowances in France
represent a large proportion of the total remuneration of the wage
earners. This is evident in the case of family allowances which
are established upon the basis of an average wage, but it is also
true of social security payments, as we shall see at the end of
this chapter.

During the nineteenth century the population of France was
predominantly rural, but this ratio has changed so that by now
the majority of the population is urban, as illustrated by the
following table:

---

3. Cf. Pierre Laroque, "From Social Insurance to Social Security: "Evolution
in France," International Labour Review, June, 1948, pp. 566-567, and "Recent
Social Security Developments in France," Bulletin of the International Social
Security Association (Geneva), XI, Nos. 1-2 (January-February, 1958), 3-18.

4. Pierre Laroque, op. cit., p. 572; Francis Netter, "Social Security Technique
and Demography," International Labour Review, 67, No. 6 (June, 1953), 550; and
S. M. Lipset, Political Man (New York: Doubleday, 1960), pp. 81, 85.

TABLE 7: URBANIZATION OF FRENCH POPULATION
IN SELECTED YEARS[5]

Active Population Over Census Age 14, in Thousands					
Year	Rural	Urban	Year	Rural	Urban
1901	8,244	11,491	1936	7,204	13,056
1906	8,910	11,811	1946	7,291	13,230
1921	9,024	12,696	1954	6,310	13,698
1926	8,200	13,194			

The system of family allowances was extended to cover all families with children; it is no longer a privilege of wage earners only. The opposition against social insurance legislation was so strong in certain groups of the population that the introduction of benefits for self-employed persons, employers, and people without an occupation had to be suspended. The self-employed felt that the required contributions would mean to heavy a burden, and were afraid that the uniform social security plan might deprive them of an imaginary superior social status. For these reasons the movement toward comprehensive coverage of the population was delayed. To secure badly needed financial aid for aged artisans, handicraft workers, independent workers in agriculture, industry, and commerce, and members of professions not eligible for old-age insurance benefits, the Régime d'allocation de vieillesse [Old-Age Allowance Act] of January 17, 1948 provides payments from funds of special organizations established for each of these occupational groups. [6]

---

5. Francis Netter, op. cit., p. 557, Table VII; Jean Marchal and Jacques Lecaillon, La Répartition du revenue National (Paris: M. - Th. Genin, 1958), I, 119 and 121; II, 8; and Annuaire Statistique de la France, 1956, p. 77, Table IV, and p. 87, Table II.

6. P. Laroque, op. cit., p. 577; Francis Netter, op. cit., pp. 555 - 556; Code de la sécurité sociale, Arts. 643 to 673.

In these pensioners' programs allowances are calculated according to past employment, although the recipients did not pay contributions to the system. Only aged needy resident citizens are entitled to these pensions, which are financed entirely by government taxes, and both allowances and insurance benefits are adjusted according to the purchasing power of the franc.

Social security benefits and family allowances, which have increased substantially since World War II, have assumed an important role in the economic and social structure of France. Although their relation to the normal wages and salaries in industry, commerce, and agriculture varies throughout the country, their total expenditure represents about 12 per cent of the gross national product, while the cost of the social security system in the United States amounts to only about 4 per cent of the gross national product, or about one-third of the economic support provided in France. While it is difficult to present an exhaustive comparison of these benefits and allowances with wages in the different industries, the French coal mining industry gives some indication of the relationship, although its fringe benefits are probably the highest of any industry in France.

SOCIAL SECURITY AND OTHER FRINGE BENEFITS AS A PERCENTAGE OF WAGE PAYMENTS IN FRENCH COAL MINES IN 1954[7]		
	Old-age insurance	8.2%
	Sickness & maternity insurance	5.5
	Workmen's compensation	7.2
	Family allowances	15.5
	Paid vacations	12.1
	Housing benefits	14.2
	Transportation	1.9
	Heating allowances	7.3
	Vocational training	2.6
	Miscellaneous indemnities	2.8
	Payroll tax	5.0
	TOTAL	82.3%

---

7. Charbonnages de France, Rapport de gestion (Paris), 1954, p. 64.

In other nationalized and private industries, social security and family allowances with some fringe benefits amount to an average of 42 per cent of the regular wages.[8] Economists and representatives of organized labor in France, though they favor in general the social security program and family allowances in their present structure, have raised the criticism that these benefits stifle initiative among workers and discourage them from assuming responsibility on the job or performing more skilled work because the potential increase in wages is too small. Some critics maintain that many workers now would rather have another child instead, since the increase in family allowance is more substantial than the wage would be for higher work skill or increased responsibility. Available data about the rise of productivity in various industries in France after the Liberation in 1944, the major reconstruction of industrial equipment and machinery, and the recent economic prosperity in France provide, however, no definite proof of the discouraging effects of social security and family allowances. Production in the coal mining industries shows a substantial increase in productivity, for example:

Average Coal Output Per Underground Miner Per Shift[9]

1930	984 kg	1949	1,099 kg
1938	1,277 kg	1950	1,203 kg
1945	893 kg	1951	1,309 kg
1946	935 kg	1952	1,364 kg
1947	959 kg	1953	1,429 kg
1948	975 kg	1954	1,519 kg

8. Warren C. Baum, The French Economy and the State (Princeton: Princeton University Press, 1958), p. 202; and Wallace C. Petersen, The Welfare State in France (Lincoln: University of Nebraska Press, 1960), Chapters 3 and 4.

9. Bernard Chenot, "Premiers résultats de la nationalisation des mines," Droit Social, July - August, 1949, pp. 242 - 246; Charbonnages de France, Rapports de gestion (Paris), 1947-1954; Warren C. Baum, op. cit., p. 195; and "La Productivité industrielle par tête en France et à l'étranger," Bulletin du Conseil National du Patronat Français, March 20, 1954, pp. 21-23.

The increased output may be in part the result of the use of skilled labor and better mechanical equipment, but it is certainly the result of reliable work as well.

The role of the social worker in this broad social security program is well defined. He is responsible for bringing individual service, advice, and guidance to the families of the insured, particularly to pregnant women, nursing mothers, infants and children, and to those adults who ask for personal aid. In the entire program, social workers are assigned to local districts where they can maintain close personal contact with the people and the existing social agencies. In the higher units of government, social workers supervise and direct professional services. On the community level, the unified family welfare unit includes this personal service for the beneficiaries of the social security payments and of family allowances.

THE SYSTEM OF FAMILY ALLOWANCES

HISTORY AND PROGRAM

France was the first country to recognize that in a modern industrial society a large number of children is no longer the economic asset for the urban worker that it was in a rural economy. Rather, a large family means a severe financial burden that tends to impoverish the parents and place them in an unfavorable economic condition in comparison with childless couples and bachelors. The normal industrial wage is not sufficient to secure adequate food, clothing, housing, medical care, and recreation for a family with several young children. Therefore, it seems necessary in the interest of the nation to supplement the income of families with children, because only with such societal support can more children be brought up with adequate health and education.

The first supplementation of wages in France was introduced in 1862 for the seamen of the Navy, the merchant marine, and the overseas fishing fleets. After a seaman had been in the service five years, regular monthly allowances were paid by the Navy Department or the ship-owner to his family for the period of his absence.[10] Similar grants to families were provided during the latter part of the nineteenth century for members of the Army and civil servants under national and departmental statutes.

In private industry, in 1884 a mine operator, an M. Klein of Vizille, took the initiative and supplemented the regular wages of workers who had three or more children. He intended to keep them as steady, reliable workers and to improve their work output by alleviating their worries about their ability to support their families adequately. Other employers in the mining and metal industries followed his example when they learned that the gratitude of the workers for this extra pay and their increased interest in their jobs were worthwhile compensation for the higher expense in wages. Some employers thought that such a so-called ethical wage, which took into account the size of the family, was morally desirable.[11]

During the First World War this practice expanded because employers needed labor and were anxious to attract skilled workers for war production. Further, high war casualties made stimulation of the birthrate a patriotic necessity, and the supplementary payments for children encouraged parents to produce them. Employers granting wage supplements had the advantage of securing a stable and cooperative labor force for their establishments.[12] In the beginning, employers engaged individually in this practice, but in 1918 at Grenoble Emile Romanet encouraged the regional mining and engineering industries to establish a

---

10. Decree of the Ministry of Marine of December 26, 1862; Roger Picard, "Family Allowances in French Industry," International Labour Review, 9, No. 2 (February, 1924), 161-162.

11. Dominique Ceccaldi, Histoire des prestations familiales en France (Paris: Union Nationale des caisses d'allocations familiales, 1957), Chapter 1.

12. The payments were called sur-salaires familiales [family supplement wages], indicating their character as voluntary additional payments to bridge the gap between wages and the cost of living of families with several children.

pooled fund for the payment of supplements to workers with large families. Industries in other parts of France noted the success of this experiment and established caisses d'équalisation [equal-ization funds] either for a territorial district, or nation-wide for some types of mines or metal and textile factories.

The contributions of employers were based upon the amount of the payroll, the number of workers, or the number of annual working days. Family supplements were scaled according to the number of children under working age. To avoid the jealousy and discontent of workers who did not merit the supplement, the allowances were mailed directly to the wives of the workers who did. The trade unions at first opposed this practice of wage supplements vigorously because it weakened their influence and strengthened the paternalistic power of the employers. In 1919, after the end of World War I, several firms cancelled the wage supplements when workers went on strike, so that the trade unions were able to demonstrate the "manière jaunâtre" [yellow nature] of the family grants. However, beginning in 1923, government contracts included a clause providing that family allowances according to the number of children were to be paid as a regular part of the wage. Wide acceptance of this wage policy among the working class forced the Confédération des unions de travail [Trade Union Congress] to change its policy and agree to the supplements. The trade unions then urged that the allowances should not be an arbitrary benevolence of the employer, but should become a legal obligation. The Loi d'allocations familiales [Family Allowance Act] of May 20, 1931[13] and its amendment of March 11, 1932 were the legal recognition of this changed social policy. They confirmed the soundness of the preceding voluntary practice, but transformed the program into a public, compulsory scheme and expanded it gradually to all industries and occupations. The program was

---

13. It went into effect January 1, 1932. The first state-wide compulsory family allowance laws, however, had been passed earlier in New Zealand (1926), New South Wales (1927), and Belgium (1930).

further extended through the Code de famille [Family Code] of
July 29, 1939, enacted immediately before the outbreak of the
Second World War. During the war, rising prices and the black
market decreased the purchasing power of the allowances, but
they still prevented complete destitution in families with numerous children. After the war, reform legislation streamlined
the family allowances, whose structure is based upon the Loi
d'allocations familiales [Family Allowance Act] of August 22, 1956
now incorporated as Libre V in the Code de la sécurité sociale.
Its social aim is two-fold: to secure an adequate income for
families with children, and to encourage an increase of the birth
rate. Both aims have been successful.

The development of a liberal family-allowance system in
France has been influenced by certain cultural and political
factors in addition to the desire of government and parliament to
increase the birth rate. Although France is a Catholic country
it had, compared with other European countries, an unusually
low birth rate until the end of World War II, and maintained the
level of population until 1950 mainly by substantial immigration
from Italy, Spain, and Central and Eastern European countries. In
her desire to increase the birth rate, France had the full moral
support and backing of the Catholic Church.

Another element that favored the development of family allowances was the coalition of conservative parties that had been in
power since the Liberation of 1944. This resulted from the
split of the labor parties and trade unions into communists and
communist-dominated trade unions on one side and socialists
and non-communist trade unions on the other. By this lack of
unity, no left-oriented government could be established, and
as a result the labor movement was not able, in spite of continuous inflation, to obtain an increase in real wages. With
the support of the Catholic Church and of leading industrial
circles the various governments could, however, expand and
liberalize both the family allowances and the social security
benefits at the expense of an increase of real wages in private
industries, major banks, and insurance companies, and in the
nationalized industries, such as coal mining, railways, electric

and gas companies, public transportation, and sea and air transport. [14]

Workers in industry, commerce, and agriculture, and self-employed persons having two or more children under the age of 15 are eligible for family allowances. [15] Allowances are paid for adolescents up to the age of 17 when in school, training, or apprenticeship, and to 20 years of age when they are attending an institution of higher learning. Crippled children are included without age limit, whereas in the United States a child has to have become totally and permanently disabled before his 18th birthday to benefit under Old-Age Insurance upon the retirement, death, or disablement of the family's primary wage earner. The family allowance for the second child is 20 per cent of the average wage in the département, and that for the third and each subsequent child in the same family is 30 per cent. The calculation of the allowance was originally based upon the minimum wage of a metallurgical worker in the Département of the Seine and its relation to the living costs and average wages in the département of residence. Since 1947, however, the basic salary must be determined annually by decree. The allowance is uniform within any given community, but varies among the different regions and between rural and urban areas according to the average cost of living. [16]

---

14. Warren C. Baum, op. cit., pp. 268 - 274; Val R. Lorwin, "French Trade Unions Since Liberation, 1944 - 1951," Industrial and Labor Relations Review, 5, No. 4 (July, 1952), 524-539; and S. M. Lipset, op. cit., p. 81.

15. An automatic adjustment of family allowances to actual wages instead of to the basic wage is recommended by Antoine Zelenka, "Ajustements des prestations de la sécurité sociale aux variations du coût de vie," Droit Social, 21, No. 3 (March, 1958), 170-179.

16. The Ministry of Labor and Social Security determines by ordinance the basic wage for the calculation of family allowances. See Hubert C. Callaghan, The Family Allowance Procedure (Washington, D. C.: Catholic University Press, 1947), pp. 39-60, and Dominique Ceccaldi, Histoire des prestations familiales en France, cited in Footnote 11. Adjustments are made either by increases of the basic wage or by an increase of the rate of the percentage of the family allowance.

If there is only one wage‑earner in the family, a higher allocation de salaire unique [single wage allowance] is paid even for the first child. [17] It amounts to 20 per cent of the average wage for the first child under five years of age, and for a child over five if one parent alone supports the family; for a single child over five years of age, the single wage allowance is 10 per cent. The maximum amount of the single wage allowance is 50 per cent of the average wage, regardless of the number of dependent children in the family. This supplementary allow‑ance, in contrast to the regular family allowance, is limited to wage‑earners; it cannot be paid to self‑employed persons. [18]

When both parents are able to accept gainful employment or are working, no family allowance is paid for the first child. The mother of a young child under five, however, who remains at home to care for her child, is entitled to a monthly allocation de la mère au foyer [allowance for the mother at home] of 10 per cent of the average departmental wage until the child's fifth birthday.

At the birth of the child the mother receives a maternity grant from the Caisse d'allocations familiales [Family Allowance Fund] to pay for the necessary supplies for the new baby. She is entitled to a birth premium of three times the average monthly wage for the first child and double the average monthly wage for subsequent children. It is paid in two installments: the first immediately after the birth of the child, and the second when the child is six months of age.

In addition to the birth premium an allocation de maternité [maternity allowance] is paid to a working mother for a period of six weeks before and six weeks after confinement; it amounts to one‑half of her wage or salary, with maximum payments

17. Alain Girard and Henri Bastide, "L'Action sociale de caisses d'allocations familiales et le salaire unique," Informations Sociales, 12, No. 3 (March, 1958), 2-150. This research justifies the objective and social effect of the salaire unique family allowance.

18. Ibid.

determined for the various regions. The mother may not be employed for a period of eight weeks, six of which must be after confinement. Illegitimate children are treated like legitimate offspring; their mothers receive the same maternity allowance. At confinement free medical, nursing, and midwife care, and free admission to a maternity hospital or maternity home are provided for securing the mother's and child's health.

An allocation familiale prénatal [prenatal allowance], equal to the regular family allowance, is paid to eligible mothers during the period of pregnancy. This prenatal allowance requires that the woman agree to undergo medical examinations at the local clinic of the Service des allocations familiales [Family Allowance Service] and to follow dietary and health measures prescribed by the physician. The amount of the prenatal allowance is increased for the third and each subsequent pregnancy, another measure aimed at encouraging procreation.

A serious problem for the family allowance program is the severe housing shortage in France. Although departmental funds give subsidies for low-rent public housing projects to help young families, there were in 1954 more than 90,000 young couples without homes of their own.

The funds also support the higher education of gifted young students up to the age of 20 to permit them to attend secondary schools and universities. If their progress is satisfactory, scholarships are frequently continued from other funds. In addition, the caisses d'allocations familiales subsidize private agencies for welfare services such as open-air schools, kinder-gartens, child-care centers, and summer vacation camps for children and for families.

Home economics courses are offered through the caisses d'allocations familiales for girls who have left elementary school and work in shops and factories, and there are more advanced courses for young mothers and housewives who might profit from a practical knowledge of skillful home management, sewing, and cooking. These courses are particularly important in small communities without municipal facilities for adult education.

In the United States we would consider the task of such adult education a function of the local school district. In France the family allowance system fills an important need by providing home economics training.

ADMINISTRATION OF FAMILY ALLOWANCES

Family allowances are administered in each département either by a public caisse d'allocations familiales [family allowance fund] or by a private, non-profit caisse d'équalisation [equalization fund] established by industrial or commercial firms who employ 3,000 or more workers. [19] A caisse d'allocations familiales needs a license from the Ministère Nationale de travail et de sécurité sociale [National Ministry of Labor and Social Security] before it may begin operations. Traditionally the administration of the caisses d'équalisation was in the hands of the employers. For many years the trade unions had clamored for a share in the funds' administration. They contended that the family allowance payments did not represent a generous gesture on the part of the employers, but that the workers paid for these allowances by accepting lower wages and paying higher prices for industrial products. At present the workers' representatives hold one-half of the seats on the administrative councils of the caisses d'équalisation. The councils also include representatives of the public, as a rule members of the Conseil général of the département, city councils, private family-welfare associations, and experts in the field of economics, health, and social welfare. For agricultural workers and self-employed persons special caisses d'équalisation are organized.

---

19. There are 111 private licensed caisses d'équalisation in France. The plan of a unified administration under the primary social security funds was abandoned by the Loi des caisses d'allocations familiales [Law on Family Allowance Funds] of February 21, 1949.

General policies and technical procedures in the administration of family allowances are determined by the Conseil supérieur des allocations familiales [Superior Council of Family Allowances] in the Ministère de travail et de sécurité sociale on which representatives of public family allowance and private equalization funds serve. In each of the 18 regions and in each département a council of family allowances is in charge of local and regional policies. A national Fédération des caisses d'équalisation [Federation of Equalization Funds], whose membership comprises all family allowance agencies, contributes to public information on the health and social effects of family allowances, carries on scientific research and demographic studies, and organizes regional, national, and international conferences.

THE FINANCING OF FAMILY ALLOWANCES

The entire cost of family allowances paid to families of gainfully employed persons is borne by the employers.[20] The employer's contribution is a legally determined percentage of the worker's wage.[21] The contributions are calculated on a uniform basis for the entire system of social security, comprising family allowances, social insurance, and industrial accident insurance. They are collected in one sum through the primary social security funds in each region. Annual salaries that exceed a legally announced maximum amount are disregarded.[22]

---

20. The French methods differ from the financial basis of family allowances in Great Britain and Canada where they are paid entirely out of general taxation. The contribution of the employer amounts to 16.75 per cent of the wage or salary, not counting the amount exceeding a maximum for computation.

21. The contribution may be paid either to the family allowance or to an equalization fund (Code de la sécurité sociale, Art. 128).

22. The payments of the firms which employ ten or more workers and the payments of independent self-employed persons are due within two weeks after every four-month period; those of smaller firms, after each month.

The cost of family allowances for self-employed persons is paid in part by their own contributions, and in part by public subsidies. Self-employed people pay a contribution assessed at a rate of the basic wage of an unskilled worker in the capital of the département according to the categories of occupations. Under special circumstances, such as low earning power, advanced age, or if the person has raised four children, the contribution of the independent worker is waived. As a rule, the government meets 40 per cent of the contributions of self-employed persons.

The family allowances in agriculture and forestry are financed on a different basis. Here the contributions are computed on the basis of the taxes paid on agricultural products and on the officially assessed rental value of the farm or the forestry or fishing unit, and a substantial proportion of the expenses is raised by a special surtax on alcoholic beverages. [23]

SOCIAL SERVICES UNDER FAMILY ALLOWANCES

For many years family allowance agencies have organized social welfare units with a staff of doctors, trained social workers, nurses, guidance counselors, and home economists. They operate consultation centers and arrange for home visits to families who seem to benefit from individual counseling service. The funds provide free medical examination, clinical and hospital treatment, placement in rest and convalescent homes, and in children's summer vacation camps for the school-age children of their members. [24] Since 1938, social workers and nurses employed in public or private family allowance funds are required to hold a state diploma.

---

23. Statute of January 3, 1952; Marcel Boret, "Les budgets limitatifs de gestion des organisations de sécurité sociale," Droit Social, 16, No. 8 (September - October, 1953), 360.

24. Yves Martin, "Le niveau de vie des familles suivant le nombre des enfants," Population (Paris), No. 3 (July-September, 1956), pp. 407 ff.

In the largest caisse d'allocations familiales [family allowance fund] in Paris, the social service division is divided into six districts, each under a supervisor of social service with a staff of 30 or more trained social workers. The division administers three health centers, each of which has medical, dental, and nursing staffs, and a central vocational guidance bureau open to all members. In other family allowance funds, experiments are conducted with marriage loans in addition to public rent supplements, and school tuition fees and railroad fares are paid to large families to enable them to take summer vacation trips.

In Paris, the social service division of the Conseil des allocations familiales [Council of Family Allowances] in the six districts is organized into four sections. (1) The Service social aux familles [Family Service Department] takes responsibility for necessary home visits to the families of the members of the funds; (2) the three health centers provide free medical examinations and clinical treatment to patients under the funds' jurisdiction; (3) the home economics division offers free courses in economical home management, food preparation and preservation, and modern diets (it instructs annually over 10,000 women and girls); (4) the vocational guidance bureau of the Conseil furnishes members of the families belonging to the funds with vocational and placement information, job analyses, vocational and aptitude tests, and occupational guidance. [25]

The functions of the social worker in the family allowance program include advising the members about their legal rights, counseling in family problems, and clarifying educational and health questions. Social workers inform the family of available community resources, private agencies, foundations, and social insurance claims; and they serve as members of the coordinated family welfare unit established in the district of their service.

---

25. Jacques Hochard, "Prestations familiales et consommations des menages," Droit Social, 21, No. 2 (February, 1958), 106-116.

As families under the family allowance plan are usually self-supporting, the social worker is able to offer them, on a basis of right of membership without any reference to charity, such professional services as counseling, guidance, and referral to community resources. The home visits of the social workers are used, in special instances, to determine whether the allowances are being reasonably spent. If children are severely neglected, undernourished, or endangered in health or morals, the allowance may be withheld by court decision.[26] This provision is designed to prevent unscrupulous parents from staying idle and living on the family allowances that are paid for the support, health protection, and education of the children. If the court rules a suspension of the allowance, the judge appoints a custodian to receive the allowance for the children and to administer the money for their education, care, and health.[27]

Since the custodian appointed by the court is usually an untrained volunteer, difficulties occasionally arise concerning home management, education, and child care. Recently, therefore, family allowance agencies have assigned social workers to deal with these problems, and some courts appoint social workers as custodians at the suggestion of the family allowance agency.

A very important function within the social welfare programs of the family allowance funds is carried on by a service domestique en famille [homemaker service] which is conducted in the départements. The departmental board of the family allowance fund makes decisions on welfare measures, particularly on the organization of a homemaker service. During recent years more

---

26. Marcelle Risler, "La tutelle aux allocations familiales et ses résultats," Les Cahiers du Musée Social, 1958, No. 4 (July-August), 119-122.

27. The Family Allowance Council in Paris employs male social workers for whose training the Council has established a special school of social work. In 1956, family allowance funds in France employed 1,225 social workers of whom 359 were on their staffs in Paris. Mlle L. Tournier, "Un service social familial: Le service social de la caisse d'allocations familiales de la région parisienne," in J. Illiovici, Le Service Social, pp. 17-19.

than six thousand homemakers have been given a four - month course by the family allowance funds. As a result, the funds are able to assign them to homes with children where the mother is seriously ill, to permit the father to continue his work, so that the family can stay together while the mother is in a hospital or convalescent at her own home. In contrast to the United States, where such service is frequently offered by private family service agencies and in a few instances by public welfare departments, the family allowance funds in France assume this responsibility. They also provide young girls to help in homes where the mother, for reasons of convalescence from childbirth, disability, or illness, needs assistance with household tasks.

THE SOCIAL INSURANCE SYSTEM

The first program of social insurance was introduced in France through the Loi des pensions aux travailleurs et paysans [Workers and Peasants Pension Law] of 1910 which provided pensions to retired workers and farmers at 65 and, after an amendment of 1912, at the age of 60. Permanently disabled persons received a disability pension and their widows and children under 16 got survivors' benefits. The contributions for this program were so low that the state was forced to grant annual subsidies in order to keep it solvent. The plan was administered by departmental pension agencies and approved mutual-aid societies established by labor unions or employers' associations under the supervision of a Caisse nationale des pensions [National Pension Fund].

In 1928 the plan was integrated into the new general social insurance program comprising old age, disability, and survivors' insurance, and health and maternity insurance for employed persons with an annual income of less than 15,000 francs. [28]

---

28. Law of April 5, 1928; later statutes have adjusted all nominal amounts in francs according to changes in purchasing value. In 1928 the maximum income was equal to about $2100 in today's purchasing power.

Several amendments increased the maximum wage limit until, in 1946, it was eliminated, so that social insurance for all employed and self - employed persons is now compulsory. The annual wage, salary, or earnings, however, are considered for contributions and for the computation of benefits only up to a certain amount which is determined by national decree of the Ministère de travail et de sécurité sociale.[29] Not covered are workers with an annual minimum income, school children, and children working for their parents.

In the social insurance program the Caisse de sécurité sociale [Social Security Fund] is now responsible for the administration of old age, disability, and survivors' insurance, health and maternity insurance, and workmen's compensation.[30] The mutual-aid societies cooperate with the government social security funds and are encouraged to develop new health and welfare activities for the preventive protection of their membership.[31]

Contributions and benefits differ in the two parts of the social insurance scheme, but the same basic principles apply to both. Members of rural mutual - aid societies and employees of agricultural cooperatives are covered in the agricultural division. In both parts of the insurance scheme contributions are compulsory for wage-earners up to 60 years of age.[32] Those who

---

29. Loi de la sécurité sociale of May 22, 1946, Code de la sécurité sociale of December 10, 1956, and decree of February 6, 1957. Annual income in excess of a statutory maximum is not considered; the maximum amount may be changed by decree.

30. The unification of administration was achieved by the Décret National of October 4, 1945, and the Loi de la sécurité sociale of August 22, 1946, but had been advocated already by the Resistance movement. Henri Michel and Louis Mirkine-Guerevitch, Les idées politiques et sociales de la Résistance (Paris: Presses Universitaires, 1954), p. 187.

31. National Order of October 19, 1945; Georges Desmottes, "Threats to Self - Help," Self - Help in Social Welfare (Bombay, India, 1954), pp. 24 - 38.

32. The contribution to the unified social insurance plan was, in the beginning, 8 per cent of the pay-roll, equally divided between employer and worker. It was first computed on the basis of five wage classes, but in 1936 this system was changed to the computation of straight percentages of the wage. Exceptions are made for

continue to work beyond the age of 60 no longer have to pay contributions, while the employers continue to contribute their own share. For domestic workers a flat rate is paid by the employers alone.

At first contributions were collected by means of insurance stamps placed on cards, but the stamp system was abolished in 1935 and contributions are now paid, as in England and the United States, by the employer in quarterly installments to the caisse de sécurité sociale. The employer deducts the worker's share from his wage or salary. A stamp system is used only for the self-employed, who purchase regular postal stamps and affix them to an insurance voucher as payment and proof of contribution.

The social insurance program is financed by payments of employers and workers. Originally their contributions were the same, 6 per cent of the payroll of each, but the employer now has to pay an additional tax of 4 per cent of the payroll for the insurance benefits of retired workers. Furthermore, the employer pays a contribution of 3 to 4 per cent of the payroll to meet the expenses of workmen's compensation (employment injury insurance) benefits, which raises the employer's social insurance tax to about 13.5 per cent of the payroll, while the worker pays 6 per cent which is deducted from his wage or salary.[33] Since the cost of family allowances is also charged to the employer at the rate of 16.75 per cent, management carries about 30 per cent of the payroll for social security. Persons who are self-employed pay the same contribution, but for certain groups government subsidies alleviate the financial burden.[34]

---

made for agricultural workers, self-employed persons, and housewives. The French system has gradually included more categories than those first covered. It extends now to self-employed persons and to employees whose salaries are higher than the maximum amount on which contributions are assessed.

33. Paul Durand, "Les équivoques de la distribution du revenu par la sécurité social," Droit Social, 16, No. 5 (May, 1953), 293-294.

34. J. Boulouis, "La tutelle du Ministre du Travail sur les Caisses de Sécurité sociale," Droit Social, 22, No. 1 (January, 1959), 35-40.

The calculation of the payments of the self-employed is based upon the income they declare for tax purposes, but is no less than the wage of their own highest-paid worker or that of the lowest-paid worker in the departmental capital. Housewives pay the minimum contribution. Insurance payments are not required from unemployed or retired workers, or from disability pensioners or children. [35]

The contributions for workmen's compensation insurance are borne by the employer, and are computed for each industrial and commercial establishment; the contribution is assessed on the basis of the degree of risk of industrial accidents. Since a decrease in risk reduces the assessed contribution, each factory and workshop is induced to provide the best possible safety protection for the workers. The rate of the contribution, which is paid by the employers alone, differs among the various industries; the average is 3.5 per cent of the payroll.

In the agricultural scheme the contributions are a flat rate of 4 per cent of the wage. For the employed agricultural and forestry workers, including share-croppers, the contributions are equally divided between employer and worker.

OLD-AGE AND DISABILITY INSURANCE

The unified social insurance program provides benefits to a large percentage of the entire population when persons retire or are permanently disabled. Eligible for the benefits are workers and employees, persons who were members of the voluntary old-age pension plan of 1910, and self-employed persons after they have contributed to the social insurance program for at least three months. The self-employed group includes craftsmen, artisans, artists, shop-keepers, businessmen, and members of the liberal professions.

---

35. Although the social insurance program and the family allowances are segregated, the national coordination of both systems permits the use of surplus income of the equalization funds to compensate for deficits in the social insurance program.

Assurance vieillesse [Old-Age Insurance Benefits]

The benefits are composed of a basic allowance (which varies, though not below a legally defined minimum amount, according to region or département) and increments for dependents. The classification of the département is made with regard to the local cost of living. The increments include an allowance for the dependent spouse and a bonus for beneficiaries who have reared three children to the age of 16. Supplementary allowances are paid to beneficiaries living in Paris and a few industrial districts with high living costs. If both husband and wife are entitled to old-age insurance benefits, the benefit of the wife is reduced by one-half.[36]   An insured person's widow who was not, herself, insured is entitled to a widow's allowance for life that equals one-half of her husband's basic allowance and one-half of the regional residence supplement. The insured person may at the time of retirement request the conversion of his benefit claim into a capital payment to establish a business of his own or to purchase a farm. In case of a capitalization, the retired insured person still receives a legally determined monthly cash benefit. Retirement is also possible as early as 55 at a reduced benefit rate.

As a measure of national economy, the payment of old-age insurance benefits is suspended for persons whose income exceeds an amount determined by legislation for individuals and married couples. This restriction of eligibility changes the fundamental character of the old-age pension plan almost into a social assistance scheme, though it is financed by insurance contributions.

For a worker who retires at the age of 60 after 30 years of contributions,[37] the old-age pension is 20 per cent of his average

---

36. The reduction of the wife's benefits is a measure of economy that differs from the provision in the United States and Great Britain, where the insured wife may elect to obtain her own old-age retirement benefit.

37. Code de la sécurité sociale, Art. 331-350; S. Lacombe, "L'Action sociale des caisses vieillesse du régime générale," Droit Social, 21, No. 5 (May, 1958), 305-311.

wage for the past ten years, if this amount exceeds the minimum insurance payment for the département. A worker retiring at 65 years receives a pension of 40 per cent of the average wage he earned during the past ten years. After the age of 60, the insured worker's pension claim rises each year by 4 per cent of the average wage, but a worker who retires at 65 is guaranteed a minimum pension which is equal to the pension of a low-paid, retired public employee.[38] Disabled workers, who have been employed for 20 years in strenuous or dangerous work, may retire at the age of 60 and receive a pension based upon 40 per cent of the average wage earned during the past ten years.

A serious problem in the operation of the French social insurance program, and of the old-age assistance allowances granted to persons not covered under old-age insurance, is the low amount of benefits in both programs. Therefore, in 1956 a supplementary system was introduced. It supplies, under the title Fonds national de solidarité [National Solidarity Fund], a flat-rate supplementary benefit to persons whose pensions or allowances do not exceed a determined amount (Law of June 30, 1956, Code de la sécurité sociale, Art. 684). The supplementary payment is a significant economic aid, since it increases the old-age benefit nearly 50 per cent and the old-age assistance allowance by 100 per cent.

The Fonds national de solidarité supplements are not raised from employers and workers, but are financed from general taxation. They are paid only to persons with low incomes. The taxes for the Fund are based upon a proportionate tax on annual incomes and a surtax on incomes over specified amounts, an increase in corporate taxes on business, and special taxes on alcohol, automobiles, stock market transactions, luxury sales, donations, and gifts.

The benefits under the Fonds national de solidarité are paid to French citizens over 65, or over 60 if unable to work. In the computation of the income limit, social security benefits, family

---

38. For agricultural workers, farmers, forestry and fishery workers who receive the same old-age pension, special minimum allowances are decreed. If the worker has paid contributions for less than 15 years, his benefits are reduced.

allowances, war invalids' and military pensions are not considered, and for war widows only 25 per cent of their pension
is counted. The supplement benefits about 4.2 million of the
5.2 million French citizens over 65. [39]

Pensions d'invalidité [Disability Insurance Benefits]

Disability benefits are paid to people whose working capacity
has been reduced by two-thirds by accident or disease. For
the first six months the patient receives a cash allowance and
free medical and hospital treatment under the health insurance
program; thereafter he is transferred to the disability insurance
program. The condition of the disabled person must be certified
by a licensed physician. The disability insurance benefit varies
from 30 to 40 per cent of the average wage earned during the last
ten years, depending upon whether the disabled person is still
capable of gainful work. The invalid receives an additional benefit
if he is in need of constant attendance or nursing care. For
each dependent child under 16 years of age an allowance is
added to the pension. [40] Pensions de vieillesse and pensions
d'invalidité [old-age and disability insurance benefits] are
reassessed annually to maintain their purchasing power. The
recipients of old-age and disability insurance are entitled to
receive the same medical benefits from the health insurance
program as the active insured population.

Eligibility for disability insurance benefits begins after
two years of social insurance contributions. During the first
five years of invalidism free medical treatment by general
practitioners and medical specialists, hospitalization, surgical
operations, and rehabilitation training are provided. If the
invalid does not regain one-half of his working capacity within
five years, he is considered permanently disabled.

---

39. F. Montès, "L'aide aux vieillards," Vers la Vie, July-August, 1957; and
"Le Fonds national de solidarité après quinze mois de fonctionnement," Droit
Social, January, 1958, pp. 38-45; Code de la sécurité sociale, Art. 684-711.

40. Minimum disability benefits vary for industrial and agricultural workers,
but they are adjusted to the cost of living.

Assurance décès [Death Benefits]

Survivors of an insured person who was covered for at least one year and who paid 60 daily contributions during the three months preceding his illness, accident, or death, receive an assurance décès [death benefit] equal to 90 times the daily basic salary of the deceased. A minimum sum is assured by law, and is increased for each child under 16 years of age. The death benefit is provided to cover the expenses of the funeral and incidentals, and is paid only to the spouse, children, grand-children, or parents of the deceased person. [41]

After the death of the insured person his widow receives a pension equivalent to 50 per cent of the deceased's pension, provided he was 60 years of age or permanently disabled. Children under 16 are entitled to an orphan's allowance equal to one-half of the father's old-age insurance pension. The same allowance is paid after the death of an insured mother who supported her children. Children, as a rule, receive an orphan's allowance until their 16th birthday, but apprentices and students attending school full-time may receive the allowance beyond this age limit.

HEALTH AND MATERNITY INSURANCE

Assurance de maladie [Health Insurance]

Health insurance in the unified French program covers the insured persons, their spouses, and children under 16 years of age. [42] Children under 20 who are students or apprentices, and other relatives engaged in the rearing of children or in household duties who are living in the home of the insured person are included. Self-employed persons, disabled war veterans, and survivors are also covered by the health insurance plan.

The benefits in health insurance include compensation for medical and hospital treatment, medicine and appliances, and dental services, as well as a cash allowance during the period

---

41. In the United States and Great Britain death benefits may be paid to other persons, such as neighbors or friends who took care of the funeral expenses.

42. Code de la sécurité sociale, Art. 283-295.

of illness when the insured patient is unable to work. A characteristic feature of the French health insurance plan is that it
does not directly provide medical treatment, hospitalization,
drugs or appliances, but only partially reimburses the patient
for his expenses. The reimbursement does not exceed 80 per
cent of the bills from the physician, dentist, pharmacist, and
hospital. In the original operation of the health insurance plan,
computation of these reimbursements was made according to a
national scale issued by the Ministère de santé publique, but the
practitioners and hospitals were not bound by the fee schedule
and often charged considerably higher fees than those announced
in the official scale. Thus, patients sometimes had to pay as
much as 50 to 60 per cent of the entire cost, while the health
insurance fund met only the remaining part of the charge. These
restrictive reimbursement schedules prevented many patients
from receiving necessary medical, dental, and hospital care. The
reform legislation of 1946 abolished the right of practitioners
and hospitals to charge arbitrary fees under the health insurance
plan. Agreements have been reached between the social security
authorities and the medical associations which stipulate that the
fees the doctors charge the patients have to be identical with the
reimbursement tariff for the area. [43] Physicians are allowed to
charge higher fees only after informing the patient and gaining
the permission of the local medical society, which is responsible
for providing another physician willing to treat the insured
patient under the regular schedule as required.

The fees are determined by an official schedule that is
agreed upon in each département between the comité régional
des assurances [regional insurance committee] and the local
medical association. The patient is reimbursed by the Caisse
des assurances de maladie [Health Insurance Fund] at the rate
of 80 per cent of his actual expenses, so that he is able, in most
instances, to get the required treatment. The patient must still

---

43. Dr. J. Bing, "La Limitation des dépenses supportées par la sécurité sociale
en matière d'hospitalisation," Droit Social, 21, No. 6 (June, 1958), 364-375.

pay 20 per cent of the medical expenses, medicines, appliances, and auxiliary services such as X-ray treatment, laboratory tests, and physiotherapy. This principle is maintained to prevent an abuse of the benefits, particularly of expensive drugs, medicines, and appliances. Doctors and hospitals are not permitted to require the patient to pay fees in advance. In emergency cases, the Caisse des assurances de maladie may grant a special advance loan to the patient to help him meet urgent expenses.

The personal, private relationship between physician and patient is maintained. The patient has a free choice of physician or dentist. He may go to the pharmacist from whom he prefers to buy the medicines, drugs, and appliances prescribed. He is allowed to select a private or public hospital for his treatment when the physician certifies the need for hospitalization. Certain major surgical operations, dental plates, dental surgery, and expensive appliances, however, require the authorization of a supervisory physician of the insurance fund to entitle the patient to reimbursement.

In general, the patient pays his medical bills like any private patient, and then is reimbursed by the Caisse de sécurité sociale [Social Security Fund] for 80 per cent of his expenses. In case of industrial accidents and occupational diseases, however (and in all cases of treatment in a public hospital), the Caisse de sécurité sociale pays the fee directly to the physician, dentist, pharmacist, or hospital. The fund in these cases pays for the entire treatment of industrial injuries and occupational diseases; the patient does not have to pay a proportion of these expenses. The fund may also assume the full payment in cases of maternity care, protracted illness exceeding a period of six months, and major surgery if the economic circumstances of the patient warrant this arrangement.

In cases of an extended illness lasting longer than six months, the insured persons and members of their families received medical benefits up to a period of three years until

1955.[44] This Assurance pour la maladie de longue durée [Long-
Term Sickness Benefit] was granted in the case of pathological
conditions for which protracted treatment was likely to forestall
permanent disability, as in tuberculosis, diabetes, syphilis,
rheumatic disorders, psychoses, neuroses, and cancer in the
early stages. The Caisse de sécurité sociale could assume the
entire expense of this care, including that for sanatorium or
convalescent - home placement when the physician considered
it necessary. During the period of inability to work because
of protracted illness, the insured patient received a monthly
indemnité monétaire de maladie [sickness indemnity] that was
determined by the social security fund after a social investigation
and a consultation between the family physician and the fund's
medical officer. In the adjudication of the cash allowance, the
economic and social conditions and the size of the patient's
family were considered. The benefits were not restricted to
medical treatment and cash allowances, but included occupational
guidance, vocational retraining, rehabilitation services, and job
placement for purposes of rehabilitation. In 1952, 26 per cent
of the patients under this program were cured and supporting
themselves, but more than 50 per cent were returned to the
Assurance d'invalidité [Permanent Disability Insurance] program.

An amendment of the Loi des assurances sociales [Social
Insurance Law], effective May 20, 1955, abolished the distinction
between regular health insurance and protracted illness insurance; experience had shown that therapy should be made available

---

44. Before the legislation of 1946, the social insurance benefits were limited to
a period of only six months. The problem of medical fees in the health insurance
program has not been fully solved; an agreement between the French confederation
of medical societies and social security authorities of 1953 was not adopted by
legislation.

45. National Decree of October 10 and November 2, 1945. Old-age pensioners
receive medical treatment under the health insurance program without waiting
periods (Law of March 27, 1956 and Decree of July 30, 1956). Clément Michel,
"Long-Sickness Insurance in the French Social Security System," Bull. International
Social Security Association, VII, No. 4 (April, 1954), 115-124.

to all insured persons for a longer period. The Caisse de
sécurité sociale no longer assumes the entire expense of
treatment; the patient again pays 20 per cent of the cost, but
the Ministère de travail et de sécurité sociale may decree that
for certain severe illnesses the patient is not required to pay
this share. These exceptions include mental illness, tuberculosis, cancer, polio, major surgery, and X-ray and radium
treatment. Applications for treatment longer than six months are
considered carefully in order to exclude fraud and malingering.

Preventive health services are part of the activities of the
program. Insured persons and their families receive free
medical examinations at specified intervals, thus facilitating
the early diagnosis of diseases. The social security agencies
carry on health education, particularly in the field of infant and
maternity care, tuberculosis control, and the training and
rehabilitation of cured tubercular patients. They are also
active in the improvement and modernization of hospitals and
rehabilitation facilities for victims of industrial accidents. They
make special efforts to aid in the prevention of industrial
injuries and occupational diseases by informational campaigns
for workers, instruction in the use of safety devices, and the
development of precautions. These activities are performed in
systematic cooperation with the government factory inspectors
who help to bring them to the attention of foremen and workers in
factories, mines, and shops. Fines may be assessed for unsatis-
factory safety conditions that are not removed by management
upon notification while, on the other hand, subsidies and special
premiums may be granted for outstanding safety improvements.

The cash allowance paid to the insured patient during his
illness amounts to one-half of his last wage with minimum and
maximum amounts fixed by law. Patients with three or more
dependent children are entitled to receive two-thirds of the last
wage with an increased maximum sum beginning the 31st day of
the illness. Self-employed persons and family members of the
insured receive reimbursement for medical, dental, and hospital
treatment, medicines and appliances, but no cash allowances.

The French compulsory program, like other health insurance systems, has been criticized. The regional and departmental medical societies have objected that the official fee schedules should provide higher compensation to physicians.[46] Representatives of the patients have complained that many patients have a hard time paying 20 per cent of the fee and that frequently doctors charge their patients far more than is stipulated by the schedule agreed upon by the regional insurance committee and the local medical society. Sometimes physicians charge for two visits or home calls when only one was made, so that the patient, reimbursed for two services, is thus enabled to pay a higher fee to the doctor. Occasionally such fees are split, by agreement, between the doctor and the patient. While the financial burden to the patient is small or none, the loss to the insurance funds is heavy if such practice becomes widespread, and complaints about the rising cost of the health insurance program are numerous. Another source of complaint is that some doctors refer patients with simple or minor illnesses to another physician and occasionally to a third specialist, thereby charging the government for two or three doctors when one could have given the entire treatment. After secret agreement with druggists, some doctors prescribe unnecessarily expensive medicines and drugs and receive a substantial kickback on them from the pharmacies. Another kickback is sometimes arranged between the two physicians when a patient is referred for further treatment.[47] It is extremely difficult for the administrators of the health insurance program, if not impossible, to detect and prevent such abuses, since the patient calls for the doctor as

---

46. An objective exploration of the economic situation of French physicians is presented by Philippe Michaux, "La Revenu du groupe médical," Revue Economique, X, No. 1 (January, 1959), 93-108, which shows a reasonable increase in average medical income.

47. See "Le déséquilibre financier de l'assurance-maladie," Droit Social, 13, No. 10 (December, 1950), 417-422. The voluntary health insurance plans, particularly the Blue Cross plans in the United States, report similar experiences and problems, including the unnecessary use of hospitalization for financial motives.

any other private individual does, and the reimbursement is requested after treatment is completed. Since a large proportion of the French population is covered by health insurance, it is not surprising that about one-half of the total income of the French medical profession is obtained through treatment of the members of the health insurance system. [48]

Despite these drawbacks, the provisions for medical treatment and medicines under the French program have proved a real and most valuable asset for the population. Before the enactment of the health insurance system, people had far more inferior medical services, in part under the medical assistance plan. The new provisions give the entire population better medical care, allow early visits to the doctor, and permit the maintenance of a family - doctor pattern -- with a concomitant personal relationship between doctor and family that has shown good health results which are reflected in the statistics.

Assurance de maternité [Maternity Insurance]

Maternity insurance benefits include free medical examina - tions and treatment, nursing service, midwife care before and after confinement, and free admission to a maternity home or the lying-in ward of a general hospital. Insured women and the wives of insured men who have paid their contributions to the social insurance program for at least ten months before the expected confinement are eligible for maternity benefits. To secure the benefits, a medical certificate of the pregnancy has to be presented to the Caisse de sécurité sociale [Social Security Fund] not later than three months before the expected time of birth. The provision of maternity ward care in hospitals and maternity homes under the health insurance program has led to

---

48. The author was unable to obtain reliable data about the frequency and the total amount of malpractice, fraud, and abuse of the health insurance program as indicated above. But personal discussions with patients, doctors, and administra - tors indicate that they are substantial. See also Philippe Michaux, op. cit., pp. 105-107.

a substantial decrease in the number of formerly frequent home confinements. [49]

In addition to maternity benefits, insured working women who leave their jobs during pregnancy are entitled to an indemnité journalière de repos [per diem maternity-leave indemnity] equal to the cash sickness allowance for a period of six weeks before and six weeks after confinement. A mother receives, therefore, at least one-half of her regular income without having to work. An additional prime noutricière [nursing bonus] is paid to those mothers who nurse their infants, usually for a period of four months; it may be continued at a decreased rate up to 11 months. The law prohibits the employment of mothers two weeks before and six weeks after confinement. The mother who is not gainfully employed but whose husband is insured, and the self-employed mother, are not entitled to maternity allowances, but they receive the medical and institutional benefits of the health insurance plan.

EMPLOYMENT INJURY INSURANCE (WORKMEN'S COMPENSATION)

Under the French Code civil a worker injured on the job could sue his employer for damages only if he could prove negligence on the part of the employer or his representative. The Loi de résponsabilité des employeurs et d'assurance des accidents [Employers' Liability and Workmen's Compensation Law] of April 9, 1898 established the legal responsibility of the individual employer to pay compensation for any industrial injuries in his factory, mine, or plant, but did not have a mandatory insurance provision. At first the law applied to industrial workers only, but amendments later extended its coverage to commercial and white-collar employees, and to agricultural workers. In 1947 the workmen's compensation system, Assurance d'accidents du travail et maladies professionnelles, was radically reformed and integrated into the unified social insurance program. It is

---

49. Francis Netter, "Social Security Technique and Demography," International Labour Review, 47, No. 6 (June, 1953), 550. Code de la sécurité sociale of December 10, 1956, Art. 296-303.

now a compulsory plan through which industrial, commercial, and domestic workers are protected against the dangers of employment injuries and occupational diseases. [50] The law does not cover farm workers, except those using power-driven vehicles, but farmers may arrange for voluntary insurance against accidents to agricultural workers with public social security funds, mutual-aid societies, or commercial insurance companies.

The protection against employment injury includes both work accidents and occupational diseases. The benefits provided are:

1) Free medical treatment by a physician, surgeon, or medical specialist whom the patient may select; hospitalization; all necessary operations; medicines, drugs, nursing, surgical and orthopedic appliances, and their maintenance and repair;

2) Cash indemnity compensation for temporary or permanent disability, and survivors' benefits if the accident or occupational disease causes the death of the insured worker;

3) Renewal of benefits in case of recurrence of occupational diseases;

4) Rehabilitation, including vocational counseling, vocational guidance, retraining or functional re-education;[51] and

5) Funeral benefits in case of the death of the injured worker.

Occupational diseases must be reported by the sick worker within 15 days after he leaves the job. The cash indemnity allowance is one-half of the previous wage for the first 28 days of the illness, and two-thirds for the subsequent period of incapacity.

If the worker is permanently disabled by occupational disease or injury, he receives a rente d'une incapacité permanente

---

50. The legislation did not follow the pattern of the German industrial accident law of 1884, but that of the British workmen's compensation. It is regulated by Libre IV of the Code de la sécurité sociale of December 10, 1956.

51. See Dr. R. Breton, "Une Expérience de réhabilitation et réadaption fonctionnelle des blessés du travail," Droit Social, 21, No. 4 (April, 1958), 246-248.

de travail [permanent employment-disability pension] computed under a formula in accordance with the last annual earnings of the injured worker, the degree of his disability, and his age, health, and occupational qualifications. Minimum and maximum pensions are determined by the statute. The worker receives a supplementary benefit when he is in need of constant care by an attendant.

Survivors of a worker who dies as the result of an injury or occupational disease receive a survivors' pension. The total amount of the survivors' pensions in one family is limited to 75 per cent of the deceased father's last wage. During recent years there have been approximately 1,700,000 injuries per year in France resulting from serious industrial accidents; about 50,000 workers are permanently maimed annually, and 3,700 killed per year by industrial accidents.[52]

The law requires the organization of comités de santé et de sauvegarde [health and safety committees] in each factory employing 50 or more workers, and in commercial firms with 500 or more employees. These committees develop measures to prevent industrial accidents and, in cooperation with management, control the maintenance of safe working conditions. Whenever an industrial accident or a serious occupational disease occurs, the committee makes an inquiry and reports on whether the legal provisions have been properly observed. The committee trains commissions de surveillance [safety teams] for first-aid and accident prevention, and advises the workers on industrial dangers and the value of safety measures.

An industrial medical service is organized to give a free medical examination to each newly hired worker and to repeat such examinations at regular intervals. The examinations are performed in the factories and plants, where medical officers

---

52. Law on Employment Injuries Insurance of October 4, 1945, and July 23, 1957; Code de sécurité sociale, Arts. 434, 448-463; L. Gerson, "Adaptation à la maladie et réadaption professionnelle," Le Médecin d'Usine, 1957, Nos. 1-3, 319-326.

can observe whether health and safety provisions are carefully carried out. [53]

Characteristic of the approach to industrial accidents and occupational diseases in France is the full administrative integration of this program into the social security system and the emphasis on the prevention of accidents and occupational diseases rather than merely on treatment and financial compensation. In the area of industrial pathology, medical inspectors conduct inquiries into the cause of individual cases of occupational disease and industrial accident requiring medical evidence not revealed by the investigation of the labor inspector. Other inquiries are directed toward the occurrence of certain typical occupational diseases caused by particular hazards, such as those in chemical industries. Industrial medical services personnel cooperate with labor inspectors for the full information of physicians, employers, and workers.

In order to encourage rehabilitation of injured workers, French legislation provides a special grant on completion of the process of vocational rehabilitation to assist the victim of an industrial accident in his resettlement. The managing board of the Division d'assurance d'accidents du travail [Industrial Accident Insurance Division] decides on the amount of the award and whether it is to be paid in a lump sum or in three monthly installments. In addition, a loan may be granted to enable the injured worker to open an industrial or commercial business or to purchase a farm on condition that he promises to operate it until the loan is repaid. The loan carries interest at 2 per cent and is to be repaid in 20 years, but a rebate is granted on the birth of each child of the recipient.

Victims of industrial accidents and other severely handicapped persons receive priority in employment. Private, public,

---

53. Loi des services médicaux de travail [Law on Medical Labor Services] of October 11, 1946; Loi des services médicaux industriels [Law on Industrial Medical Services] of October 11, 1946; Decrees of November 26, 1946, January 16, 1947, and December 27, 1950; Jacques Bousser and Jean-Jacques Gillen, "Medical Inspection of Labour and Industrial Medical Services in France," International Labour Review, 65, No. 2 (February, 1952), 184-210.

and semi-public firms have to employ a certain percentage of disabled workers which is determined annually by decree of the Ministère de travail et de sécurité sociale. Certain types of full- and part-time occupations are reserved for categories of disabled workers; "emploi facile" [light employment] is allotted to disabled persons who cannot work at a normal rate or full-time. Sheltered workshops and distribution centers for home work supplement the occupational opportunities of the disabled person.

ADMINISTRATION OF THE SOCIAL INSURANCE PROGRAM

The administration of the unified social insurance system is divided among the three upper levels of the government: the national, the regional, and the departmental.

The Departmental Administration

In each département a caisse primaire de sécurité sociale [primary social security fund] administers old-age, disability, health, and maternity insurance; long-term sickness benefits; and indemnity compensation for industrial injuries and occupational diseases. Certain approved non-profit mutual-aid societies may participate in the operation of health and maternity insurance in the département, but their administration remains under the control of the primary departmental caisse primaire de sécurité sociale and the caisse régionale de sécurité sociale [regional social security fund]. Workers are at liberty to choose which of the various primary insurance organizations of the département they want to be insured by. Their selection, as a rule, is made according to the recommendation of the labor unions.

A social service division of the caisse de sécurité sociale provides individual casework services to families. The division organizes consultation centers and health clinics in the larger cities; the caisse de sécurité sociale and caisses d'allocations familiales of the département share between them the expenses of these facilities.

The Regional Administration

In each of the 16 regions of France a caisse régionale de sécurité sociale [regional social security agency] administers social insurance operations under the jurisdiction of the regional unit and supervises the primary departmental caisse de sécurité sociale.

The regional funds operate the payments of those old-age and disability insurance benefits that are not directly distributed by the primary funds in the départements.

In the field of employment injury insurance, the regional funds arrange the assessment of contributions for employers and firms according to legal provisions and collect the assessed contributions. They pay industrial accident pensions to disabled workers, their families, and survivors, and reimburse medical and rehabilitation costs of industrial accident insurance to doctors, dentists, pharmacists, hospitals, and clinics.

Aside from the caisse régionale de sécurité sociale, a separate direction régionale de sécurité sociale [regional social security administration] is organized in each regional district. Its staff is responsible for the control, supervision, and auditing of all operations under the jurisdiction of both the regional and departmental agencies in the realm of social insurance and family allowances. It controls the compliance with legal requirements and the economy and efficiency of the various services, as well as the necessary cooperation between the branches of the social insurance administration with the caisses d'allocations familiales.

The National Administration

At the national level the social insurance system is administered by the Direction générale de sécurité sociale under the Ministère de travail et de sécurité sociale. The Conseil supérieur de sécurité sociale [Supreme Council of Social Security] functions as an advisory board whose members are appointed by the Ministre de travail [Minister of Labor]. Its objectives are to study problems of social security referred to the Conseil and to advise the Minister, the administration, and its staff regarding legislative action and administrative measures. A subcommittee of the Conseil, the Comité technique d'hygiène et des services sociaux [Technical Committee for Health and Welfare Services], assists the ministry in the development of policies for the integration of the facilities and cooperation between the caisses de sécurité sociale and caisses d'allocations familiales with other public and private health and social welfare services.

At the national level again, a special staff unit independent of the general social insurance and family allowance operations is set up under the title Direction générale de sécurité sociale [General Social Security Administration]. It is in charge of the supervision and auditing of social security operations -- the coordination of the facilities of the caisses d'assurances sociales and caisses d'allocations familiales, and the legal and financial control of the entire program.

The organization of these separate regional and national units of administration is considered necessary in France because of the legal and structural complexity of the social security and the family allowance funds. Each agency at these various levels of government is an independent, incorporated organization with guaranteed substantial rights of self-government, directed by its own board. These boards consist mainly of lay persons who are elected by that portion of the population covered under the social insurance and family allowance legislation, with particular representation from trade unions and mutual aid societies. The principle of self-government in these organizations, according to French tradition, assures to the beneficiaries responsible management of social insurance and family allowance payments. Workers, employers, and self-employed persons are very conscious of the values of the social security program, and at the same time aware that its benefits are their own achievement and responsibility. Therefore, technical, objective control and supervision by the professionally trained staff of the Direction de sécurité sociale in the Ministère de travail and in the 16 regional districts is deemed necessary to secure an objective, economical, and efficient management of the social security system.[54]

FINANCIAL OPERATION OF THE SOCIAL SECURITY PLAN

Current contributions to the social insurance and family allowance programs cover the full operating costs, including benefits and administration.   Even the expenses of supervision and control in the départements, regions, and the Ministère de travail are met from the contributions, so that no general tax revenues are used to maintain the system.

The financial administration of the social security plan is unified, but is divided into three branches, each with independent operation and accounting: social insurance, industrial accident insurance, and family allowances.   The three maintain a caisse jointe d'action [joint action fund] for the financing of all health, medical, and welfare services in the various programs.   They are financed upon the same principles.   The workers contribute only to the first branch (social insurance); the other two are financed by the contributions of employers and self-employed persons only.[55] The operation does not try to make a profit and does not apply the actuarial methods of commercial insurance companies, but attempts instead to balance the program on a pay-as-you-go basis. The contributions levied upon wages, salaries, and the income of the self-employed are calculated to meet the expenditures for cash benefits, medical, social, and welfare services, and the cost of administration, but they are not designed to produce additional income for the establishment of reserve funds.   As a rule, there is no direct relationship

54. Pierre Laroque, Réflexions sur le problème social (Paris: Editions Sociales Françaises, 1953), pp. 25-28; and Wallace L. Petersen, op. cit., Chapters 5 and 6.

55. Public subsidies are necessary to supplement the family allowance contributions of self-employed persons in the lower-income brackets.
   The costs of the social security program in France before the 1959 devaluation of the franc is illustrated in Table 8 and the relationship of the expenses for social security to the gross national product in Table 9.

between the amount of the contributions paid by or for an insured person and the benefits to which he is entitled under the various circumstances in which benefits are due. However, minimum periods of membership are required before an individual can be eligible for benefits in the program.

SPECIAL SOCIAL INSURANCE PROGRAMS

The general social insurance plan covers the vast majority of the French population, but some categories of workers are protected by separate social insurance programs which started earlier -- civil servants in national, regional, departmental, and municipal government service; railroad workers and employees; miners; seamen; gas and electrical workers; employees of large banks; and actors, singers, dancers, and technical staff employed in theatres and opera companies. Each of these groups has the protection of its own separate scheme, with varied contributions and benefits. In these plans, the representatives of the insured workers and employees participate in the administration of the program. In the special insurance program for miners, work-men's compensation for this particularly endangered labor group is included.

Benefits in these separate plans are at least equal to, and usually higher than, those in the general insurance system. The separate plans are financed by contributions of employers and workers with supplements from the government.[56] In these special schemes the workers are either protected against all social risks (which is the goal of the social security plan), or only against the long-term risks of old age, disability, and death.[57] Coordination rules permit insured workers to change occupations without loss of their insurance rights.

---

56. For instance, in the miners' social insurance plan, the employer contributes 12 per cent of the wage; the insured miner, 10 per cent; and the national government, 8 per cent from general revenues.

57. Special retirement plans have been developed for various professional groups. See Ivan Martin, "Le régime de retraites des cadres," Droit Social, 21, Nos. 9-10 (September-October, 1958), 484-495, and No. 11 (November, 1958), pp. 556-565.

TABLE 8

COST OF SOCIAL SECURITY IN FRANCE, 1954-1958 (IN MILLIONS OF FRANCS)[58]

	Social Insurance	Industrial Accidents	Family Allowances	Pensions, Annuities	Total
1954	355	66	624	691	1,736
1955	400	84	672	743	1,899
1956	458	96	731	832	2,117
1957	527	110	788	1,004	2,429
1958	561	163	878	1,153	2,755

TABLE 9

COST OF SOCIAL SECURITY AND ITS RELATION TO GROSS NATIONAL PRODUCT AND NATIONAL INCOME IN FRANCE, 1954-1957 (IN MILLIONS OF FRANCS)[59]

	Cost of Social Security	As % of Gross National Product	As % of National Income
1954	1,736	12.3%	14.6%
1955	1,899	12.6%	14.6%
1956	2,117	13.5%	14.8%
1957	2,429	14.5%	15.4%

58. Source: Ministère des Finances, Statistiques et études financières (Paris), 10, No. 113 (May, 1958), 448, Table 22, and No. 111 (March, 1958), pp. 260-261, 266-267, and 268; Jean Massé, Statistiques médicales de sécurité sociale (Paris: Revue francaise du travail, 1958).

59. Derived from Ministère des Finances, Statistiques et études financières, 10, No. 113 (May, 1958), 448, Table 22; p. 427, Table I; p. 549, Table I.

UNEMPLOYMENT INSURANCE

Unemployment insurance is not included in the general social insurance program of France, nor is there a compulsory scheme of unemployment compensation as a separate system.[60] Unemployment is not considered a major economic risk in France as it is in Great Britain, the United States, and most industrial countries, but as an exceptional situation which may be met by public assistance to unemployed people in financial need.

For several decades France has not experienced a severe unemployment crisis such as the United States had during the depression of the 1930's and England had in the 1920's. For this reason there has been little pressure from the trade unions, the mutual-aid societies, or other consumers' or merchants' groups for a compulsory unemployment insurance program to be incorporated into the social security system. An important economic custom of long standing in France, which is also protected by legislation, provides for separation or severance pay based on length of service in case of the dismissal of a worker or salaried employee. In many instances this separation pay may amount to a full year's wage, and in general it is equal to six months' earnings. It is easy to understand that French workers under these circumstances fare no worse than workers in the United States or England, who rarely receive unemployment compensation for more than six months.

During the nineteenth century, mutual-aid societies and trade unions organized voluntary plans whereby their members were paid benefits when out of work. They usually received supplements from the local community, since these benefits relieved the public relief budgets. In 1905 a national law on subsidies to labor union unemployment funds provided national grants to

---

60. The French approach differs widely from the concept of social insurance in Britain and the United States; in these countries compulsory unemployment compensation played a decisive role in the legislation of 1911 (England) and 1935 (United States).

these mutual - aid and union funds. In 1914, a Caisse nationale d'assurance de chômage [National Unemployment Compensation Fund] was established which received annual grants for distribution for the relief of the unemployed. [61]

At present, voluntary unemployment insurance plans are based on the free initiative of labor unions or employers' associations. Organizations planning to set up an unemployment fund must have their program and policies approved by the Ministre de travail et de sécurité sociale. General rules are prescribed for them by the Ministre de travail for standards, methods of management, and investment of reserves. Each unemployment compensation fund has to provide free placement service for its members, but it may use the local public employment service. A local unemployment compensation fund may be licensed by the municipal government. The by - laws of each unemployment compensation fund must specify conditions of eligibility, contributions, benefits, and provisions for administration. Financial solvency must be secured. Benefits are not paid to workers until they have been members for 12 months and have paid their contributions regularly, nor to those who refuse to accept suitable employment offered them by the placement services of the fund or public employment office. Fraud or attempted fraud excludes the member from claiming benefits for a period defined in the by-laws of the fund. Special benefits may be granted to members working part-time. The self-employed, such as artists, craftsmen, artisans, shopkeepers, and writers may become members of an unemployment compensation fund. They are entitled to compensation, however, only when entirely out of work and without income, and after they have registered with the public employment service for a job in line with their training, skill, or experience.

Since unemployment compensation is paid only by some labor unions and mutual-aid societies to their members, these

---

61. "L'Assistance aux Chômeurs," Liaisons Sociales, No. 1367 (April 23, 1954), pp. 8-9.

organizations receive government subsidies, the amount of which
is determined by the proportion of unemployed persons in the
area to the total members of the voluntary society insured against
unemployment. Most unemployment compensation funds grant
additional benefits for the wives and dependent children of the
insured workers during the period of unemployment.

For wage earners who are not protected by a voluntary unemployment insurance plan, an unemployment assistance program
operates under the title of Service d'aide aux travailleurs sans
emploi [Voluntary Unemployment Assistance Service]. 62 The
communal and departmental appropriations for assistance de
chômage [unemployment assistance] for persons who have lost
their jobs, are willing and able to work, and have registered
with the public employment service, are supplemented by national
grants-in-aid. The individual assistance payments made to
unemployed workers vary according to the number of dependents
the worker has, but are, in general, inadequate. To be eligible
for unemployment assistance the worker must be deprived of
sufficient resources or income for the maintenance of himself
and his family, and must have had three months' residence in
the community and six months of employment prior to his claim
for assistance. In larger communities a residence of six months
is required, and a worker in Paris or its environs must have
resided there for a full year. Not eligible are workers who
voluntarily leave their jobs, those dismissed because of a strike
or industrial lock-out or incompetence, those who refuse to
accept offers of suitable employment, and those physically unfit
to work. 63

---

62. This type of categorical assistance to unemployed persons and to their
families has its parallel in the British legislation on unemployment assistance to
workers who had exhausted the unemployment insurance benefits or were not
eligible for them, created by the Unemployment Act of June 28, 1934. See also
Val R. Lorwin, "Trade Unions, 1945-1949," in E. Earle, Modern France, p. 216.

63. Blind persons, severely disabled persons, and invalids classified as incapable
of gainful employment are entitled to receive unemployment assistance if they
comply with special legal requirements.

Assistance de chômage [unemployment assistance] consists of a daily basic assistance allowance for the unemployed adult head of a household and a supplement for his unemployed spouse and children under 21 years of age who do not receive family allowances. After one year of unemployment the assistance is reduced by 20 per cent and thereafter by 10 per cent more. This reduction represents an attempt to reduce chômage professionnel [permanent (deliberate) unemployment], but it also makes unemployment assistance a still more inadequate measure of income maintenance for workers who cannot find new jobs. If the public employment service refuses to grant an applicant unemployment assistance, he may appeal his case to a local and a departmental commission which makes the final decision.

Unemployment assistance benefits for independent "intellectual workers" -- painters, sculptors, actors, dancers, musicians, composers, writers, and journalists -- are given upon a special certificate: Aide des travailleurs intellectuels. The applicant must prove that he has made his living from his professional work for the past three years. The departmental employment service decides upon the application after consultation with representatives of the applicant's professional organization. Workshops for unemployed intellectuals are organized by the Ministère de travail in which activities such as classification of scientific and technical collections, cataloguing of libraries, and laboratory services are performed. [64]

Vocational training and retraining, as well as a systematic expansion of the apprentice-training program, are used to supply some of the urgently needed replacements in industries with serious labor shortages. Adult workers and juvenile apprentices are trained in public vocational-training centers and workshops, particularly in the metal trades, building, construction, and textile manufacturing. So serious was the labor shortage in the mining industry after the Liberation that Polish refugees and German prisoners of war were encouraged

---

64. A national decree of July 15, 1949, Art. 4, provides subsidies for local facilities that employ intellectual workers who are out of a job.

to remain permanently in France to work as miners. Miners are granted special privileges because of their vital importance to the national economy and the exhausting working conditions. Pay increases for seniority, procedures for contract and dismissal, classification of the various types of work, and the protection of union rights of the miners are guaranteed. Retirement with full pension is possible for them at the minimum age of 50, provided they have completed 30 years of work in the mines, which must include 20 years of work underground. 65

OUTLOOK ON SOCIAL SECURITY

Despite the impressive progress the French social security system has made during the past two decades, it is not yet a comprehensive program and is still far from its final goal. Unemployment compensation, which has become a vital and integral part of the social insurance plans in most industrial countries of the world, has not yet been incorporated into the compulsory, unified social insurance scheme. Unemployment has not been a serious social problem in France (in contrast to the experiences of the United States, England, and other nations) so that France is planning to allow about one and one-half million foreign workers to settle there to offset her labor shortage. This acceptance of foreigners should help to supply badly needed agricultural workers and to aid the general demographic policy of the government.

Since there is no compulsory unemployment insurance, it has not been possible to integrate the traditional operation of public assistance fully into the new scheme of social insurance and family allowances. In the field of family allowances, which is particularly important in France, the influence of the mutual-aid societies as self-governing bodies has been so strong that a unified administration of these allowances has not been achieved, although family allowances are financed on the basis of compulsory contributions from employers. The social security

---

65. Loi des pensions aux mineurs [Law on Miners' Pensions] of March 6, 1946.

system does not yet cover the entire population. There are still inequalities in coverage and benefits among the various groups, and there is no inclination to give up what each considers its privileges in favor of a unified plan.

Reforms in the field of social security tend in the direction of a comprehensive, compulsory, and unified program. The coordination of administrative and financial operations, the broad interpretation of the concepts of social security as including preservation of health and working capacity by means of medical and social services, and by industrial health and safety measures, is characteristic of the French system. Plans for future reforms must attempt to combine wage regulations and more liberal social legislation designed to guarantee a minimum living standard for all with the achievement of a satisfactory relationship among the people of different income levels. Continuous increases and expansion of social benefits in France have been accepted as necessary for the protection of the population against poverty, malnutrition, disease, and despair. On the other hand, the people have been unwilling to accept health and welfare services such as medical protection, school lunches, and vacation camps for children as a supplement to their family allowances, as has been done in Great Britain. The French tend to consider the provision of regimented services for the family or children an infringement upon the personal liberty of the parents, and particularly an affront to the prestige of the father.

There is still some resistance among certain groups of the population to the idea of a really comprehensive system of social security that will protect everyone. Political unrest and strikes, rising prices, and the opposition of groups unwilling to give up special privileges or to assume a heavier burden for the aim of social security, are retarding factors in the development of social reform in France.[66] The self-employed groups, businessmen,

---

66. P. Laroque, op. cit., p. 587; see also Francis Montès, "L'Etat a prélevé plus de 400 milliards à la Sécurité sociale," Vers la Vie, January, 1958; and Wallace C. Petersen, op. cit., Chapter 8.

manufacturers, and members of the liberal professions do not want to be identified with the broad masses of workers and salaried employees. But the masses are themselves very individualistic, and harbor a deep-seated suspicion of a state-sponsored program, even one devised for the benefit of the entire population. French workers refuse to accept the guardianship of the government, just as they reject the guardianship of the employers. This attitude is widely shared in the United States.

There have been experiments in the development of improved management-worker relations in France, although the scope of this study does not allow detailed discussion of them. The need for better human relations in industry has not been overlooked. An organization, Action pour les structures humaines, was founded in 1945 for the purpose of developing methods of capital-labor partnership. Professor Georges Friedman of the Sorbonne University in Paris has investigated the results of this movement.[67] He found that about 2,500 small- and medium-sized enterprises in France were operating on a salaire proportionné [proportional wage] system in which workers and salaried employees share the profits according to agreements with the employer and participate in management through elected works committees. In a few industrial firms the entire personnel -- workers, employees, and managers -- have been transformed into a société coopérative de travail [labor cooperative] which directs production, in the form of self-governing workshops, as a collective enterprise. Customers are brought into the partnership in order to increase business and regulate prices, a move designed to secure labor stability and further expansion of production.

The provision of family allowances and social insurance benefits has been necessary to compensate for the general impoverishment resulting from the war, the Occupation, and the post-war economic crisis. The program entails substantial

---

67. "Some Experiments in Industrial and Human Relations," International Labour Review, 71, No. 1 (January, 1955), 79-85; and Où va le travail humain? (Paris: Gallimard, 1953).

sacrifices on the part of employers and wage-earners in favor of those unable to work -- the old, infirm, and sick, and mothers with several children. Social insurance benefits and family allowances provide only a modest amount of social and economic security, in view of the decreased purchasing power of the franc and the rising prices of most commodities.[68] Contributions to social security have, in fact, largely replaced other taxes. It remains necessary to achieve a higher standard of economic security for the old and disabled, as well as for children, after the economy of the country has fully recovered and can provide the funds required for such expansion.

In the line of international social security, France has concluded bilateral agreements with Belgium, the Netherlands, and Switzerland which secure the preservation of social insurance rights and benefits for persons moving to these countries or to France.[69] In October, 1958, France and the other five nations of the European Coal and Steel Community -- Belgium, the Federal Republic of Germany, Italy, Luxembourg, and the Netherlands -- by common consent incorporated in the Treaty of the European Economic Community a provision that all categories of workers would, for social security purposes, be treated as citizens of the country of residence. Thus migrant workers, immigrants, the stateless, and refugees have full rights in old age, disability, and survivors' benefits, maternity and health insurance, funeral grants, workmen's compensation and unemployment insurance. Family allowances in France are excluded from the provision because in this area France exceeds the allowances of all the other European countries. All periods during which an individual has paid towards social security coverage in any country within the European Economic Community are credited on his behalf

---

68. Pierre Dieterlein, "La répartition du revenue national," Revue Economique, X, No. 1 (January, 1959), 73-92.

69. P. Laroque, op. cit., pp. 588-590; Marc Dégas, "Les accords internationaux dans le domaine de la protection vieillesse," Droit Social, 22, No. 1 (January, 1959), 50-55.

toward the accumulation of final benefits in the country in which he becomes eligible for insurance payments or benefits.[70]

The economic importance of social security benefits and family allowances in France is generally recognized, but there are still differences of opinion whether the present program presents the most desirable method of redistribution of income for the entire population. When the system of social insurances was established, its primary aim was to equalize the risks of an industrial society among the various classes so as to protect the victims of industrialization and changing social and economic conditions, particularly the aged, the sick, persons injured by industrial accidents and occupational diseases, and their families. Social insurance legislation applied the experience and principles derived from those developed by the commercial insurance companies, and used their calculations and techniques. The large volume of contributions made by employers and workers to the various social insurance programs permitted benefits to be paid to those groups receiving the most immediate impact of a changing technology. Basically, however, they transferred funds from one group -- employers and workers -- to another group (the aged, sick, disabled) among the insured population.[71] The resulting redistribution of income through the payment of benefits is a consequence, not the aim of social insurance. Family allowances and public assistance, however, follow a different policy. They are also devised to aid the poor, the sick, the handicapped, the disabled, and particularly families with numerous children, in order to secure a minimum subsistence for all. However, public assistance and social services transfer substantial parts of the national income from the upper social classes, favored by property, birth, and material economic success, to that part of the population that is in financial need.

---

70. Daniel S. Gerig, European Multi-Lateral Social Security Treaties (Social Security Administration, Research and Statistics, No. 43 [Washington, D. C., December, 1958].

71. Paul Durand, "Les Equivoques de la rédistribution du revenu," Droit Social, 16, No. 5 (May, 1953), 292; and Wallace C. Petersen, op. cit., Chapters 1-3.

The family allowances perform the same economic function by the transfer of tax-collected funds to those families with two or more young children; by this transfer of money, they intend to secure a healthy, decent up-bringing of the children, thus helping the parents to meet their own responsibilities for the children by sharing them with the community.

The pattern of redistribution of income imposes a heavier financial burden on the employer than on the worker in France. Social insurance contributions are 6 per cent of the payroll each for the employer and the worker. But the employer has also to pay an additional 4 per cent tax for the aged, between 3 and 4 per cent of the payroll for workmen's compensation insurance, and a 16.75 per cent tax for family allowances, so that management contributes about 30 per cent of the payroll for social insurance and family allowances. Since these taxes are calculated as costs of production, the high level of prices in France is a partial result of these social contributions.[72] For certain groups of self-employed persons with modest incomes and for public servants in all levels of government, special sub-sidies are granted to alleviate the burden of social taxation.

As the contribution of the employers is based upon the wages and salaries of their workers, not upon the financial success and profits of their enterprises, the redistribution of the national income through social taxation does not represent a very fair charge on the firms and individuals who are best able to carry the burden of social security. The same has been said for the rural family allowance contributions, which are mainly based upon agricultural production, not upon profits from farms, fisheries, etc. On the other hand, it is felt in France that this pattern still represents a more effective method of income distribution than the flat-rate contributions that form a major part of the English social security system, although family allowances in Great Britain are paid from general taxation.[73]

---

72. G. Laurent, "La measure de l'évolution du coût de la vie," Droit Social, 21, Nos. 9-10 (September-October, 1958), 452-458.

73. Paul Durand, article cited in Footnote 71, pp. 293-294.

The contributions to social security and family allowances in France are limited by consideration of a legally determined maximum amount of wages, salaries, and earnings for the computation of taxes. The same principle is used for the social insurance contributions for old - age, survivors', and disability insurance, and for unemployment compensation in the United States. These arrangements limit the function of redistribution of income to some extent, but do not totally prevent it.

The French imposition of high taxes for social insurance and family allowances upon the employers has led to an increase in prices that burdens all consumers, and has stifled the attempts of labor unions to obtain higher wages. These results may, in fact, prevent a fair redistribution of the national income and therefore cause renewed demands for higher wages, in spite of the recent stabilization of the franc. The entire operation of the social security system and family allowances, however, cannot be held responsible for increasing prices and temporary inflation, because many other factors influence the economic situation of France.[74] Among these elements are the high cost of military operations in Algiers, competition among producers, various economic monopolies, the interaction of national and international markets, particularly in respect to the new European common market policies, production costs and wages. Under these circumstances, the cost of social security is only one of many elements to be considered in the economic recovery of the country for which careful research will be necessary in order to find the best solution.

---

74. Etienne Antonelli, "La Sécurité sociale," Revue d'Economie Politique, 68, Noş. 4-5 (July - October, 1958), 970-985; Pierre Lassegue, "La situation sociale," Droit Social, 22, No. 1 (January, 1959), 32-34.

SELECTED BIBLIOGRAPHY

Armstrong, Barbara N. The Health Insurance Doctor, His Role In Great Britain, Denmark, and France. Princeton: Princeton University Press, 1939

Baum, Warren C. The French Economy and the State. Princeton: Princeton University Press, 1958.

_____. "The Marshall Plan and French Foreign Trade," in E. M. Earle, Modern France: Problems of the Third and Fourth Republics. Princeton: Princeton University Press, 1951, pp. 382-402.

Besse, Fernand. "L'amélioration de la Sécurité sociale et des allocations familiales," Droit Social, 13, No. 10 (December, 1950), pp. 436-441.

Bonvoison, G., and G. Maignam. Allocations Familiales et Caisses de Compensations. Paris: Receuil Sirey, 1930.

Boret, Marcel. "Les budgets limitatifs de gestion des organisations de sécurité sociale," Droit Social, 16, No. 8 (September-October, 1953), 357-363.

Bourgeois, Léon. La Politique de la prévoyance sociale. 2 Vols. Paris, 1914 and 1919.

Bousser, Jacques, and Jean-Jacques Gillen. "Medical Inspection of Labour and Industrial Medical Services in France," International Labour Review, 65, No. 2 (February, 1952), 184-210.

Bremme, Gabriele. Freiheit und soziale Sicherheit. Motive und Prinzipien sozialer Sicherung dargestellt an England und Frankreich. Stuttgart: Ferd. Enke, 1961. [Published after the completion of this study.]

Callaghan, Hubert C. The Family Allowance Procedure. Washington, D. C.: Catholic University of America Press, 1947.

Callebat, Georges. Assurances sociales et allocations familiales en agriculture. Lons-le-Saunier: M. Declume, 1953.

Ceccaldi, Dominique. Les institutions sanitaires et sociales. Paris: Foucher, 1953.

Clark, Marjorie R. "Organized Labor and the Family Allowance System in France," Journal of Political Economy, 39, No. 5 (August, 1931), 526-537.

Code de la Sécurité Sociale (Décret no. 56-1279 du 10 décembre 1956). Paris: Journal Officiel, 1956.

Cohen, Wilbur J. "Foreign Experience in Social Insurance Contributions for Agricultural and Domestic Workers," Social Security Bulletin, 8, No. 2 (February, 1945), 7-8.

Doublet, Jacques and Georges Lavau. Sécurité Sociale. Paris : Universitaires de France, 1957.

Douglas, Paul H. "French Social Insurance," The Annals of the American Academy of Political and Social Science, 164 (November, 1936), 211-248.

"Le déséquilibre financier de l'assurance-maladie," Droit Social, 13, No. 10 (December, 1950), 417-422.

Durand, Paul. "Les équivoques de la rédistribution du revenu par la sécurité sociale," Droit Social, 16, No. 5 (May, 1953), 292-298.

_____. La Politique Contemporaire de Sécurité Sociale. Paris: Dalloz, 1953.

Earle, Edward Mead (ed.). Modern France: Problems of the Third and Fourth Republics. Princeton: Princeton University Press, 1951.

Ehrmann, Henry W. "The Decline of the Socialist Party," in Edward M. Earle, op. cit., pp. 181-199.

Falk, I. S. "Medical Services under Health Insurance Abroad," Social Security Bulletin, 3, No. 12 (December, 1940), 11-20.

_____. Security Against Sickness: A Study of Health Insurance. New York: Doubleday, Doran & Co., 1936 (Chapter XI).

Feraud, Lucien. Actuarial Technique and Financial Organisation of Social Insurance (International Labour Office, Studies and Reports, Series M [Social Insurance] No. 17 [Geneva, 1940], pp. 167-270).

Fooner, Michael. "The Use of the Stamp System for Social Insurance in France," Social Security Bulletin, 2, No. 6 (June, 1939), 18-22.

Friedman, Georges. "Some Experiments in Industrial and Human Relations," International Labour Review, 71, No. 1 (January, 1955), 79-87.

Gauthier, Louis. "L'organisation d'un service enterprise de médecine du travail," Droit Social, 13, No. 2 (February, 1950), 73-77.

Gourdin, André. Les Sociétés de Secours Mutuel. Paris: Paul Dupont, 1920.

Hoffner, Claire. "Recent Developments in Compulsory Systems of Family Allowances," International Labour Review, LVI, No. 4 (October, 1947), 337-370.

"Industrial Relations in France," International Labour Review, LVI, No. 4 (October, 1947), 454-456.

International Labour Office. Approaches to Social Security, An International Survey (Studies and Reports, Series M [Social Insurance], No. 18 [Montreal, 1942]).

_____. Economical Administration of Health Insurance Benefits (Studies and Reports, Series M [Social Insurance], No. 15 [Geneva, 1938], pp. 169-185).

_____. "Family Allowances Schemes in 1947," International Labour Review, LVII, No. 4 (April, 1948), 315-333; and LVII, No. 5 (May, 1948), 456-477.

_____. International Survey of Social Services, I, Geneva, 1936, 219-284.

Kirk, Dudley. "Population and Population Trends in Modern France," in Edward M. Earle, op. cit., pp. 313-333.

Lajugie, J. "La rédistribution du revenu national," Droit Social, 13, No. 3 (March, 1950), 109-118.

Landes, David S. "Observations on France: Economy, Society, and Polity," World Politics, IX, (1957), 329-350.

Laporte, Marie-Madeleine. Les Allocations Familiales dans le Commerce et l'Industrie en Droit Française et Etranger. Paris: Dalloz, 1938.

Laroque, Pierre. "From Social Insurance to Social Security: Evolution in France," International Labour Review, LVII, No. 6 (June, 1948), 565-590.

_____. Réflexions sur le Problème Social. Paris: Editions Sociales Françaises, 1953.

Lebel, Roland. La Généralisation de la Protection Sociale. Paris: Documentation économique, 1953.

Levasseur, G. "Chronique de jurisprudence en matière de sécurité sociale," Droit Social, 16, No. 1 (January, 1953), 54-57, and No. 3 (March, 1953), 178-183.

Lipset, Seymour Martin. Political Man. New York: Doubleday, 1960.

Lorwin, Val R. "The Struggle for the Control of the French Union Movement," in Edward M. Earle, op. cit., pp. 200-218.

Maras, Pierre. Le Fondement de l'obligation aux Allocations Familiales. Paris: Sirey, 1936.

Matthews, Ronald. The Death of the Fourth Republic. New York: Praeger, 1954.

Monnin, R. Famille et Sécurité Sociale. Paris: Editions Familiales de France, 1944.

Paillat, Paul. "Structure démographique des cadres français," Sociologie du Travail (Paris), III (July-September, 1960), 246-256.

Petersen, Wallace C. The Welfare State in France. Lincoln: University of Nebraska Press, 1960. [Published after the completion of this study.]

Picard, Roger. "Family Allowances in French Industry," International Labour Review, IX, No. 2 (February, 1924), 161-176.

Pinte, Jean. Les Allocations Familiales. Paris: Receuil-Sirey, 1935.

Quatremarre, Pierre. "La gestion administrative des organismes de sécurité sociale," Droit Social, 16, No. 8 (September-October, 1953), 493-496.

Rockwell, Almon F. "Social Insurance and Related Measures in Wartime Europe," Social Security Bulletin, 3, No. 6 (June, 1940), 21-24.

_____. "Social Insurance for Special Groups in France," Social Security Bulletin, 4, No. 10 (October, 1939), 11-18.

Rodgers, Barbara. "Social Security in France," Public Administration (London), XXXI, No. 4 (Winter, 1953), 377-398; and XXXII, No. 1 (Spring, 1954), 99-116.

Romanet, Emile. Les Allocations Familiales. Lyons: Chronique Sociale de France, 1924.

Ruggles, Richard. "The French Investment Program and Its Relation to Resource Allocation," in Edward M. Earle, op. cit., 368-381.

Sachet, Adrien. Traité Théorique et Pratique de la Législation sur les Accidents de Travail et les Maladies Professionnelles. Paris: Recueil-Sirey, 1937.

Sawyer, John E. "Strains in the Social Structure of Modern France," in Edward M. Earle, op. cit., pp. 293-312.

Siegfried, André. "Approaches to an Understanding of Modern France," in Edward M. Earle, op. cit., pp. 3-16.

_____. Guide Pratique des Lois Sociales. L'Aide à la Famille, L'Aide aux Travailleurs. 2nd ed. Paris: Musée Social, 1943.

Vibart, Hugh H. R. Family Allowances in Practice. London: P. S. King & Son, 1926.

Villey, Dr. "Sécurité sociale et prestations familiales: le contrôle médicale," Droit Social, 16, No. 5 (September-October, 1953), 485-493.

Willoughby, Gertrude. "Social Security in France and Britain," Political Quarterly (London), XIX, No. 1 (January-March, 1948), 49-59.

_____. "Population Problems and Family Policy in France," Eugenic Review, Vol. 45, No. 2.

Woog, C. and Damarchid M. Bardon. L'Indemnisation des Accidents du Travail. Paris: Presses Modernes, 1939.

CHAPTER 6

PROFESSIONAL STANDARDS AND EDUCATION FOR SOCIAL WORK

DEVELOPMENT OF SOCIAL WORK EDUCATION

The forerunners of social work in France were the members of the religious orders of Saint François de Sales, Les Dames de Charité, and Les Filles de Charité, created on the initiative of St. Vincent de Paul during the seventeenth century. Modern professional work developed rather late in France, as shown by the founding in 1911 of the first Catholic school of social work, L'Ecole normale sociale, in Paris by Mlles Novo and Butillard. Since this start in professional education, French social work has been oriented mainly toward health and family protection.[1] It is characteristic of professional social work in France that for many years training as a registered nurse was a prerequisite for social work education, and until recently visiting nurses were considered to be as truly social workers as the assistantes sociales who correspond to the trained social workers in England or the United States. Visiting nurses[2] are still employed instead

---

1. In 1899, the first European school of social work was established in Amsterdam, one year after the New York Charity Organization Society opened a training course in social work.

2. The visiting nurses still represent a majority of all professional persons employed in social work activities in France. They perform not only nurses' duties

of social workers in numerous agencies primarily concerned with the care and rehabilitation of sick persons.

The development of principles in French social work resulted in a practice in which certain concepts of casework, respect for the dignity of the person in need, and the necessity of individualized treatment have been accepted. Public welfare agencies began employing trained social workers in the 1930's. These social workers are engaged in casework with families and children, and with juvenile and adult delinquents, and in medical social work for patients and their families. The surintendantes d'usines [industrial social workers] are an important group of social workers who serve in connection with industrial plants, workers, and their families. A third group of social workers is employed in recreational and social group-work and in institutions; among them are the résidentes sociales [group workers in settlement houses]. First the private agencies, and later the public welfare authorities and social security organizations (such as the family allowance agencies) became aware of the value of trained social workers; both now employ an increasing number of women and men.

CURRICULA AND METHODS OF SOCIAL WORK EDUCATION

The importance of professional training for social work in France is evident from the rapid growth of institutions for education in this field. In 1923, the existing five professional schools and the Directeur du comité central d'assistance publique et d'hygiène publique de Paris [Director of the Paris Board of Public Assistance and Hygiene] asked for official regulations for the curriculum of social work education. The Conseil supérieur d'assistance publique [Superior Council of Public Assistance] in

---

in hospitals and clinics, but also functions which are assigned to social workers in other countries. The visiting nurses are organized in a separate national federation, Association des Infirmières Visiteuses de France; their number is about 138,000. They are grouped into three divisions: child health nurses, social hygiene nurses for tubercular patients, and general hygiene nurses.

the Ministère de travail et des services sociaux [Ministry of Labor and Public Welfare] answered that since social work hardly existed as a profession in France, regulations for training were impossible.[3] In 1928, however, the schools of social work themselves founded the Comité d'entente des écoles de service social, a national association which in 1932 succeeded in convincing the government that an officially approved program of social work training was necessary. By government decree a state diploma giving the social worker the official title of assistante de service social was introduced.[4] Schools meeting government standards were legally recognized, and a national system of uniform supervision of all such schools, with annual centralized examinations for their students, was instituted. At the outbreak of the Second World War in 1939 there were 12 professional schools of social work in France, six of them in Paris. In addition there were 30 visiting nurses' training schools which, after the Liberation, were authorized to train both social workers and visiting nurses. During the Second World War and the Occupation several schools of social work were temporarily closed or transferred to other cities. After the Liberation in 1944 the number of schools increased rapidly, since urgent social and health problems required a large number of trained workers. In 1950 there were 66, and at present there are 70 recognized schools of social work in France, 18 of them in Paris and the surrounding Département de la Seine. Accreditation of the schools is granted by the Ministère de santé publique et de population [Ministry of Public Health and Population].

These recognized schools have the character of technical colleges; they are not incorporated into the universities. Many of their part-time instructors, however, are faculty members of universities, and include professors of medicine, psychiatry, law, psychology, and political science. The curriculum at the

---

3. Alice Salomon, Education for Social Work (Zurich: Verlag für Recht und Gesellshaft, 1937), p. 9; and P. F. Armand-Delille, L'assistance sociale et ses moyens d'action (Paris: Alcan, 1926).

4. Decrees of January 12, 1932, and December 13, 1933.

schools covers a three-year period. Eligible for admission are French citizens between the ages of 19 and 35 who can pass an admission examination and are in good health.[5] Candidates who have a high school diploma or university degree are admitted without special examination. The first year is devoted primarily to medical subjects, social hygiene, and public assistance legislation. The academic training, with a minimum of 367 hours of theory, is combined with field work in hospitals,[6] maternity homes, children's institutions, and child health centers. The second and third years emphasize the study of social legislation and social, economic, and administrative problems. Included in the curriculum are family and child welfare, economic and social conditions, civil and criminal law, labor laws, public assistance legislation, professional ethics, and the history, organization, and administration of social agencies. During the second and third years, field work and observation visits are offered in various social agencies, social insurance and family allowance agencies, settlement houses, factories and railroad agencies that maintain social service departments, recreation services, and youth centers. Only women were admitted to most schools until 1944, but the Comité central des caisses d'allocations familiales [Central Committee for Family Allowances] established at that time a separate school for male social workers in Paris.[7] A number of schools have a few residential facilities available for out-of-town students. The schools also recommend to students investigated and approved families who are willing to furnish board and room. Scholarships are granted under the auspices of the Ministère national de santé publique [National Ministry

5. Foreign students may be admitted by the schools with the approval of the Ministère de santé publique. French registered nurses who have completed two years of training may be admitted to the second year of studies, so that their social work training lasts two years.

6. M. Santy, "L'organisation des services hospitaliers," Pages Documentaires, 1958, No. 5 (June-July), 323-350.

7. The Ecole de préparation aux carrières sociales masculines.

of Public Health], the Entr'Aide française, and some students' associations, but are given only on the recommendation of a recognized school. 8

The main orientation in social work training continues to be directed toward medical and health problems. In field work in hospitals, clinics, and dispensaries, and in home visits, the social work student pays special attention to illness, diet, health education, sanitary conditions, medicines and appliances, and clothing. There is less emphasis than in the United States on economic questions, relief payment, rent, employment, the responsibilities of relatives, and emotional problems. 9

PROFESSIONALIZATION AND ORGANIZATION
OF THE PROFESSION

The development of social casework in the United States and Canada has recently influenced the thinking in social work education in several European countries, including France. The schools of social work and their faculties have assisted in the arrangement of a number of institutes and seminars, some of them under the auspices of the United Nations and the specialized international agencies. One of the limitations of the study of casework stems from the limited academic education in theories of psychology and psychiatry of many students in the schools of social work in France compared with students in graduate schools in the United States and Canada. They often do not have

---

8. Decree of the Ministère de santé publique of March 27, 1945; Yvonne Bougé, Préparation et Activités de l'Assistante Sociale (Paris: Bloud and Gay, 1947), p. 40.

9. An interesting discussion of the application of scientific principles in social and psychological investigations is offered in Didier Anzieu's article, "Divers types d'enquêtes psychosociologiques," Informations Sociales (Paris), 8, No. 7 (July, 1954), 765-770.

sufficient knowledge of psychological and emotional factors for the development of casework skills. 10 Traditionally the programs of the schools emphasize health, medical problems, and legal and administrative questions rather than human relations and skill in dealing with other people's needs. Most French schools of social work have general curricula and educate their students for social welfare rather than for specialized skills in child casework, psychiatric social work, or social group work. The field of community organization is dealt with only slightly, and then in connection with social welfare legislation. Another factor which makes it difficult to introduce into the French schools the American tradition of casework is the lack of trained faculty members with experience in casework practice, supervision, and teaching. The directors of social agencies and some who have supervised young graduates in such agencies have complained that in many schools the curriculum has little relation to the problems their graduates will face in social work practice. This lack of integration was particularly apparent recently when some schools introduced social casework courses into their curricula. 11

The present method of field work is more like an apprentice-ship, and is carried on under the supervision of agency personnel who are not on the faculty of the schools. An instructor from the school pays an occasional visit to the agency and has some conferences with the students and supervisors, but this visit establishes only a tenuous relationship compared to the intensive education and coordinated supervised field - work practice that students get in schools of social work in the United States and Canada. The question of field - work supervision presents a particularly difficult problem for the French curriculum. But it seems that concepts of social casework are slowly finding

10. M. Colin, "La phénoménologie et l'enseignement de la psychologie dans les Ecoles sociales," Service Social dans le Monde, Vol. 1958, No. 1.

11. Myriam Davis, "L'application des principes du Casework à l'entretien individuel utilisé comme méthode de formation des élèves assistantes sociales," in Erna Sailer et al., New Trends in European Social Work (Vienna: Astoria, 1955), pp. 49-54.

their way into the schools' academic programs, and that a sincere appreciation of casework principles is growing. This growth has been stimulated by the international exchange of teachers and students of social work, and by the experience of the Paul Baerwald School of Social Work in Versailles, which was operated under the sponsorship of the American Joint Distribution Committee and under the direction of American professors from 1949 to 1953.[12] It will probably be necessary to include on the teaching staffs more persons well trained in casework methods if the understanding of social casework is to be broadened.

The cultural exchange program of the United States and the United Nations which enables French social workers to observe or study American methods of social work education has proven to be valuable for France. These methods are now applied with modifications in several schools of social work in France. A more personal relationship between the instructor of the school and the individual student has been introduced. One of the first results has been the development of personal discussions on a regular basis to clarify questions and problems and to direct the individual student's learning process. The problems discussed in these personal conferences relate in part to the object of study, such as social conditions, and in part to the attitudes of the student and his sociological and psychological problems. The conferences help him to overcome doubts and insecurity, and permit him to apply theoretical knowledge to practical problems he has encountered in his field work.

In the experience of the schools, applying psychological theories to patients in field work results in disturbance for some students who had felt, on the basis of their academic courses, that they knew how to categorize patients, but found the problems more involved than they expected. Theoretical knowledge is occasionally used as a defense against an anxiety about practical field work.

---

12. See Philip Klein, "The Paul Baerwald School of Social Work," The Jewish Social Service Quarterly, 26, No. 4 (June, 1951), 544-553.

One of the major problems facing the student is his difficulty in reaching a complete understanding of social service. Frequently he arrives at the school with definite ideas and opinions that are more closely connected with the motives that led him to choose this study than with a real knowledge of social conditions. In field work he is confronted by the reality of human social problems, and is often perplexed and deeply confused when he finds them difficult to solve because of the complexity of human behavior and the inadequacy of resources for aid and rehabilitation. The disappointment the new student almost inevitably feels as a result of these difficulties has to be overcome.

The first problem is centered in the understanding of various forms of human behavior and maladjustment. The student must change from an attitude of moral judgment to one of tolerance and understanding, without imposing his own values. This process requires a deep change of personal attitude and endangers the normal system of defenses which most human beings develop. For instance, most people strongly resent lying because honesty and sincerity are considered to be moral or ethical values which occupy an important place in our total personality, and guilt is produced if truth is not respected. In general, we try to persuade others to avoid lying and cheating also, but a social worker must accept such actions on the part of his patient without blaming him and without immediately attempting to educate and change him. Similar experiences make it essential that the student learn to give up his formerly rigid attitude of disapproval, based upon his ethical and religious standards, and to become more understanding and flexible. Understanding of human behavior is also necessary with regard to other manifestations such as severe anxieties, withdrawal, and feelings of depression.

The second major problem which the student faces in social work education is the necessity of recognizing certain inadequacies, such as lack of material funds for aid, lack of decent housing, inadequate wages, unsanitary working conditions, inflexible and impractical rules in the school, the apathy of clients in social agencies, and related experiences. The normal student refuses to accept such inadequacies as inevitable, and is inclined to attempt at once to change the conditions and improve the situation of the client. But he has to learn that the acceptance of many limitations is part of life in modern society, and that he cannot continually identify himself with the client without endangering his ability to learn his profession and his function as part of the social agency. The growth of self-discipline is part of the maturation process of the student in social work.

It is in these problems that the conferences with the instructor or supervisor can be of greatest help to the student in alleviating his emotional reactions and bringing about a better understanding of social reality. In some ways the relationship of the instructor to the student is the same as that of the social worker to his client. Each student is, of course, an individual case and differs from every other. Just as with the client in casework, progress here can be made only if instructor and student share a feeling of confidence and mutual trust. Adjustment has to be made in the light of professional growth. The instructor permits the student to discuss freely his general problems, as well as the structure and operation of social services, and encourages rather than criticizes. The instructor's task is to understand the student's difficulties, and to help him to overcome the barriers to his professional growth.

The schools keep a record of the academic and field work of each student. These records are submitted to the Commission d'examens [Board of Examiners] before the final examination of the student. The members of this board are appointed annually by the Ministre de santé publique, and are selected from the Ministères de santé publique, de travail et de sécurité sociale, d'instruction publique, and de la Justice [Ministries of Public Health, Labor and Social Security, Education, and Justice] from faculty members of the medical schools of the universities, from social agencies, and from schools of social work. The annual examinations are held only in cities where there is a university with a recognized medical school. 13

---

13. In contrast to the French system where the certificate of a social worker is issued by the Ministère de santé publique, social workers in Belgium receive their

Specialized training for social work in industry is offered in several of the schools of social work, with a curriculum in social legislation, factory management, personnel work, and industrial hygiene. [14] The field work training includes the placement of the student in a factory, usually for six months, as a regular unskilled worker. When he completes this period, his field work includes the counseling of workers in a factory or department store on personal and family problems, hygiene and education. He is taught to interpret the workers' complaints and social needs (especially those of women and children) to the manager, and to achieve for the workers a better adjustment to their working conditions. Since industrial social workers are employed by the company, the student must learn to serve the needs of the workers and their families within the limits of his duty to the owner as his employer. It is often difficult to convince a business executive or his assistants that paternalistic favors to workers are ineffective and humiliating, and that economic or personal crises within a worker's family must be handled with a due regard for the individual's dignity. The student learns to investigate the causes of absenteeism, but regular home visits are not considered to fall within his proper province and are referred to a family agency or the municipal united family services. He must therefore learn, as well, how to make proper contact with factory inspectors, public assistance authorities, and with social insurance and family allowance agencies. [15]

In 1932, at the suggestion of the schools, a Conseil de perfectionnement des écoles d'infirmières et d'assistantes sociales

---

certificate from the Ministère de la Justice [Ministry of Justice]. From the American point of view this seems little warranted by the nature of social work, which has little relation to specific legal aspects, but it is explained by the fact that in Belgium social work has mainly served in the field of juvenile delinquency and as probation and parole services for various types of courts.

14. The first school for the training of industrial social workers was opened in 1917 by Mlle Marie Diemer and Mlle de Montmort.

15. M. J. Staercke, "La formation des assistantes sociales d'industrie," Bulletin Social des Industriels, 29, No. 241 (November, 1957), 367-370.

[Supervisory Council of Schools of Social Work] was established to advise the Ministère de santé publique in the field of education for social work.   It is composed of representatives of those ministries concerned with social questions, representatives of the faculties of the Université de Paris (Sorbonne), of the schools of social work, and of members of social agencies. The annual examinations given at the same time each year for students of social work as they complete the first, second, and third year of study are prepared with the assistance of a subcommittee of the council. [16] Each examination consists of a written essay, a practical demonstration, and an oral examination. Since 1946 the student has received his state license as assistante sociale [social assistant] after he has completed his studies and passed his final examination. Formerly the student, after passing the examination, had to work for two years in a full-time, paid social work position before the license was issued. [17] To retain experienced workers during the transitional period, persons with more than ten years of practical social work experience were admitted to the final examinations although they had not attended one of the recognized schools of social work. However, these candidates still had to pass the examinations that the students are given after three years of study.

An advanced education in social work has been established by admitting licensed graduates of the recognized schools of social work to a new post-graduate social work career which qualifies them for civil service positions with the chance for promotion to higher supervisory and administrative positions. Among these tenure positions are the direction of coordination of social services and assignment as technical social work consultant. In France, as well as in other Central European countries, there has been a demand for well-trained and experienced social

---

16. The council -- Conseil de perfectionnement des écoles sociales -- was created by a decree of 1932; amendments were made by decrees of August 28, 1936, and October 7, 1940, and by the law of April 8, 1946.

17. Law of April 8, 1946.

workers to supervise students and undertake research in social welfare, and to assist the schools of social work and public and private social agencies in the development of their organization and policies. [18]

Special courses for supervisors in public and private social agencies have been offered since 1951 at the Ecole nationale de la santé publique in Paris and as in-service training courses and refresher courses for social workers employed in the social insurance and family allowance administrations, as well as for other personnel of the family allowance funds.

In 1946, social work was made a licensed profession by the law of April 8, Article 1. The titles of "assistante sociale" or "aide d'assistante sociale" are reserved for licensed social workers. [19] Social workers, like physicians, clergymen, and members of the bar, have to maintain professional secrecy on confidential information obtained from their clients. Violation of professional secrecy is punishable under the provisions of the Code pénal, Article 378. A Commission consultative pour l'exercise de la profession d'assistante sociale [Advisory Board on the Exercise of the Social Work Profession] has been organized under the Ministère de santé publique. [20] The Commission consultative [Advisory Board] examines the licenses presented for recognition and the records of social workers applying for an examination to continue in their profession.

If a social worker accepts a professional position, he has to register within one month at the office of the prefect of the département, with his state license and official title. If he moves to another département, a new registration is required. Social workers who have interrupted their professional activity

---

18. United Nations, Bureau of Social Affairs, Training for Social Work, Second International Survey, 1955, p. 51.

19. Special examinations for social workers with five years' practice employed before January 1, 1941 were possible within three months. Without an examination, social workers have not been permitted to work since April 9, 1948.

20. Decree of June 21, 1946.

for more than two years have to re-register, although they have
not changed their residence. The prefect of each département
publishes annually a list of all licensed social workers and
visiting nurses. The list contains the date and character of the
license and title, and is kept in the file of the Directeur d'hygiène
publique [Director of Public Health]. A special badge for social
workers and visiting nurses is approved by the Ministère de
santé publique and is worn exclusively by the members of these
two licensed professions.

In the field of industrial social work, a special license as
conseiller social de travail [industrial social consultant] and
as conseiller assistant social de travail was established by a
decree of March 17, 1942. Social workers are eligible for
these positions if they have had supplementary training in one
of the schools of social work offering a six-months' curriculum
approved by the Ministère de travail and have had two years of
successful experience in social work after receiving the license
as social worker, or hold a graduate degree in law, political
science, medicine, pharmacy, literature, or philosophy.[21]

Since only large factories, industrial and mining concerns, and
department stores can afford to employ an individual industrial
social worker or an industrial social consultant, services sociaux
entre-usines [inter-factory social services] have been organized
in which a number of small- and medium-sized workshops and
factories cooperate. The owners of a group of such industrial
establishments who want to have a social worker available for
the workers and their families organize a joint service. If the
number of these industrial and commercial firms is substantial, a
director of social services or an industrial social consultant is
frequently employed under whose supervision several industrial
social workers are active. As a rule, industrial social workers
are assigned to a number of factories or workshops of the same
industrial branch. Their office hours in each factory and shop
are held once a week at a regular time, but home calls and

---

21. Decree of March 17, 1942, on admission to institutes for industrial social
consultant training.

contact with other community agencies are also provided as in larger plants.[22] The social worker attends meetings of the shop council, assists in the management of factory canteens, health services, clinics, consumer cooperatives, and summer camps for the workers and their children. Most of the joint services insurance companies, chemical plants, and laboratories.[23] Some larger firms employ an industrial social worker under the title of ingénieur social [social engineer]. He is engaged in the same activities as the industrial social worker, but he assumes responsibility for the adjustment of legal, health, and family problems of the employees and serves as liaison officer between the company and community resources which may be helpful in meeting the individual needs of the factory workers and their families. Thus, the social service division of the Association national des compagnies de chemins de fer [National Association of Railroad Companies] organizes first - aid stations at large railroad centers with physicians, nurses, and a social worker in attendance. The service also provides periodic free health examinations for employees, vacation camps for children, and referral for special free treatment to other agencies. Additional social workers are employed in housing projects constructed by the railroad companies for their workers.[24]

The Association des travailleuses sociales [Association of Social Workers], a professional organization, was founded under the direction of Mme Gervais-Courtellement, Mme Jacob, and Mlle Delagrange in Paris in 1922. The association established a club in Paris, and organizes regular meetings and observation

22. M. Ginet, "Les fonctions des travailleurs sociaux dans l'entreprise," Feuillets de l'Association Nationale, Vol. 1957, No. 36.

23. Yvonne Bougé, op. cit., p. 193.

24. Ibid., pp. 199-203. The railroads had first asked the assistance of the French Red Cross and other social agencies, but found that a special social service of their own was needed for their activities.

visits to furnish its members cultural and professional stimulus.
It also grants an annual scholarship for study in a foreign country
to one of its members.

The Union catholique des services de santé et des services
sociaux, a denominational association, has both nurses and
social workers as its members. [25]   Its activities emphasize
religious aspects, moral problems, and the conflicts of modern
life.   Annual reunions and retreats, regional conferences, study
groups, and pilgrimages to Rome and Lourdes are among the
functions of this professional association.

In 1944, after the Liberation, the Association nationale des
assistantes diplomées d'Etat [National Association of Licensed
Social Workers] was organized. [26]   It comprises professional
social workers of all regions of France, and is directed by a
national board composed of 22 members elected from regional
districts.   A national staff assists in developing standards of
service in consultations, and in making recommendations for
employment contracts with public and private agencies.   An
annual conference, usually attended by more than one thousand
delegates, directs the policies of the association.   All of the
organizations of social workers, including the sections of social
work in the two main labor union federations, the C. G. T. and
the C. F. T. C., and the denominational associations, have a
comité d'entente [coordinating committee] which represents the
professional interests of social work before the government and
the parliament.

---

25. The union was founded in 1922 by Monseignor Gerlier and Mlle d'Airolles;
it has 15, 000 members in 135 local chapters (Yvonne Bougé, op. cit., pp. 295-
296).

26. The national association has about 5, 000 members, probably more than
two-thirds of the licensed social workers in France.

SELECTED BIBLIOGRAPHY

Anzieu, Didier. "Divers types d'enquêtes psychosociologiques," Informations Sociales, VIII, No. 7 (July, 1954), 765-770.

Armand-Delille, P. F. L'Assistante Sociale et ses Moyens d'Action. Paris: Alcan, 1926.

Association Nationale des Assistantes Sociales. Action Sociale et Service Social. Paris: L'Association, 1957.

Association Nationale des Assistantes Sociales Diplomées d'Etat. Service Sociale et Culture Humaine. Paris: Editions Sociales Françaises, 1948.

_____. "Etude sur le secret professionnel et son application à la profession d'assistante sociale," Progrès Social, No. 29 (September, 1946), pp. 3-7.

Aubrun, H. Guide Pratique d'Aide Sociale. Paris: Musée social, 1957.

Baur-Halbwachs, Mlle. "Recours à l'action sociale," Informations Sociales, XI, No. 2 (February, 1957), 188-190.

Bougé, Yvonne. Préparation et Activités de l'Assistante Sociale. Paris: Bloud & Gay, 1947.

Calvet, Henri. La Société Française Contemporaire. Paris: F. Nathan, 1956.

Chabert, A. Les Salaires dans l'Industrie Française. Paris: Armand Colin, 1955.

Chauvel, A. "La profession d'assistante sociale," Pages Sociales, No. 29 (September, 1947), pp. 7-9.

_____. "La coordination des services sociaux," Pages Sociales, No. 25 (March, 1947), pp. 12-16.

Clery, P. "Social Work in France," Social Welfare (Manchester), October, 1951.

Combes, Paul. Niveau de Vie et Progrès Technique en France. Paris: Presses Universitaires de France, 1956.

"Contribution à l'approfondissement des méthodes de service social," Informations Sociales, XI, No. 10 (November, 1957), 1193-1201.

Cordelier, Susanne F. Service Social Féminin. Paris: Librairie Plon, 1948.

Danty - Lafrance, Louis and Jean. Pratique de la Rémunération du Travail. Paris: Editions d'Organisation, 1956.

David, Myriam. "L'application des principes du Casework," in Erna Sailer, New Trends in European Social Work. Vienna: Astoria, 1955, pp. 49-54.

_____. "Perfectionnement en psychologie des assistantes sociales," Actualites Sociales, October, 1957.

De Buyst, C. "Le rôle de l'assistante sociale au cours du traitement de certaines catégories de délinquants," Service Social dans le Monde, Vol. XVI, No. 3 (July, 1957).

De Gourlet, Apolline. Cinquante Ans de Service Social. Paris: Editions Sociales Françaises, 1947.

De Hurtado, Isabelle. "La formation du personnel," Informations Sociales, XI, No. 7 (July, 1957), 716-722.

Dériol, Claudius. "Les carrières sociales," Chronique Sociale de France (Paris), July-August, 1950.

Dubois, Mlle. "Hierarchie Professionnelle," Informations Sociales, XII, No. 2 (February, 1958), 36-46.

Foliet, J. "Simples réflexions sur les carrières sociales," Chronique Sociale de France, July-August, 1950.

Getting, G., and Edouard Rist. "Principes et organisation du service social à l'hôpital," L'Hygiène Sociale, No. 98 (May 10, 1938), pp. 1927, ff.

Joubrel, Henri. "L'éducateur de jeunes socialement inadaptés," Educateurs (Paris), No. 55, 1955.

Laborie, Paul. Précis d'Assistance Sociale à l'Usage des Infirmières et des Infirmières Visiteuses. Paris: Poinat, 1928.

Léon, A. "Problèmes actuels de l'orientation professionnelle en France," Avenirs, January, 1958.

_____. Psychopédagogie de l'Orientation Professionnelle. Paris: Presses Universitaires de France, 1957.

Liberman, R. et al. "Les relations de travail à l'intérieur du service social," Informations Sociales, XII, No. 2 (February, 1958), 2-46.

Macadam, Elizabeth. The Social Servant in the Making. A Review of the Provision of Training for the Social Services. London: George Allen & Unwin, 1946.

Manuel, P. "Une expérience internationale: Atlantique," Informations Sociales, XII, No. 4 (April, 1958), 49-57.

Marshall, T. H. "Le rôle des sciences sociales dans la formation des travailleurs sociaux," Service Social dans le Monde, XVII, No. 4 (October, 1958), 156-164.

Martin, Ivan. "Le régime de retraits des cadres," Droit Social, XXI, Nos. 9-10 (September-October, 1958), 484-495; and No. 11 (November, 1958), 556-565.

Molina, Manuel (ed.). Guide Pratique de Travail (Social, Juridique, Administratif). Paris: Eyrolles, 1956.

Moutillard, Th. "Service social rural Bonnetable," Pages Sociales, No. 16 (March, 1946), 6-8.

Nampon, Mlle et al. "Séminaire sur le Casework," Informations Sociales, XI, No. 10 (November, 1957), 1113-1201.

Première Conférence Internationale de Service Social, Deuxième Section: Enseignement dt Service Social. Paris, 1928.

Racine, Aimée. "L'évolution de l'enseignement du service social dans les différents pays," Le Service Social (Brussels), XXV, No. 4 (July-August, 1947), 83-91.

Robert, August. Le Service de Santé Scolaire et Universitaire. Paris: La Technique de Livre, 1954.

Sailer, Erna et al. New Trends in European Social Work. Vienna: Astoria, 1955.

Salomon, Alice. Education for Social Work: Zurich: Verlag für Recht und Gesellschaft, 1937.

Selver, Henry et al. "La formation d'un travailleur social," Informations Sociales, VII, No. 2 (February, 1953), 12-153.

Simonnet, G.-L. "Le régime général de la sécurité sociale et la rééducation professionnelle," Droit Social, XIII, No. 10 (December, 1950), 436-441.

Sparake-Guillaume, Louise. Le Service Social dans l'Industrie. Liège: Descer, 1943.

Termant, Suzanne. Service Social. L'Assistante Sociale -- sa Mission. Paris: B. Pichon & R. Durand-Aurias, 1945.
_____. Service Sociale. L'Assistante Sociale. Paris: Librairie Générale de Droit et de Jurisprudence, 1947.

Turpin, Yvonne. "L'adaptation du personnel médico-social au progrès de la médecine, " Informations Sociales, XI, No. 11 (December, 1957), 1336-1344.

Veil, Claude. "La reclassement professionnel, " Informations Sociales, XI, No. 10 (November, 1956), 1207-1213.

Viollet, Abbé Jean. Petit Guide du Travailleur Social (formation morale et méthodes d'action). Paris: Confédération générale des familles, 1931.

glossary

A

abri de réception transitoire
transition hostel (for the homeless and persons newly released from prison)

accident du travail
industrial accident; work injury

Action pour les structures humaines
organization for the promotion of good labor-management relations

Administration générale de l'assistance publique
General Public Assistance Administration (in Paris)

Administration nationale des prisons
National Prison Administration

adoption ordinaire
ordinary adoption

aide d'assistante sociale
licensed assistant social worker

Aide des travailleurs intellectuels
Aid for Intellectual Workers

Aide familiale
visiting housekeeper service

Aide morale de la jeunesse
Moral Aid for Youth (agency licensed for probation services for girls)

aliéné
insane, mentally ill

allocation de la mère au foyer
allowance paid to non-working mother of a child under age 5

allocation de maternité
maternity allowance paid on birth of a child; also paid to a working mother six weeks before and six weeks after confinement

allocation de salaire unique
allowance paid for children of single-wage-earner families

allocation familiale
family allowance

allocation familiale prénatale
prenatal family allowance paid during pregnancy

ambassadeur de service social
ambassador of social work (social welfare attaché), appointed to represent the Entr'Aide française, q.v., in foreign countries

asile d'enfants
a children's home; orphanage

assesseur
assessor, lay member of Tribunal pour enfants, q.v.

assistance de chômage
unemployment assistance

assistance aux familles nombreuses
  assistance to large families

assistance aux femmes en couches
  maternity benefit paid for six weeks before
  and six weeks after confinement

Assistance publique
  public assistance

Assistance publique centrale
  central public assistance agency in Paris

assistante de service social
  official title of social worker earning a
  state diploma; shorter form, assistante
  sociale, is commonly used

assistante sociale
  licensed social worker (masc. form is
  assistant social)

assistante sociale déléguée à la
coordination
  supervisor of coordination of social work
  within a district or département, responsible to the district Comité de coordination de service social
  aux familles, q.v.

assistante sociale scolaire
  school social worker (visiting teacher)

Association amicale des délégués
à la liberté surveillée
  National Child Protective Association,
  furnishing probation services

Association des infirmières visiteuses de France
  Association of Visiting Nurses of France

Association des travailleuses
sociales
  Association of Social Workers (professional organization)

Association du service social à
l'hôpital
  Association for Social Service in Hospitals

association familiale
  family association (cooperative)

Association médicale régionale
  Regional Medical Association

Association nationale des assis-
tantes diplomées d'état
  National Association of Licensed Social
  Workers

Association nationale des companies de chemins de fer
  National Association of Railroad Companies

Assurance d'accidents du travail
  Employment Injury Insurance; workmen's
  compensation

Assurance d'accidents du travail
et maladies professionnelles
  Employment Injury and Occupational Diseases Insurance

Assurance décès
  Death Benefit Insurance

Assurance invalidité
  Permanent-Disability Insurance

Assurance maladie
  Health Insurance

Assurance maternité
  Maternity Insurance

Assurance pour la maladie de
longue durée
  Long-Term Sickness Insurance

Assurance vieillesse
  Old-Age Insurance

atelier de charité
  charity workshop

auberge de la jeunesse
  youth hostel

aveugle
  blind

B

bagne d'enfants
  children's penitentiary

banque populaire
  nonprofit credit and loan association

biens des pauvres
  poor-relief chests

bureau d'addresses
  employment bureau

bureau d'aide sociale
  bureau of social aid (public welfare department)

bureau d'assistance publique
  public assistance bureau

bureau de bienfaisance
  welfare bureau (public or private charity office)

bureau de charité
  poor - relief committee

bureau de rencontres
  confidential social service exchange

bureau des pauvres
  poor - relief bureau

bureau d'hygiène publique
  bureau of public hygiene(local health office)

bureau régionale d'hygiène publique
  regional bureau of public health

C

Caisse d'allocations familiales
  Family Allowance Fund

Caisse d'assurances sociales
  Social Insurance Fund

Caisse de compensation
  Social Insurance Compensation Fund

Caisse d'équalisation
  [industrial] Equalization Fund

Caisse des assurances de maladie
  Health Insurance Fund

Caisse de sécurité sociale
  Social Security Fund

Caisse jointe d'action
  Joint Action Fund

Caisse nationale d'assurance de chômage
  National Fund for Unemployment Compensation

Caisse nationale des pensions
  National Pension Fund

Caisse primaire d'assurance de maladies industrielles
  Primary Workmen's Compensation Fund

Caisse primaire de sécurité sociale
  Primary Social Security Fund

Caisse régionale des assurances de maladies industrielles
  Regional Workmen's Compensation Fund

Caisse régionale de sécurité sociale
  Regional Social Security Fund

Cartotèque sanitaire et sociale
  Central Sanitary and Social Registry

centre d'accueil et d'observation
  reception and observation center (established by a département under a 1950 decree of the Ministère de la Justice)

centre d'accueil pour les enfants pré-scolaires
  a day nursery for pre - school children; receiving home

centre communal de jeunesse
  community youth center

centre d'observation
  (1) agency making social investigations of juvenile offenders for the Tribunal pour enfants; (2) a correctional institution

centre d'orientation éducative
a specialized child-guidance clinic for
children brought before the juvenile court
on complaint of their own parents

Centre laïque des auberges de
jeunesse
Lay Center of Youth Hostels

centre psycho-pédagogique
child guidance clinic organized by the
Ministries of Education and Public Health

centre social
settlement house (may also be called
maison sociale or résidence
sociale)

chômage
unemployment

chômage professionnel
permanent (deliberate) unemployment

cité-jardin
garden city

classe de perfectionnement
class for retarded and handicapped children

clinique externe d'orientation
child guidance clinic (as out-patient department of a hospital)

Code civil
the Civil Code of Napoleon

Code de famille
Family Code (1939)

Code de la sécurité sociale
Social Security Code (1956). Libre V
concerns family allowances

Code de travail et de prévoyance
sociale
Code of Labor and Social Welfare

Code pénal
the Penal Code of Napoleon

colonie correctionnelle
correctional school, industrial school

colonie de vacances
vacation camp

colonie pénale
penal colony, penitentiary

Comité central d'assistance publique et d'hygiène publique de
Paris
Central Public Assistance and Public Hygiene Committee of Paris

Comité central des caisses d'al-
locations familiales
Central Committee of Family Allowance
Funds

Comité d'aide aux prisonniers
libérés
Discharged Prisoners' Aid Committee

Comité de coordination de service
social aux familles
Committee on Family Service Coordination: the governing body of the unified
family service agencies of a district within
a département, as enacted by the Règlement intérieur du service
départemental de coordination
des services sociaux, q.v.

Comité d'entente
(1) coordination committee; (2) Committee of Coordination (association of private
social agencies in Paris)

Comité d'entente des écoles de
service social
National Association of Schools of Social
Work

Comité de propagande et d'action
contre le taudis
Slum Clearance Committee

comité de santé et de sauvegarde
committee of health and safety

comité de secours et patronage
a special parole committee of a maison
de l'éducation surveillée, q.v.

comité de surveillance
supervisory committee

Comité national des écoles en
plein air
National Committee for Open-Air Schools

Comité national pour la défense contre la tuberculose
National Tuberculosis Committee

comité pour la protection des mineurs délinquants
committee for the protection of delinquent minors (a local child-protective agency)

Comité régional des assurances
Regional Insurance Committee

Comité technique d'hygiène et des services sociaux
Technical Committee of Hygiene and Social Services

commissaire de police
police commissioner

Commission consultative pour l'exercice de la profession d'assistante sociale
Advisory Board on the Exercise of the Social Work Profession

Commission d'apprentissage et de l'éducation professionnelle
Commission on Apprenticeship and Occupational Training

Commission de la jeunesse
Youth Commission (advisory commission of the Haut Comité de la jeunesse, q.v.)

commission de surveillance
safety team (in factories and mines)

Commission d'examens
Board of Examiners

Commission générale des rapatriés
General Commission for Repatriated Persons

commission sanitaire
sanitation commission

commune
community, city

Confédération des unions de travail
Trade Union Congress

Conférence internationale du service social
International Conference of Social Work

Conseil départemental des allocations familiales
Departmental Council of Family Allowances

Conseil de famille des pupilles
Family Council for Public Wards (départemental)

Conseil de perfectionnement des écoles d'infirmières et d'assistantes sociales
Supervisory Council of Schools of Nursing and Social Work

Conseil de surveillance
Supervisory Council of the départemental bureau for coordinated social services. The Conseil is appointed by the Conseil général of the département

conseil d'hygiène publique
council of public hygiene

Conseil d'instruction publique
Board of Education

Conseil général
General Council of the département (its legislative body)

Conseiller assistant social de travail
licensed Assistant Industrial Social Consultant

Conseiller pour la protection de l'enfance
Counselor for the Protection of Children (appointed to the Cour d'appel in cases of appeals against the decision of the Tribunal pour enfants)

Conseiller social de travail
licensed Industrial Social Consultant

conseil municipal
municipal council

Conseil régional des allocations familiales
Regional Council of Family Allowances

Conseil régional de sécurité sociale
  Regional Council of Social Security

Conseil supérieur
  Superior Council

Conseil supérieur d'assistance
publique
  Superior Council of Public Assistance

Conseil supérieur de la protection de l'enfance
  Superior Council of Child Welfare

Conseil supérieur de l'assistance
publique
  Superior Council of Public Assistance (formerly Directoire de l'assistance
  publique, q.v., now replaced by
  the Directoire de population et
  d'assistance publique)

Conseil supérieur des allocations
familiales
  Superior Council of Family Allowances

Conseil supérieur de sécurité
sociale
  Superior Council of Social Security

correction paternelle
  special measures under the Code civil
  for apprehension and imprisonment, on
  complaint of parents, of unmanageable
  children

cour d'appel
  court of appeals

cour d'assises
  jury court

crèche
  day nursery

Croix-rouge français
  French Red Cross

D

déchéance paternelle
  abrogation of parental authority by court
  decision

Décret de protection de santé des
enfants scolaires
  Decree on the Protection of the Health of
  School Children

délégué à la liberté surveillée
  probation officer

délégué permanent à la liberté
surveillée
  official title of full-time probation officer
  appointed by the Tribunal pour enfants

délégué technique
  social worker appointed as district field
  representative of the Groupement
  d'action des services sociaux,
  q.v.

déportés
  Frenchmen deported by the Germans to
  work as "slave laborers" during World
  War II

dépôts de mendicité
  workhouses for vagrants and beggars

détenu
  convict in a penal institution

difficiles
  "difficult" children: one of the two categories of delinquent children established
  by the Loi d'assistance à l'enfance. The other, more serious, category is vicieux, q.v.

directeur
  director

Directeur d'hygiène publique
  Director of Public Health

Direction départementale de sécurité sociale
  Departmental Social Security Administration

Direction des assurances de maladies industrielles
  Workmen's Compensation Administration

Direction des assurances sociales
  Social Insurance Administration

Direction générale de l'administration pénale
Central Prison Administration

Direction régionale de population
et d'assistance publique
Regional Population and Public Assistance
Administration

Direction régionale de sécurité
sociale
Regional Social Security Administration

Direction régionale d'hygiène publique et des hôpitaux
Regional Public Hygiene and Hospital Administration

Directoire de l'assistance publique
Directorate of Public Assistance (national
relief board established in 1886), now
replaced by Directoire de population et d'assistance publique

Directoire de population et d'assistance publique
Directorate of Population and Public Assistance

Directoire d'hygiène publique et
des hôpitaux
Directorate of Public Hygiene and Hospitals

Directoire générale de sécurité
sociale
General Directorate of Social Security

dispensaire d'hygiène mentale
mental hygiene clinic

dispensaire d'hygiène sociale
social hygiene dispensary (out-patient
clinic for prevention and cure of tuberculosis and contagious diseases), a public
health clinic

Division d'assurance d'accidents
du travail
Industrial Accident Insurance Division
(Workmen's Compensation)

Division d'assistance publique
Division of Public Assistance

Division d'éducation technique
Division of Vocational Training

Division départementale d'hygiène
publique et des hôpitaux
Departmental Division of Public Hygiene
and Hospitals

domicile de secours
residence or settlement rights (giving
right to public assistance and community
services)

E

Ecole en plein air pour les enfants en danger
Open-Air School for Children Susceptible
to Diseases

Ecole nationale de la santé publique
National School of Public Health

emploi facile
light employment

emprisonnement correctionnel
imprisonment, penal commitment

enfants abandonnés
deserted children; waifs

enfants arriérés
retarded children

enfants assistés
dependent children in need of permanent
assistance (also called pupilles de
l'assistance)

enfants en garde (also called enfants
protégés)
dependent children, committed by the
Tribunal pour enfants to the care
of the bureau d'aide sociale

enfants protégés
enfants en garde, q.v.

enfants secourus
dependent children in temporary economic
or social need

enfants secourus en dépôt
dependent children under temporary institutional care

enfants trouvés
foundlings

Ensemble des communes
Federation of Municipalities

Entr' Aide française
semi-official organization financed by the Ministère de santé publique for coordinating and subsidizing private welfare and health agencies

Entr'aide sociale aux prisonniers
Cooperative Social Aid for Prisoners

établissement de rééducation agrée
licensed correctional training school

F

faubourg-jardin
garden-suburb (suburban housing development)

Fédération d'éducation nationale
National Education Federation

Fédération des caisses d'équalisation
National Federation of Equalization Funds (private family allowances)

Fédération des services sociaux à l'hôpital
Federation of Hospital Social Services (founded 1922 for medical social workers)

Fédération nationale des sociétés familiales
National Federation of Family Associations

Fonds joint d'action
Joint Action Fund

Fonds national de solidarité
National Solidarity Fund (supplies funds to supplement old-age allowances as needed)

G

gardien
guard (in a reformatory), now known as a moniteur

gardien substitut
court-appointee, in absence of parent or legal guardian

Grand bureau des pauvres
Central Relief Office (Paris, 1550)

Groupement d'action des services sociaux
Coordination of Social Services Activities, a semi-private agency established by the Ministère de santé publique in 1951 to coordinate public and private relief and health services and expand their facilities nationally

Groupement des unions d'oeuvres d'assistance et d'aide sociale
Alliance of Associations of Relief and Social Work Agencies (in Paris)

H

Haut Comité de la jeunesse
National Youth Committee, coordinating public and private agencies in recreation, sports, and social group work for adolescents

Hôtel des consultations charitables
pioneer free medical clinic (eighteenth century, Paris)

hôtel maternelle
maternity home for unmarried mothers and their children

hôtels de Dieu
formerly almshouses; now hospitals

"Hygiène par exemple"
"Hygiene by Example" -- philanthropic society for health education

hygiène scolaire
  school health services

I

incorrigibles
  hardened, habitual criminals

indemnité journalière de repos
  per-diem maternity-leave indemnity

indemnité monétaire de maladie
  sickness indemnity

ingénieur social
  social engineer (industrial social worker
  employed by large company)

institution d'éducation corrective
  institute of corrective education (correctional school)

institution d'éducation surveillée
  institute of supervised education (reformatory school)

Institution nationale des sourds-
muets
  National Institution for Deaf-Mutes

institut médico-pédagogique
  psychiatric clinic with residential facilities

Institut national de travail et
d'information professionnelle
  National Labor and Vocational Guidance
  Institute

internat médico-pédagogique
  child-guidance residential institution for
  in-patient treatment

J

jardin d'enfants
  kindergarten

juge des enfants
  judge of Tribunal pour enfants,
  q. v.

juge d'instruction
  examining magistrate (judge of inquiry)

L

légitimation adoptive
  legitimation by adoption

libérés
  released convicts or juvenile delinquents

liberté surveillée
  probation

Ligue française des auberges de
jeunesse
  French League of Youth Hostels

Ligue nationale contre le péril
vénérien
  National League Against Social Diseases

Ligue prophylactique
  Prophylactic League

livret de santé
  health book (for free medical examinations
  for a child from birth through school); also
  called carnet sanitaire

logement sanatorium
  health center for out-patient treatment
  of non-infectious victims of tuberculosis

Loi d'allocations familiales
  Law on Family Allowances (1931, amended
  1932). The later Loi d'allocations
  familiales of 1956 forms the basis of
  the family-allowance structure (as incorporated in Libre V of the Code de la
  sécurité sociale)

Loi d'assistance à l'enfance
  Law for the Assistance of Children (1943)

Loi de la sécurité sociale
  Law on Social Security (1946). Its provisions are embodied in the Code de
  la sécurité sociale of 1956

Loi de résponsabilité des employeurs et d'assurance des
accidents du travail
  Employers' Liability and Workmen's
  Compensation Law (1898)

Loi des assurances sociales
Law on Social Insurance (1928, amended subsequently)

Loi des caisses d'allocations familiales
Law on Family Allowance Funds (1949)

Loi des habitations à loyer modéré
Law on Low-Rent Housing (1953); enacted a payroll tax to be paid by employers and used for housing construction

Loi des habitations publiques
Public Housing Law (1947); provided loans at low interest for construction of low-rent housing

Loi des pensions aux mineurs
Law on Miners' Pensions (1946)

Loi des pensions aux travailleurs et paysans
Law on Pensions for Workers and Peasants (1910)

Loi des services médicaux de travail
Law on Medical Labor Services (1946) [industrial medical services]

Loi Loucheur
Low-Rent Housing Law (1928)

Loi nationale de l'assistance médicale gratuite
National Law for Free Medical Assistance (1893)

Loi pour la protection des enfants maltraités
Law for the Protection of Mistreated Children (1889)

Loi pour les tribuneaux des enfants et adolescents et pour la probation
Law on Courts for Children and Adolescents, and Probation (1912)

Loi Roussel (Loi de la protection de jeunes enfants)
Law on the Protection of Young Children in Foster Care (1894)

Loi sur les aliénés
Law on the Mentally Ill

M

maison d'éducation surveillée
reformatory school; approved correctional school

maison de la charité
house of charity (Catholic parish charity organization)

maison maternelle
maternity home

maison sociale
settlement house (may also be called a centre sociale or résidence sociale)

maladie professionnelle
occupational disease

Maquis
the French Resistance movement during World War II

Marraines sociales
Social Godmothers, Paris agency to help juvenile delinquent girls; ceased operation in 1943

Ministère de la Justice
Ministry of Justice

Ministère des anciens combattants et victimes de la guerre
Ministry of Veterans and War Victims

Ministère de santé publique et d'assistance publique
Ministry of Public Health and Public Assistance, replaced by Ministère de santé publique et de population, q.v.

Ministère de santé publique et de population
Ministry of Public Health and Population

Ministére des prisonniers de guerre
Ministry of Prisoners of War

Ministère de travail et de sécurité sociale (formerly Ministère
de travail et des services sociaux)
  Ministry of Labor and Social Security
  (formerly Ministry of Labor and Social
  Services)

Ministère nationale de l'éducation publique
  National Ministry of Public Education

moniteur
  guard in a reformatory, or counselor in
  a correctional school

Mont-de-piété
  philanthropic loan society

mutualitée familiale
  self-help family cooperative

mutuelle coopérative
  mutual-aid society

mutuelle familiale
  family association for mutual aid

observateur de comportement
  counselor (staff member of centre
  d'observation)

Oeuvre de la visite des détenus
dans les prisons
  Society for Visiting Prisoners in Penal
  Institutions

Oeuvre protestante des prisons
de femmes
  Protestant Society for Women's Prisons

Office central des habitations à
Bon Marché
  Central Office for Low-Cost Housing (public housing authority in the Ministère
  de santé publique, organized in 1912)

Office central des oeuvres de
bienfaisance
  Central Office of Welfare Agencies (association of private agencies in Paris)

orphelinat
  a children's home, orphanage

ouvroir
  workshop

Paris charitable
  Official Parisian directory of charitable
  organizations

patronage
  neighborhood or community center; orphanage

Patronage Rollet
  a child-protective agency in Paris, founded
  by Judge Henri Rollet

Pensions de vieillesse
  Old-Age Insurance Benefits

Pensions d'invalidité
  Disability Insurance Benefits

Permanence d'entre'aide sociale
  Permanent Social Coordination Service (in
  Paris) -- later replaced by Groupement
  d'action des services sociaux,
  q.v.

prévoyance sociale
  preventive social services

prime d'allaitement
  nursing bonus, paid to mother up to 12
  months while breast-feeding; also called
  prime nourricière

prison-école
  prison-school (reformatory)

procureur général
  district attorney, public prosecutor

pupilles de la nation
  wards of the state (war orphans)

pupilles de l'assistance
  See enfants assistés

pupilles vicieux
  severely maladjusted children and adolescents, considered incorrigible

R

réclusion
solitary confinement

Régime d'allocation de vieillesse
Old-Age Allowance Act (1948)

Règlement intérieure du service départementale de coordination des services sociaux
Statute of the Conseil général of a departement integrating social services of all organizations within its jurisdiction

rente d'une incapacité permanente de travail
permanent-disability pension

repos
rest; convalescence

résidence sociale
settlement house (may also be called centre social or maison sociale)

résidente sociale
group social worker in a settlement house

Résistance (Maquis)
the resistance movement during the German Occupation in World War II

restitution de droit de puissance paternelle
restitution of parental rights by the court

S

salaire proportionné
proportional wage (profit-sharing system for workers)

Sauvegarde de l'adolescence
agency for assistance of adolescent delinquents (est. 1929)

Secours national
National Relief, an organization established during the war, now succeeded by the Entr'Aide française, q. v.

secours préventif d'abandon
public assistance to prevent abandonment of children

Sécrétariat social maritime
maritime social agency for counseling and casework services to seamen

service d'aide aux travailleurs sans emploi
voluntary unemployment assistance service

Service des allocations familiales
Family Allowance Service

service de sauvegarde de l'enfant
child protective agency; may make investigations for the judge of a juvenile court

Service domestique en famille
Homemaker Service

Service social aux familles
Family Social Casework Service

Service social central de la marine
Central Naval Social Service, a voluntary social agency for seamen

Service social de l'enfance
Social Service for Children, a national association furnishing probation and child welfare services

Service social de sauvegarde de l'enfance et de l'adolescence
Social Service for the Protection of Children and Adolescents (a private agency)

service social d'usine
factory (industrial) welfare service

Service social maritime
social service agency for merchant seamen and fishermen

Service social pour l'enfance en danger moral (now Service social pour l'enfance)
Social Service for Children in Moral Danger (pioneer private agency in casework service, est. 1923)

services sociaux entre-usines
inter-factory social services

société coopérative de travail
labor cooperative for operation of self-governing workshops

Société de patronage des prison-niers libérés protestants
Society for Helping Discharged Protestant Prisoners

Société des Amis
Society of Friends (Quakers)

sociétés de secours mutuelles
mutual-aid societies (in Britain, "friendly societies")

Société des rheumatiques para-lysés
Society for Paralyzed Rheumatics (conducts vocational retraining courses)

Société pour la protection de l'en-fance
Society for the Protection of Children (est. 1887, in Paris)

Société pour l'instruction et pro-tection des sourds-muets
Society for the Education and Protection of Deaf Mutes

surintendante d'usines
industrial social worker

sur-salaire familiale
family-supplement wage, a supplemental allowance paid by private industry to workers according to the size of their families

sursis
suspension or postponement of sentence

T

transfers sociaux
social transfers (of national income to social services)

travaux forcés
hard labor

Tribunal pour enfants
official title of the Juvenile Court. The Tribunal consists of a professional jurist and two lay assessors

Tribunal pour les adolescents
official title of Court for Adolescents

tribunal supérieur
superior court

tuteur
special guardian appointed by the court

U

Union des patronages
(1) Union of Neighborhood Centers;
(2) national child-protection association furnishing probation and child-welfare services

Union familiale des pères méri-toires
Family Union of Deserving Fathers -- a cooperative self-help family association

Union national des associations régionales de sauvegarde de l'enfance
National Federation of Regional Child Protective Associations

Union nationale des sociétés fa-miliales
National Union of Family Associations, est. 1945 by government decree

Union nationale interfédérale des oeuvres privées sanitaires et sociales
National Union of Voluntary Health and Social Organizations (comparable to the National Welfare Assembly in the U.S.)

Union nationale maritime
National Maritime Union, maintained by shipowners and shipping companies

V

vicieux
incorrigible -- the more serious of the two categories of delinquent children established by the Loi d'assistance à l'enfance. The other category is dif-ficiles, q.v.

N A M E
I N D E X

S   U   B   J   E   C   T   I   N   D   E   X

Date Due

SEP 2 5 '69 FEB	SEP 30 '69		
FEB 2 5 '70	FEB 13 70		
OCT 6 '70 MAR 18 '71			
MAY 17 '71 MAY 4 '71			
OCT 4 '77	SEP 14 '77		
JUN 27 '78	JUN 7 '78		
	PRINTED	IN U. S. A.	